# Steven Gerrard, Michael Owen and .... Me

## MIKE YATES
## TELLS HIS STORY

with Keith Miller

Foreword by Jamie Carragher

ISBN 978-1-78280-160-3

All photos courtesy Mike Yates collection except where noted.
Front cover photo courtesy of LFC and Nick Taylor.
Design – Neil Barnard at 809 Design Associates Inc. Set in Garamond
Printed and bound in the United Kingdom by Butler, Tanner & Dennis

For information about this book please contact: keith@millerpublishing.net
www.stevengerrardmichaelowenandme.co.uk

This is not an official Liverpool Football Club publication. The views expressed herein are solely those of the author and do not necessarily reflect those of Liverpool Football Club.

# Contents

# Interviews

'I had already scored two good ones and I was absolutely buzzing. The conditions were ideal, the pitch was perfect and the lads were really pinging the ball around sweetly. This was football at its very best, the way it should be played.

And I wanted that third goal.

As soon as the ball broke out of our defence and I saw Steven Gerrard moving into a wide position down the right, I knew I was going to get a chance. By the time his clever first touch had brought the long pass under control and helped him to ghost past his marker, I was already sprinting towards the penalty area.

Close to the byline Stevie G whipped in a hard, flat cross that curled away from the keeper and rocketed towards a space on the edge of the six-yards box; a space that I was about to fill. Bursting past a defender at full pace, I met the ball square on and it thumped off my forehead, flew into the top corner of the net and thudded back off the stanchion. Get in!

A hat-trick at Anfield!

We were fourteen years old, signed on at Liverpool Football Club, and I was living every schoolboy's dream.

Life couldn't get any better than this.'

*Mike Yates*

# Special Thanks

To Nicola and Devon .... My two best friends. I love you with all of my heart. You are my strength, my support and my reasons to believe.

To Mum and Dad .... Now that I am a parent myself, I can really appreciate the many sacrifices you have made for me over the years. I know that you have done everything in your power to nurture my roots and help me flourish. I love you.

To my brother and sister .... Geoff, thanks for inspiring me by involving me in your football circles and fanning the flames of my passion for the game. It meant a lot. Helen, my little big sister! Thanks for making my life off the field during my younger years such fun! I love you both very much.

To Steven Gerrard and Michael Owen .... A very special thank you for your inspiration over the years and for giving your blessings to this book.

To Carra .... Thank you for your willingness to contribute the foreword. You epitomise The Liverpool Way and I admire you greatly as a player and as a person, so I was absolutely delighted to get your input.

To Liverpool Football Club .... for everything!

To Keith Miller .... Without your outstanding gift for transforming my memories and thoughts into words on paper, this book would not have been possible. Working on this project has been a great experience and even better that I could share it with somebody who has become a true friend. Your attention to detail, research, passion and writing ability would put you #1 on my team sheet every week! Thanks 'Partner'!

To all the other special people who have contributed to this project .... Your support is sincerely appreciated.

In memory of Eloise Lema Dalton

- Mike Yates

# Foreword

## by Jamie Carragher

Football is an amazing game that can provide a very rewarding career and an exciting lifestyle. So it's no great surprise that each year thousands and thousands of young players dream about becoming a professional at one of the top clubs. Unfortunately, even though many of those young players are taken on by academies all around the country, the harsh reality is that only a handful of them will ever make the grade.

It is such a highly competitive environment that the vast majority of players will eventually be released, even if they have been relatively successful. I was in the Liverpool side that won the FA Youth Cup in 1996 and the whole team was given a professional contract. This had never happened before, and it was probably mainly a reward for the lads doing so well, but they all still had an extra chance to succeed. Despite that, almost inevitably, twelve months down the line most of them were gone. At eighteen we were the best team in the country, but very few of us are still involved in the game today. And that's the reality of professional football.

I have even seen this at the highest level. When I started at the National School at Lilleshall, our coach told us: 'There are thirty-two of you here now, but only four or five are going to make it.' And he was right! Now, in my case, I always believed that I was one of those four or five. But there goes the biggest problem - all young players think they are going to make it!

Even if somebody at an academy keeps warning the players to be prepared for being released, it never really sinks in. A coach in any group can identify the top players, the middle players and the bottom players. And of course the players have already figured all of that out by themselves. But even the ones in the bottom group will still think it's going to happen for them. Maybe they are kidding themselves, but they still all have that same belief!

There is just no way around it. Once you have been trying to be a footballer for your whole life, especially when you get so close at eighteen, then you cannot stop yourself from believing that success is just around the corner.

Unfortunately statistics prove that to be totally wrong, so all young players need to take more heed of the warnings.

As far as I am concerned there is no real secret to what makes a talented young footballer become a successful professional. At the end of the day it is all about hard work and 100% commitment. Every youngster should be constantly thinking: Am I working as hard as I can in training? Am I staying behind to do extra practice? Am I in the gym often enough trying to get stronger? Am I improving my speed? Am I listening to my coaches properly? Am I putting maximum effort into my performance? Am I doing more than the other players to win a place on the team?

Earning success as a footballer is all about giving absolutely everything you have got and always being prepared to push yourself that bit extra to keep moving on to the next level. I often hear people say things like, 'Oh, he was so much better than me at fourteen, I can't believe he didn't make it.' And why didn't he make it? Almost certainly because he didn't go that extra yard!

Every year I feel genuinely sorry for the many players that get released; but then I think to myself, well why don't you now try and become a bit stronger mentally and accept more responsibility for your own future? The club can offer all the help in the world but it's the players themselves who have to take control of their life. They are the ones who have to grab whatever second chances come their way.

Many players get so disillusioned when they are let go that they lose their self- belief and the hunger to keep going, so they end up just drifting out of the game. But, at the same time, there are plenty of players who have been released but then went on to play for England. Because they kept pushing themselves!

It is obviously part of a coach's job to motivate his players, to encourage them and build up their enthusiasm. Realistically then, there is just no way that coaches can keep reminding their trainees that they are probably not going to make it. That could never work.

So the big challenge is how to encourage young players to keep working hard towards the ultimate goal of earning a professional contract, but also make them aware of the reality of being released without killing their ambition.

Somehow we have to get that important fact of life across effectively, so that players are persuaded to start thinking about other things that they might do in the future, in or out of the game, because the reality is that

90% or more of them are going to be released.

That is why I think this book is such a good idea. Mike Yates' story paints a very honest picture of the realities of being released, but it also shows how he turned his setback into an enjoyable career and a happy life.

All young players should be encouraged to read this book because they will enjoy it and learn a lot at the same time.

Maybe then the realities will hit home.

# Part One
# Growing Up the Liverpool Way

## Earliest Memories as a Young Footballer

Talk to any footballer, even the world's greatest superstars from Gerrard to Messi, and they will almost certainly tell you that their love for the game started as far back as they can remember. It is that inborn passion, fuelled by the free-spirited, fun-filled, excitement of childhood that in later life will help turn talent into success. And that is why I am going to start telling my personal football story from the very beginning. I made my Yates family debut on Wednesday 7th November 1979, joining my brother Geoff and sister Helen, as happy children of proud parents Geoff and Cheryl. Dad was a hardworking and dedicated healthcare specialist and Mum was an equally hardworking and dedicated home keeper. Our family home was a comfortable semi-detached house in the village of Burscough, close to the market town of Ormskirk, about thirteen miles from Liverpool city centre. It could never be argued that I was born into a position of privilege but, at the same time, there is no doubt that we enjoyed a good standard of living and I grew up in a happy and caring environment. The true depth of that reality was starkly driven home later in my life when eye-opening, disturbing experiences around the world showed me that I had in fact been extremely fortunate the day that destiny chose to drop me into that particular spot on the planet.

Looking back to my childhood, all of my very earliest memories seem to revolve around me kicking some kind of a ball – football, tennis ball, sponge ball, it didn't matter what. I even used to love playing keepy-uppy with a balloon inside the house. We had an archway in our living room and I used that as the goal to smash the ball in. It must have driven my mum and dad mad, but they never complained. All of my family were Evertonians, so obviously I became one too. By the time I was a toddler I was already wearing the full Everton kit. My favourite game was to pretend I was playing in a big match, usually Everton v Liverpool, and do my own commentary: 'It's Yates on the ball, he turns, beats his man and smacks the ball into the Liverpool net. Get in!'

My brother Geoff, who is ten years older, had a big influence on me with regards to football. In the early days I'd go to watch him play but instead of following the game I'd be kicking a ball around all the time. I can picture myself going to the boot of the car to get out an old case ball, with most of the panels ripped off, and then running across to the shale pitch next door. The goals had nets and I just loved smashing the ball into the roof of the net. Then at half time I'd rush on to the main pitch and blast the ball into their nets as well. That was always a real buzz for me; that lovely sound as the ball hits the net and then the swish as it runs up the back. And you know what, I still love that sound to this day. Just like when the ball smacks against the stanchion at the back of the goal. Or even when it thuds back off the post or bar. That's what it's all about really, the sheer thrill of the moment.

By the time Geoff was about fifteen he was playing for Skelmersdale Spartans and they asked me to be their team mascot. The Spartans won the league that year and, since I was the mascot, they let me pick up the trophy. I just loved being able to do that, hearing all the cheering going on around me. I am sure that positive experience must have given me plenty of inspiration for the future – by being part of a winning team, enjoying the feeling of success, expecting to do well and wanting to win my own trophies.

I was lucky to have a big brother around in those early days to encourage my passion for football. He would always find time for me, have a kick about, talk about Everton's matches and keep me generally involved in the game. I don't know if that happens so much these days amongst kids but I know for sure that it was a huge help for me.

Other than just kicking a ball around for fun or playing with my brother and dad, I had my first real taste of football at the age of six when I started going to soccer practice on Saturday mornings at my school, St John's Primary. The sessions were run by one of the fathers, Peter Croft. We all had to pay 50p to play. The money was supposed to cover costs but I suspect that it was probably also a way of giving it all a sense of value, to encourage the kids not to fool about. No danger there in my case. I was as keen as mustard to play well and desperate to impress Mr. Croft because, although he was a father and not a teacher, he actually picked the school team. I can vividly remember one morning when there was a big rumour going round the kids that a stranger standing on the line was a scout. So I spent the whole session running around the pitch like a chicken with its head cut off, busting my guts, flying all over the place like a lunatic, just doing anything to look good. I kept thinking that if I did well enough the scout might walk up to me at the end and say: 'Well played son, you should come and play for Everton'. Needless to say he wasn't a scout at all, just a new dad who'd come to watch his kid. A good job really because I was so excited and out of control I ended up getting in the way of a goal-line clearance and the ball smacked against my backside and flew back over the head of our keeper. What a brilliant start to my football career – an own goal scored with my arse! I have to laugh about that now …. but it does show that even then I was dreaming about being a professional footballer.

My first experience of participating in a proper, organized football match was playing for St John's Primary, away at St. Ann's. It was a horrible, rainy September day but I thought it was going to be the best day of my life and I couldn't wait for kick-off. The team wore a blue and white striped shirt with blue shorts and socks. I was too small to wear the kit they supplied but luckily I had brought my own blue Everton shorts and socks. I remember wishing I could have worn my Everton shirt too because the school one was really itchy. But don't mind that, what a brilliant feeling it was to pull on that shirt and run out onto the pitch as part of a team in a 'real match'!

Most of the kids on that team were eleven, while I was still only six and a lot smaller than all of them. So, not surprisingly, I spent most of the match on the bench. Finally I did get sent on for the last five minutes, hungry and ready for my big moment in time. Unfortunately reality checked in at that point and I ended up just running up and down the middle of the pitch, totally frustrated and confused, helpless to do anything other than just watch the ball flying over my head. I don't think I got a single kick and we got slaughtered. Nevertheless, it was a good first learning experience for me and one that I was fortunate to get at such a tender age: something that could not happen today due to stricter age limit restrictions.

When that group of older boys left school I moved up in the team the next season and started playing regularly, even though I was still a lot younger than all the other kids. We won the local schools cup final that year, 3 - 1, and I scored all three. To be honest, and not wanting to sound big headed, I didn't think this was anything special. Scoring goals was what I was supposed to do. I loved scoring goals. In fact I loved it all. I loved putting the kit on. I even loved just kicking a ball. But for sure, winning a trophy and scoring a hat trick in the cup final in only my second season definitely gave me a big boost in football, even if I wasn't aware of that at the time.

Didier Drogba came out with a fantastic quote when he appeared on the BBC's 2012 Sports Personality of the Year. Gary Lineker was hosting

*Me and my brother Geoff*

*Practice for Panini!*

the show and he asked Didier what it was about his character that had made him such a big game player, why did he always seem to be at his best whenever the pressure was greatest. And Didier Drogba answered: 'I just want to have fun on the pitch. You know, every time I come out on the pitch I feel like a kid. So I just want to enjoy it all. I feel like I was six years old again. I just want to start running after the ball, start kicking the ball.'

Absolutely brilliant!

## My First Football Club and The Scouts Are Already Watching

Quite early on, football also became a big part of my life outside of school as well. I wanted to play as much as possible and I was really keen to be part of what I thought was a proper team, meaning a football club rather than just the school. So my dad took me along to Burscough Dynamo and that's where I first met Tommy Galvin, who was in charge of junior football. My brother Geoff had played for Dynamo and Dad thought it was the best option for me as well. So I went for a trial and did well enough to get picked for the squad. Unfortunately, even though they thought I was a decent player, when Dad told them that I was only seven they had to turn me down for the team, as I was underage for the league rules. I still went to the practices but I couldn't play for the team on Saturdays and Sundays until the following season, the year when I turned eight.

That was a long wait for any kid but especially one that was as mad to play as I was. I can still remember the very first game I played for Dynamo, it was a home fixture against Kew Corinthians from Southport. We won 10 – 0 and I scored a few, but what I most recall about that match is that our manager, George Bond, wanted us to get there early to help put up the nets and this was the first time I'd had the chance to do that. I loved it. Mainly because while I was putting them up, I was making sure that the nets were perfect, nice and tight, so that if I scored a goal the ball would make that fantastic rippling sound that I always wanted to hear after one of my shots had gone in.

I don't think that many kids nowadays are asked to put up the nets before a game and that is a pity. Having to do those kind of jobs made us understand, even at such an early age, that there was a lot more involved in staging a football match than just turning up to play. I am sure that it

Photo courtesy of Liverpool FC via Getty Images

*'I just want to have fun on the pitch. You know, every time I come out on the pitch I feel like a kid. So I just want to enjoy it all. I feel like I was 6 years old. I just want to start running after the ball, start kicking the ball.'*

- Didier Drogba, appearing on the BBC Sports Personality of the Year 2012 helped give us youngsters a greater sense of responsibility and a better understanding of the game. That in turn encouraged us to apply ourselves more seriously and gave us a better opportunity to make progress.

Another positive offshoot I gained from the experience of getting the nets ready was that I quickly realized I also had to prepare myself in just the same way. So every Saturday night, before the game on Sunday morning, I'd clean my boots until they were spotless, get all my kit organized, go to bed early, have a good night's sleep, then get up early, well rested, ready to play and raring to go. And that is a regular routine that I maintained all the way through my football days, especially after getting picked up by Liverpool as a schoolboy. From the time I first started playing for Dynamo, I was aware that I didn't want to let anybody down, least of all myself. So I always made sure I got properly prepared for any game. Mum and Dad played their part too, by keeping an eye on me, giving me good advice and encouragement and feeding me the right kind of food. It was my dad who first got me into the habit of always keeping my boots clean and in good nick – something that later became an obsession of mine and still is to this day. He used to always remind me: 'Those boots are the tools of your trade and the state that they are in will say a lot about you.' It was valuable advice and nowadays I still have a look at the boots of young players to get a quick idea of their attitude. To be truthful I do the same thing with any coaches I work with as well. Can't help it. Tools of the trade!

Around that same time, I won my first individual football trophy at a soccer camp at Burscough FC. I was awarded Player of the Week and when the organizer presented the trophy he told the crowd: 'We have high hopes for this young boy. He has the potential to be the next Maradona.' Not true but a nice thing for him to say. I remember carrying that trophy around with me everywhere I went for a week. I drove mum and dad berserk by begging them to take me to all our relatives and friends so that we could show them the trophy. I even took it to bed with me at night and went to sleep with it clutched in my arms.

At that same camp, the South Liverpool first team goalkeeper came for a penalty shoot out competition involving all the kids. I got into the final against an older boy and we had the spectators really entertained because we just kept scoring. Both of us put away all of our first five

*Opposite: Collecting my first trophy in another Everton kit at Victoria Park, home of Burscough FC*

penalties. Keep in mind that we were both young kids, under pressure, in front of a big crowd, hitting penalties against a grown man and he was doing his best to save them. We were out there for ages and both of us scored ten straight penalties. The crowd just loved it. After that we went to 'sudden-death' and still kept going and going until eventually I hit the post and the other lad scored. Even though I didn't win that penalty competition, it certainly was another very important benchmark moment in my development as a young player, another very positive experience and a great confidence builder.

For me this was just another bit of fun in football but for my parents it was the first time that they started thinking that maybe I had a bit of talent for the game. Funnily enough, that camp was held at Victoria Park where later in life I would end up actually playing non-league football for Burscough. In fact, while playing for Burscough, I ended up banging quite a few penalties into that same goal where the competition was held. Lots of practice and lots of inbred confidence I suppose. I once even scored a good goal against Liverpool at that end!

The more I think about it now, looking back to those very early days, the more I realize that I was exposed to so many positive experiences in the game and surrounded by constant care and guidance; and that must have helped me enormously to push on. It could easily have been quite the opposite - family not bothered, teachers not interested, no footy practice - but I was lucky, I got all the right kind of encouragement that any young boy needs to inspire him to do well in any aspect of life. I think that, above all, the biggest break I got was that I was constantly surrounded by good people.

After I'd been playing for Burscough Dynamo for just one season, Tommy Galvin, who did some scouting for a number of teams in the North West, told my parents that he thought I was talented enough to be considered a prospect for signing by one of the bigger clubs. Even though my mum and dad are very grounded people, I suspect that Tommy's statement would still have given them plenty to think about. One thing that they instinctively knew, without any hesitation, was not to say a single word about it to me. So I remained totally oblivious, happily living in my football bubble and loving every minute of it!

**Starting Life as a Schoolboy Player at Liverpool Football Club**

I had no idea about all of the big club talk that had been going on behind the scenes until one Sunday afternoon, after an away match at Formby, when I got changed and went out to meet my dad. He was standing there with a man who I didn't know. It turned out to be Hughie McAuley, a Liverpool FC coach and scout. He introduced himself, told me what he did, then just came straight out with the direct question: 'How would you like to come and train at Liverpool?' After a moment of stunned silence .... I probably couldn't believe my ears .... I eventually managed to blurt out: 'Yeah, definitely. I'd love to.' Dad made some wisecrack about me being an Everton fan and Hughie joked back that it was not a problem as, 'Liverpool would soon get rid of all of that rubbish in my head.' They might have been joking but I was genuinely worried. I can even remember seriously thinking at the time: 'Oh no, what's my brother going to think of me going to Liverpool?'

It was a dream coming true in front of my own eyes but I think I was in a bit of a trance for the next 24-hours.

The reality of the massive opportunity that I'd been given didn't really sink in at all until later that Sunday evening, when we were all at home watching a Liverpool v Everton match on TV. I was sitting in front of the fire, totally absorbed in what was happening in the game, when out of the blue my dad pointed at the screen and just said: 'Heh son, just think, that's the football team who you are going to start training with tomorrow.' Wow .... talk about impact. Tomorrow! Liverpool Football Club! Anfield! The Kop! First training session tomorrow! That single, simple, short statement really thudded into my young brain and jolted me into a full appreciation of this amazing new development that was about to change my life forever. That was when the excitement really kicked in.

Needless to say, I had a very restless time in bed that night. It's difficult for a seven-year old boy to get to sleep when he is busy banging in goals from every angle at Anfield, saluting the roars from the Kop as they chant the name Michael Yates, flinging himself full-stretch for a match-winning diving header at Wembley, then lifting aloft the FA Cup surrounded by his cheering team mates, all proudly wearing that famous all-red strip. So no, not a great amount of rest involved that Sunday night. But bring on Monday afternoon quickly please. I'm going to train with Liverpool Football Club!

In hindsight, it was probably no coincidence that Liverpool invited me to start training just before my eighth birthday. They'd almost certainly been watching me for a while and were just waiting for me to reach the right age to comply with the regulations for signing schoolboys. That might have been a good thing because the particular match that Hughie McAuley had chosen to watch me for the first time had ended up with us getting battered 8 – 1 by a very good Southport team. On the positive side though, I did manage to score a blinder with a direct shot from the halfway line, something that I've always enjoyed trying at every level I have played.

The morning of that first training session with Liverpool gave me some of the most confused and frantic hours of my life. Before going to school I had to pack my kit bag and I didn't have a clue what to take. The packing was easy; it was the picking that was difficult. Do I have to take my boots or my trainers? Or both? Do I have to take my own shirt, shorts and socks? What colour should I wear? Will they give me some gear when I get there? Shin pads? Do I need my own ball? In the end I decided I needed to take a full set of kit just in case. The next problem to deal with was that virtually all of my kit was Everton gear – Everton home, Everton away and Everton third choice shirts. Even my boots were in an Everton bag! It was going to have to be Everton or my school team shirt with the big old-fashioned collar – and there was no chance whatsoever of me turning up in that! I was getting really desperate until my brother reminded me that I had a Real Madrid T-shirt that I'd got on holiday in Spain, so I took that along with some white shorts and socks.

In those days, before the Liverpool FC Academy was opened, the schoolboys trained at either the Vernon Sangster Hall or at Litherland High School, both in the city of Liverpool. I started at Litherland, with other players from areas around where I lived, such as the Southport boys. Steven Gerrard also started training with Liverpool around this same time but he was over at Vernon Sangster. I can remember that very first session quite clearly. My dad drove us there and Tommy Galvin came along as well, to introduce us to the coaching staff. On the way in I was absolutely amazed to see Kenny Dalglish, standing there in his full Liverpool Manager's kit. Kenny Dalglish! I was terrified in case he was going to run my session. As it happened, he was only dropping off his son Paul who was attending a session with one of the older age groups.

*Opposite above: Kenny Dalglish - King Kenny!*
*Opposite below: The Kop*

# Paul Dalglish

*Technical Director of Lonestar Soccer Club and Head Coach of Austin Aztex, Austin Texas, USA; former professional footballer in England and Scotland.*

Young players shouldn't give up on their dreams too soon. Although I was part of the youth systems at both Celtic and Liverpool, I didn't actually make my Premier League debut until I was twenty-one, at Newcastle United. One of my challenges was that I was a late developer. At eighteen I was tiny and still looked like a little boy. So I was one of those young players who needed more time to mature and develop physically.

People often ask me if it was hard for me to live up to the Dalglish name. Being brutally honest, I think it opened some doors for me as I got older but, as soon as those doors were open, I immediately found myself under immense pressure – much more than the other young players around me. No matter how well I played, people still automatically compared me to my dad. Most Liverpool fans rate Kenny Dalglish as the greatest player to ever represent the club, so I could never ever have matched that benchmark.

In the end I suffered a bit of a confidence crisis and found myself slipping out of the game. I stopped playing altogether for about two years. I have to credit Alan Shearer for saving me from myself. I bumped into him at Aintree Race Course and he pulled no punches: 'What's happening to you Paul? You're fat and you look a mess! You were a good young player. Stop messing around and get yourself sorted out before it's too late'.

Mike Newell was there as well and he told me to get fit and come to Luton for pre-season training. So I put my beer down there and then and stopped drinking from that point on.

Most importantly, I stopped blaming everybody else for causing my problems and finally, at age twenty-six, I took full responsibility for my own life. I went to the gym every day, trained hard, improved my diet and started to live right. The benefits were instant and my career was soon back on track.

Alan Shearer telling me the truth was the best thing that ever happened to me.

After I'd really given it my very best shot, if I'd failed I could have accepted it because I couldn't have done any better. But, in the end, I did well. And that made me realize I'd wasted so much time and opportunity when I was younger.

All young players need to fully understand that you only get what you deserve from football – good and bad! Don't blame other people or other factors for your failings, face the honest truth and deal with it. Once you work hard enough to win the battle of 'you v you', then you can be happy and look at yourself in the mirror.

Every player who gets signed on at an academy has talent. What separates the cream from the rest is their attitude and mentality.

Jamie Carragher has got to be the classic example. I have known him since we were nine. He started out as a big, gangly striker, converted to midfield and is now a top class centre-back. He has played over 700 games for Liverpool and he has squeezed every ounce of success out of his body. He had a burning desire to succeed from an early age. He never showed any fear, no situation intimidated him. He has always found a way to succeed at whatever he has been asked to do. Nobody has ever had a better attitude than Jamie Carragher. I have the utmost respect for him.

*Paul Dalglish in his days at Liverpool*

As a coach myself today, it doesn't surprise me to remember that the very first session was all about passing the ball properly. Hughie McAuley ran the session and when it was finished he spoke to my dad and confirmed that they wanted me to keep coming on a regular basis. About two weeks later, at the first session after my birthday, they officially asked me to sign. A mad keen footballer, just turned eight, I was now on a Centre of Excellence contract for the mighty Liverpool. From then on I trained with the club every Monday and Thursday, from 5:00 pm – 6:30 pm; based at Litherland High School for the first two years until I was later moved across to Vernon Sangster.

There were no actual match fixtures for the Centre of Excellence boys in those days. We spent all of our time doing skills training or playing 5-a-side amongst ourselves, to bring whatever we'd learned into an actual playing environment. More often than not the gym would be split in half and two groups of lads would do a different session, usually with Hughie McAuley, Dave Shannon or Steve Heighway himself. The two groups would then swap over and we'd finish off with the 5-a-side games. The biggest challenge in those days at Litherland was a lack of space, which is why they had to split us into groups and some lads would occasionally have to sit out a session until it was their turn. Nowadays, with lots and lots of space at the LFC Academy, all of the kids can be involved all of the time and so get maximum time on the ball. It's so much better that way.

## Introduction to Melwood and a Kid Called Steven Gerrard

By the end of that first season, even though we weren't playing actual games for Liverpool, my life was becoming increasingly occupied by football. I was training at the Centre of Excellence during the week after school, practicing and playing for the school team during the week, while still playing for Dynamo on Saturdays and Sundays. My football dream was now really starting to unfold. No more so than whenever a school holiday came along and we were invited to train two afternoons per week on the grass at Melwood, the hallowed turf of Liverpool's first team training ground. Even though I was too young then to truly appreciate the magnificent history of LFC, and understand what it meant to literally walk in the footsteps of some of the great Liverpool Legends, I can recall being blown away by the quality of the pitches and the general facilities.

*Me and another great young player,*
*Mark Beesley, winning the Trisconi Cup!*

*Me, age 9 & Steve Heighway*

*Me, age 9 training at Melwood*

I can also remember arriving at Melwood early one afternoon, walking into what I thought was an empty changing room, tossing my bag onto the bench, turning around to rush back outside and literally bumping into what felt like a brick wall. It was John Barnes! And he was huge. John Barnes .... a colossus on the pitch and a giant off it! I panicked, mumbled a bit of an apology and legged it as fast as I could out of there. Once I'd managed to catch my breath and calm down though, it soon became a different story. By then I had convinced myself that I had 'met' John Barnes and that's what I told the other lads when they arrived. Fortunately for me, John Barnes would crop up again at various later stages of my football life. He has always been a very positive influence on my development.

One of the other things that really sticks out in my mind about those early days at Melwood is the famous Shankly 'sweat box' and the boards with all the numbers on that were used for passing and shooting practice. If you had a ball at your feet when you passed by those boards and nobody was using them it was just impossible not to fire a shot at them and try to hit a number. I literally could have spent hours there if they'd let me. As I understand it, the great Liverpool manager Bill Shankly designed this facility as a way to develop and improve rapid and accurate passing skills, quick reactions, good endurance and the ability to accurately hit the target at the end of a fast-paced, physically demanding period of play. The coach would call out a series of random numbers and the player would have to turn and shoot at the correct target each time. There was even a line across the boards, about a quarter of the way up, which I suppose was also used to practice passing the ball directly to feet. Former players like Phil Neal have told me stories about just how tough those 'sweat box' sessions used to be. As youngsters we never used the boxes like that but we did play 5-a-sides on them. Later in life, I also used them to do rehabilitation work alongside first team players like Patrick Berger. Those Shankly boards have now been dismantled.

While I was hugely impressed by Melwood, the thing that really made by far the biggest impression on me was the day that I first came into contact with Steven Gerrard. Our football paths had never crossed before because he was from Huyton, a different area of Liverpool to me, and so he had been training with the Centre of Excellence at Vernon Sangster while I was at Litherland. Even though we were only eight, by the end of the season I'd already heard a few stories about this lad Steven Gerrard and how good a player he was. When we actually met for the first time at Melwood, I can remember straight away thinking that there was just something about him, something different to the rest of the kids. Later, when we all got changed and went outside and I first saw him strike a ball, I then knew for sure that there was definitely something special about him.

Just before we started playing an 11-a-side game on the B pitch, Steve Heighway sat us all down to give us instructions, including announcing who would be each player's opposite number. As the coach gradually worked his way through the list of names, my eyebrows must have shot up when I heard the words: 'Steven Gerrard, I want you to mark man-to-man on Michael Yates.' OK, no problem. As we kicked off I was actually looking forward to the challenge. Even though I'd heard he was a good player, I was full of confidence because I'd become accustomed to scoring goals whenever I played, regardless of whoever I was playing against, and I'd already enjoyed a fair amount of success. Truthfully, up until that point I hadn't come across anybody who could stop me scoring. But by the time that game was over I knew that I'd just entered a brand new world; a tougher, more demanding world with a whole new set of higher standards to be achieved and harsher challenges to be met.

From the very first contact, Steven made it abundantly clear to me that he was only interested in one outcome for our personal battle, that he was going to win it and prove that he was a better player than me. Steven ran me ragged. He hit me hard with every tackle, he held me down for headers, he kicked me, he tripped me, he pulled my shirt, he did whatever was necessary to stop me playing. That was a real shock to my system. It was the first time that I'd ever played against somebody who simply drove himself relentlessly to victory and even knew how to use a few tricks of the trade to help him get there. Before Steven, I had never come across any player who had grabbed my shirt or bib to stop me getting to a ball before him. And if there was any 50/50 ball to be won there was only ever going to be one winner. Plus he had loads of ability and could play. In every sense of the word, it was a real education for me.

That experience of being marked one-on-one by Steven Gerrard became my first big lesson in football and totally opened my eyes to what real competition was all about.

Nowadays whenever I watch Steven play and hear people's comments about how his incredible determination has done so much to help Liverpool win so many lost causes, including that legendary night in

Istanbul, it always makes me think back to that very first time I came across him at Melwood. He was only a boy then but he already had that iron resolve and unstoppable drive. Significantly, it wasn't just me and the other kids who could see that he was going to be a winner; it was blatantly obvious that he himself knew it too. As early as age eight, Steven Gerrard already had the power and courage of total self-conviction.

In retrospect, it's now easy for me to think that Steve Heighway knew exactly what he was doing when he chose Steven Gerrard to mark me in that match, because he would have known for sure that I had never ever played against anybody like him. He probably thought it would be a good wake-up call for me, as well as a solid test of my own character and commitment.

Steve Heighway knew both of us as players and he also knew we were from different social backgrounds. I grew up in the rural village of Burscough, in a comfortable middle class environment, while Steven was born and raised in the much tougher, working class Blue Bell Estate in Huyton, an area that has produced a long list of professional footballers. There is no doubt that at age eight I would have been a bit on the naive side and generally accustomed to playing against 'nice kids' on good, grassy pitches. Steven, on the other hand, would have already experienced having to fight his way through many of the football games he found himself playing in; often in the street or on rough ground and usually against older and bigger kids who were ever willing to knock him about if required.

The steely backbone in Steven Gerrard the footballer was first forged in the heat of matches battled out on the Blue Bell Estate. From day one in football he had to learn to deal with physical contact and aggression as an everyday part of the game. So when I got such a big shock that first time I faced Steven, with his aggressive style that I'd never come across before, he actually would have just been playing his normal game. This strong competitive element was clearly something that I now needed to add to my character.

*Opposite: Man of steel ...*

Photo courtesy of Liverpool FC via Getty Images

# Tom Culshaw

*LFC Academy Elite Coach, former Liverpool Reserve Team captain and Lilleshall graduate*

I have known Steven Gerrard ever since we were born. We both grew up on the Bluebell Estate in Huyton and played most of our early football in the little square in front of Steven's house on Ironside Road. Later on we both played for the same junior team. I was a year younger than the other kids in our squad but Stevie was so good he was playing two years above his own age group! At age eight, around the same time that he was signed on by Liverpool, I joined Everton. When they let me go at ten I moved across to Tranmere Rovers and was soon made captain of the Liverpool City Schoolboys team. Within a year, Liverpool FC moved in for me and I was happy to join Steven at the Vernon Sangster Centre of Excellence.

For my last two years of secondary school I was invited to attend the F.A.'s National School at Lilleshall. When I went there Jamie Carragher was in the year above me and when I was in my final year Michael Owen was in the age group below me. I really enjoyed that Lilleshall experience and it gave me a good platform start my YTS years at Liverpool.

The club gave me a professional contact at seventeen. I played regularly for the Reserves and things went well for me under Roy Evans and Sammy Lee. By the time I was made captain of the Reserves and was going for nights out with first team players, who were now my mates, I really started to believe that I was there. Unfortunately, when Gerard Houllier took over, he brought in a new regime and I found myself being pushed out by more and more foreign players. In the end I was released.

*Tom Culshaw with goalkeeper Ian Dunbavin*

That really knocked the heart out of me. From the time I was just a little kid, my dream had always been to be a professional footballer and get to play at Goodison Park, Anfield and Wembley. I achieved all of those targets but never made the big one – I never played first team football for Liverpool.

When you get as close as I did, it comes as a huge shock when you are let go. Especially when, as in my case, I felt that I was playing better than some of the fringe players in first team squad. It seemed to me that their places were safe because they'd already crossed the line, not because they were better players than me. That's very tough to deal with. The reality is it's not good enough to just be a very good player; you have to be truly exceptional.

Of course, I tried to make it at other clubs but playing football was never the same again for me. I'd been spoiled at Lilleshall and I'd been spoiled at Liverpool. After those wonderful experiences I wasn't able to maintain my enthusiasm elsewhere, so my career gradually lost momentum. Eventually I drifted out of the game. So much so that I stopped playing altogether. At the age of twenty-two, I couldn't even watch a match on TV! This is very hard for any youngster to handle. Some of my mates ended up with drinking problems and other issues after being let go.

Today I have enormous respect for any players who get released and then manage to make a successful comeback. Steven's cousin, Anthony Gerrard, is a good example of that. He was released by Everton but kept going and he has since enjoyed a good career as a professional, even playing for Cardiff in the 2012 League Cup Final against Liverpool.

Looking back on it now, I can see that I took the rejection too personally, so I didn't have the sense to see straight. I should have pushed myself to keep on playing or find some other way to stay in the game. But at that awkward age you think you know everything, which of course is completely wrong.

After drifting along for a while, working with some of my mates who had their own business, I finally started listening to the sensible people who were encouraging me to get back into football where I belonged. Steven gave me plenty of encouragement and helped me a lot mentally. In the end I started doing some coaching work with English kids in Spain and that was my first step towards returning to football full-time.

Now that I am back at Liverpool, the club that I love, I am really enjoying my life as a coach. I know that I can give a lot to the current crop of young players because I've been there myself and can share all my knowledge with them. There are certain qualities you can't teach a player, you can only describe them. So it's powerful that I can call upon my personal experience and tell them about the young Steven Gerrard: the kid who'd do slide tackles on the gravel road outside his house; the kid who wanted to win every game he ever played, including sock-ball in the dressing rooms; the kid who could have played in any position on the team; the kid who had enough mental strength and ambition to one day outboss Patrick Viera and Roy Keane.

The kind of kid who becomes a great player.

## Making Good Progress as Michael Owen Bursts Onto the Scene

Looking back on those first few years at the Centre of Excellence, while I was totally impressed with Steven Gerrard and also rated some of the other lads, I can't remember being overshadowed by anybody, which seems to suggest that I was more than holding my own as a player. I was certainly scoring lots of goals and I felt very much at home and comfortable in that environment. I knew I belonged there on merit and I truly enjoyed playing with those better quality players. It was so much more advanced than playing for the school or Dynamo because there were other players of the same level of ability who knew how to play properly. They could zip in a pass, they knew how and when to release the ball and they understood positional play better. Playing with Dynamo there would be lots of running around all over the place but with Liverpool we were taught how and where to operate on the pitch, with a better sense of structure and more defined roles. My job was to score goals and I just absolutely loved that idea. Give me the chances and I'll bang them in for you! It was great. I was happy, I wanted to do well, I wanted to impress.

One early report from Steve Heighway praised my technical ability but said that I'd still always be judged by my capacity to score goals. So I just kept on scoring goals. Another report mentioned that I needed some extra pace. So my dad went out and bought some rope and an old tyre so I could work at home to try to improve the strength in my legs. Whatever was asked of me I tried my hardest to give – and more!

Despite my overall good performance, after each year of training and the summer session at Melwood had finished, I always seemed to find myself a bag of nerves wondering if I'd get signed on again for the following year. Even when I was called into the office and told, 'Well done son, you had a really good year, see you at Certificate Night', I'd still be terrified that I wouldn't get re-signed. This didn't really make sense at the time, and it certainly doesn't make sense now, because I knew I was doing well. The coaches often praised me and regularly picked me to demonstrate the right techniques. I can remember a really good example when Steve Heighway asked me to demo a long pass, the kind that has enough back spin that it just drops into the targeted player or area. He wanted me to find him with a pass over a distance of about 45-yards: 'Right, come on then Yates, find me. Hit the right nipple preferably.' And I did, bang on the button!

*Frank Skelly looks on as I dream of lifting this one day for real!*

*This is the best club in the world ...*

Even though the coaches generally reassured me about my progress, there was still some concern deep down inside me, some nagging inner fear. After the Certificate Night the club would send us a letter in the post letting us know whether we'd been invited back for the following season. That week or two's wait for the postman was always an absolute nightmare for me because I couldn't stop myself fearing the worst. I suspect that it was simply a case of me wanting it so badly that I was petrified to be turned down. I loved what I was doing so much that the mere thought of losing it sent me into a nervous spin of lingering doubt.

Needless to say, when those letters did arrive year after year, inviting me back to Liverpool the following season, there was no happier person in the world than me. My dream was to play for Liverpool Football Club and with each passing year I was getting closer and closer to fulfilling that dream. Bring on the next season!

My first encounter with Michael Owen came in 1991 when he was selected to play his first game for our Liverpool under-11 side, against a Welsh Select XI. I can remember that it was a rainy day and we played on the B Team pitch. When that Welsh Select XI arrived at Melwood they brought with them a fantastic reputation as a very strong team that hadn't been defeated for over a year. It's a sign of how good a side we had at Liverpool in those days that we absolutely thrashed them. I actually think the score was 11 – 1 in the end.

It was the first time Michael and I ever played upfront together as strike partners and, as usual, I scored a couple of goals but Michael immediately made a huge impact by scoring four or five. I know for sure that he scored more than me because that immediately set off all the alarm bells ringing in my head. Keep in mind that before Michael Owen came along I had always been the #1 striker on our Liverpool team. So all of a sudden I had another new challenge, a battle to keep my place! I had been scoring loads of goals for Liverpool for a few years and then along came this new lad to play his first game for us and he banged in a bag full and amazed everybody with his electrifying pace. It was all the more impressive because before the game there had been a lot of buzz going on around him – partly because some of our coaches obviously knew about him but also because a lot of the Welsh lads had already come up against him in school football. In fact, that same year, Michael broke Ian Rush's seemingly unbeatable goal scoring record for Deeside Primary Schools in North Wales when he netted 92 goals in about thirty games. But what a player!

Just like when Stevie G. first arrived on the scene, you could see straight away that Michael was something very, very special indeed.

I think that Michael had been trialling at other clubs before coming to Liverpool, without wanting to commit to anybody. But the fact that we produced such a classy and dominant performance against a really good Wales team, seemed to convince him, and obviously his dad as well, that Liverpool had the best facilities, best coaches and a very strong squad. By then our team had a nucleus of really good young players: Ian Dunbavin in goal, who still plays for Accrington Stanley; Neil Murphy, who played at right back, and became a pro with Blackpool; at left back we had Mattie Cass or Michael Ball, who went on to play for Everton and Rangers; Stephen Wright played centre back and was always very solid and mentally very strong from a young age and he went on to play for Liverpool; Layton Maxwell was a well-built lad and a powerful presence in midfield, who also played for Liverpool; Jason Koumas, who was a great passer of the ball, always able to find players when they made a run, and he eventually played for Tranmere, West Brom and Wales; Richie Partridge, a really fast right winger who went on to play for Liverpool and a few other clubs (and married Michael Owen's sister); Mike Garrity (who is now a coach at the LFC Academy); Gareth Evans, a midfielder who went on to coach at LFC; plus Stevie G of course, weaving his magic and driving the team forward; and finally me up front, happily taking whatever chances I could, banging in goals all over the place. So when Michael Owen joined that very strong side then it just became even stronger.

Looking back to those days I know that we played some brilliant football on that team. In the end we earned ourselves the nickname 'The Dream Team' and we were the first, probably the only, group that Steve Heighway took charge of himself every year, moving through all the age groups with us, instead of just sticking with one age group like he normally did. Sometimes one of the other coaches would run a session but Steve would always be there in the background, keeping an eye on things. He also watched all of our matches, including Sunday games, all the way from the under-11s through to the YTS years when we reached sixteen. This was very unusual and, when you remember that Steve Heighway was the Head of the Centre of Excellence and then the Director of the Academy when it was started, it really shows how very much he and Liverpool valued that particular squad.

## Mike does battle for Burscough

Dynamo's Michael Yates took his personal goal tally to over the 50 mark in his team's 10-1 win against Deansgate. Yates netted five times, with Phil Miller (2), Mark Beesley (2), and Joseph Taylor adding to the score. In the Under 13s Rufford Colts re-claimed top place when they beat second placed Formby 4-2.

Neil O'Farrell's Craven B...

## Michael blasts cup warning

THE Southport Craven Minor League under 12 representative team continued their progress in the Liverpool County FA inter-league competition with an impressive 5-0 victory over the Skelmersdale League.

Michael Yates scored four of the goals and had an outstanding match. Stuart Clare scored the other goal.

In the Under 10s ... Yates ...

### RESULTS

**Under 10s:** Ainsdale 2, Ormskirk 1; Birkdale 8, Holborn 0; Formby 4, Dynamo 3; St Patrick 2, Alexandra 3; Hesketh 2, Rufford 8; Town Green 4, Deansgate 3; YMCA 0, SP Trinity 3.

**Under 11s:** Formby 5, Dynamo 4; Ormskirk 11, Deansgate 4; Rufford 5, Hesketh C 1; SP Trinity 1, Birkdale 6; YMCA 8, Mawdesley 0.

**Under 12s:** Rufford 11, Deansgate 0; Holborn 5, Hesketh 0; Ainsdale 3, Ormskirk 2.

**Under 13s:** Hesketh C 2, Rufford 5; Red Star 2, Dynamo 3; Redgate 5, YMCA 1; Holborn 4, Ainsdale 0; SP Trinity 6, Deansgate 0; Town Green 5, Birkdale 2.

**Under 14s:** YMCA 3, Ormskirk 3; Aabacas 1, Crosby St 7; Dynamo 2, Birkdale 1; Stuart Junior 2, Town Green 3.

**Under 15s:** Dynamo 2, Town Green 6; Ormskirk 4, SP Trinity ...

## Yates notches No.50

TWO goals from Craven Minor League Birkdale United's under 10 ace Glen Crowder and one apiece from Peter Clarke and Steven Miles secured the points by beating Ormskirk West End 4-0.

A hat-trick from Mark Blakey and two from Paul Docherty helped Formby J.S.C. to an outstanding 10-0 win over a luckless Hesketh Bank.

A goal from Deansgate under 10's Andrew Hall couldn't stop Dynamo beating them 6-1.

At under 11, Ormskirk W.E. overwhelmed Ainsdale 10-1 with four goals each from Mike McGinn and Neil Ramsden, John Armstrong and Lee Shirley also scoring.

Rufford Colts (Steven Warwick 4, William ...

... two and securing the points for his team in their 3-4 win over table leaders and previously unbeaten Formby J.S.C.

Gareth Simpson and Mark Beesley also scored for Dynamo whilst Formby's scorers were James Houlihan, Stuart Morton and Paul Duffy.

### JUNIOR SOCCER

In the same division Holborn Boys (Matthew Fagan) drew 1-1 with Ainsdale.

A Robert Lawler goal and excellent performances by Steve Leggett and Wayne Rimmer put Birkdale United's under 14 side in the final of the Langfield Trophy with a ...

... Crosby Stuart side.

**Under 10**
Ormskirk 0 Birkdale 4, Sp. Trinity 2 Hesketh C 1, YMCA 1 Rufford 0, Formby 10 Hesketh 0, Dynamo 6 Deansgate 1, Ainsdale 6 St. Patrick 1.

**Under 11**
Deansgate 0 YMCA 1, Dynamo 12 Hesketh C 1, Formby 1 Birkdale 2, Ormskirk 10 Ainsdale 1, Rufford 11 Mawdesley 0, Southport Trinity 5 Town Green 2.

**Under 12**
Holborn 1 Ainsdale 1, Ormskirk 15 Hesketh C 5, Birkdale 4 Town Green 0, Rufford 2 Southport Trinity 3, Formby 3 Dynamo 4.

**Under 13**
YMCA 2 Redgate 4. Hes-ket ...

## Goal king Yates runs riot

MICHAEL YATES scored six for Dynamo in their 18-2 win against Ormskirk West End in the Craven Minor League under-13 division, John Peckham (3), Gareth Simpson (3), Mark Beesley (2), Joe Taylor (2), Glynn Forshaw and Mike Hawksby also netting.

Rufford (Ryan Bell 2, Kevin Leadbetter, Mike Roe) won 4-0 against Town Green and Holborn Boys (Stuart Wright 5, Ian Granite 4, Danny Ritchie 2, Ian Savage, Barry Leadbetter) won 13-0 against Hesketh CC.

Under-11: Ainsdale 2, Ormskirk 0; YMCA 2, Southport Trinity 2.
Under-13: Redgate 2, Birkdale 2; Southport Trinity 8, YMCA 2.
Under-15: Birkdale 3, Ormskirk 0; Dynamo 0, Southport Trinity 1; YMCA 2, Aabacas 2.
Under-10: Ainsdale 4, Dynamo 1; Ormskirk 7, Hesketh Bank 4.
Under-12: Formby JSC 5, Town Green 3; Hesketh CC 2, Southport Trinity 8; Rufford 1, Ainsdale 4; Birkdale 3, Ormskirk 1.
Under-14: Birkdale 3, Town Green 0; YMCA 1, Redgate 4; Crosby Stuart 5, Rufford 1.

LED superbly by Joe Cain, Boundary chalked ...

... up a thrilling 2-1 success against Playhouse (Spike) in the Edge Hill Junior League under-13 division Trophy tussle, Terry Smith and Ronnie Lloyd hitting the target.

ANFIELD Junior League under-13 division leaders Oakfield had to battle hard for their single goal success over Anfield, Steve Thompson scoring.

BRUNEL won 5-0 against Orrys in a cracking Scotland Road Junior League Under 11 Everton Park Cup clash, Williamson scored four and Williams adding the fifth.

OLD XAVS pegged back Wavertree Youth Alliance Under 18 leaders Arthur 5-2 to narrow the gap ...

## UNDER 13s

**MANAGER:** George Bond.
**ASSISTANT:** Alec Blakeman
**SQUAD:**
Stephen Huyton, Carl Johnson, Michael Yates, Glyn Forshaw, Mark Beesley, John Penkman, Joe Taylor, Gareth Simpson, Mark Nolan, Chris Trotter, Ian Luya, Philip Simpson, Joe Carroll, Liam Kershaw, Michael Hawksby, Danny Blessington, Stuart Pennington, Anthony Stafford, Philip Miller

**HONOURS:**
Mahood Cup; Easter Festival of Football national winners, Bognor.

**MANAGER'S REPORT:**

George and Alec would like to thank all the boys for a great season. In the finals played at Bognor Regis and at Burscough FC's ground the boys played fantastic.

Just a special thanks to Michael Yates, who has been with me since he was under nine, for the great goals that he has scored during that time. I am sure that one day we will see him presenting the trophies to the boys.

**TOP GOALSCORER:**
Michael Yates (56 goals).
**Manager's Player** of the Year:
Chris Trotter
**Players' Player** of the Year:
Chris Trotter
**Most Improved** player:
Mark Nolan

### TABLE

Under 13s

| | Team | PLD | W | D | L | Pt |
|---|---|---|---|---|---|---|
| 1 | Lmd Jub | 24 | 22 | 1 | 1 | 45 |
| 2 | Rufford | 24 | 21 | 0 | 3 | 42 |
| 3 | Dynamo | 24 | 17 | 2 | 5 | 36 |
| 4 | Tn Grn | 24 | 14 | 0 | 10 | 28 |
| 5 | Holborn | 24 | 12 | 2 | 10 | 26 |
| 6 | Redgate | 24 | 11 | 3 | 10 | 25 |
| 7 | Birkdale | 24 | 10 | 3 | 11 | 23 |
| 8 | Ainsdale | 24 | 10 | 2 | 12 | 22 |
| 9 | Formby | 24 | 8 | 5 | 11 | 21 |
| 10 | YMCA | 24 | 9 | 1 | 14 | 19 |
| 11 | Spt Tr | 24 | 6 | 2 | 14 | 18 |
| 12 | Dsm Wl | 24 | 3 | 1 | 20 | 7 |
| 13 | Hesk | 24 | 0 | 0 | 24 | 0 |

# Frank McParland

*Academy Director, Liverpool Football Club*

I have been a Liverpool supporter all my life. I was at Wembley as a fan in 1974, when Shankly's side beat Newcastle 3-0, and I was there as a member of staff in Dortmund and Istanbul. Great days, great wins. But here at the Academy it's not necessarily all about winning. The most important thing is about getting the players through to Melwood. We're helping them to grow up, training them for life really. We don't just want good footballers; we want good, well-rounded individuals.

So much has changed at Academy level since I was a young lad. In my day there were one or two kids in the city who were at Liverpool or Everton, but it was very rare that you knew anyone who was actually in the game. It was much more elite in those days. There were a lot of very good players back then who did not get near playing for Liverpool when they could have been stars.

Nowadays we have to watch thousands of young players. Everton and Manchester United do the same. If you don't do it, then when it comes to the time you can sign a player, at nine, you won't know who the best ones are and they could end up signing for other clubs.

Football today is a global business and that starts at the academy level. We've got probably over sixty staff in our Academy, full and part time. We've got scouts who go out and search for talent. We've even got five analysts, just for the Academy, looking at the way the kids play and develop.

We start studying players from as early as five. At that age you are looking for someone who stands out in terms of co-ordination, who is very quick or very athletic. As they get older, talent and ability are the obvious first points of attraction; but we also want a winning mentality, a strong character - someone who can stamp their personality on a game.

Our number one aim is to get as many local, Scouse kids into the first team as possible. In the meantime, we are going to continue to bring the best players in England and from abroad to Liverpool.

Brendan Rodgers gives fantastic support to the young players - that's evident with who has figured in the first team this season. We've had six academy players involved so far, not including Raheem Sterling as he was involved last year. And when we see the likes of Sterling, Suso and

*Frank McParland*

Wisdom playing first-team games, it's fantastic. The best moment for me personally came during my first year back at the club, when Jack Robinson came on at Hull to make his debut at age sixteen. It was one of the most memorable occasions of my entire career.

On the flip side of the coin, the hardest part of my job is having to release players, telling someone that we are letting them go. Whether it's a nine year-old or a nineteen year-old, it always leaves me with a very heavy heart.

That is definitely the toughest thing I ever have to do.

## Playing Alongside the Steven Gerrard and Michael Owen Combination

It was a massive coup for Liverpool to sign Michael Owen for the Centre of Excellence and the best news about all of that for me was that I didn't lose my place! On the contrary, they played Michael and me upfront together as strike partners. I don't suppose he remembers this as much as I do but before each game started, just as we were about to kick-off, he'd always turn to me and say: 'Come on partner, let's go to work.' It was a compliment to me that Michael was always happy if we were selected to play alongside each other in any kind of match. I guess he knew my game, I knew his game, we understood each other and we both knew how to gel effectively to score goals.

Although Michael Owen was a relatively small lad he was still very strong. He was also extremely determined and equipped with an incredible ability to bounce back up off the floor. Even when running at top speed, with bigger defenders trying to knock him off balance, he had this uncanny ability to come out the other side of the tackle on his feet and with the ball under control. As well as making the most of the good service he got from the midfield players, he could also make lots of chances for himself out of nothing. And he was always a very cool finisher. Before games he didn't just think he was going to score, he knew he was. And whenever he didn't score he was totally gutted.

I remember his dad, Terry Owen, who had played professional football, teaching him how to swap around the studs on his boots, so he could be faster off the mark in a sprint for the ball. Instead of having just two long studs at the back of the boot, he'd replace the two short studs in the middle with two more long ones, to get the extra purchase on the grass when pushing off. It must have worked because nobody could beat him for pace over the first few yards. Funnily enough, I can also remember that Terry used to clean Michael's boots for him, which would have stood out in my mind because I was so manically obsessive about cleaning my own boots. It wasn't just that I was being particularly fussy about my boots, it was actually part of my pre-match ritual, one of the ways that I'd think about the job ahead and prepare myself mentally.

Steven Gerrard was another one who always made sure his boots were totally spotless. The very first thing he'd do when he got into the dressing room after a game would be to slip off his boots and start scraping the mud off the bottom. I can still visualize him sitting there for ages cleaning

*Age 12 with Graeme Souness*

*One of my first games at Melwood, played on 'the pigs'. Me in the front row in the blue top and Stevie G fifth from right in the middle row.*

them with a sock, even the soles underneath, making sure that no bits of grass were stuck around the studs. He was like that with his trainers too. Any time they had any kind of mark that he couldn't scrub off then he'd get a new pair. So, as you can imagine, he had lots of trainers! You could also say that was yet another of his many positive attributes, his pride in his kit and his own appearance.

Whenever Steven and Michael were both playing on the same team then it was instant carnage. The two of them played so brilliantly together that they literally tore opposing teams to shreds. Even from the very beginning, from as early as age eleven, their awareness of each other on the pitch was phenomenal. They were both totally on the same wavelength. As soon as Steven picked up the ball in midfield he would instinctively know where Michael was; Michael would instantly start his run and Steven would automatically slot the ball into the right space. As a coach today I often find myself saying 'the best players make the best decisions', and I saw that happen time and time again over the years from the Gerrard-Owen combination. It was really incredible link-up play by any standards. Having said that, I can also remember Steven threading the ball through to me a lot too, with me then converting the chances into goals. It really was a fantastic experience to play in that side. I never felt phased by the idea of playing in the same team as these two fantastic players; quite the opposite, I relished it. That was what I loved most in life, not only playing football but also actually playing it at a very high standard. It was exhilarating and I couldn't get enough!

Interestingly, I have a video recording of a match that the three of us played in together for Liverpool when we were about eleven: and for one of the goals Steven picks up the ball in the right centre of the pitch, hits it first time towards the box, right into the path of Michael's early run, who then goes on to smack it past the keeper. Great goal! Now fast-forward about ten years to 2001 in Munich .... yes, that memorable night when England beat Germany 5 -1 .... and have a look at the third goal of Michael's fantastic hat-trick. Exactly the same story, same sequence of play – and same result! If you play the video clips of those two goals side by side on the same screen the similarity is uncanny. The sequences of play are almost identical. The only real differences are the age and size of the two players involved, plus the importance of the occasion of course! And

*Opposite above: Michael Owen • Opposite below: Steven Gerrard*

Photos courtesy of Liverpool FC via Getty Images

what a brilliant night that was for the whole of England but, if I am allowed to be a bit selfish, especially Liverpool with Stevie G and Emile Heskey also scoring.

From day one, Michael Owen demonstrated the same sort of ruthless streak as Steven Gerrard. He was able to zone in on the job at hand and do whatever was necessary to come out on top and win. Off the pitch he was an easy-going lad who enjoyed a joke or two, but on the pitch he was a totally different person; very focused, with that same steely determination that typified Steven. If Michael went in for a 50/50 tackle you knew he was going to win it. In fact he was totally fearless going into any kind of tackle, even when the odds were stacked against him. And when we were anywhere around the box he was always a man on a mission – he had to score, even if it meant him shooting from a ridiculously tight angle instead of laying it back for me for an easy tap-in. In a situation like that, whenever somebody tried to score himself instead of passing to a team-mate in a better position, our coaches, all of them from Ronnie Moran down, would always ask if we'd seen the other player. If you answered yes, then they'd just say OK. But if you admitted that you hadn't been aware of the easier chance then there was hell to pay!

I always loved to score goals but Michael was truly obsessed. I'd like to think that I created a lot of chances for him but it rarely worked the other way around. However, that ambitious, selfish streak was part of his character as a young player and it certainly worked in his favour in those days. Of course as he got older the coaches encouraged him to be more aware of the other players around him and to release the ball if one of his teammates had a better chance to score. But, throughout his entire career, Michael has been a great goal scorer and all great goal scorers thrive on being a bit selfish; that deep seated hunger to be the one who bangs the ball into the back of the net. A good example of that would have to be his amazing, solo 'wonder goal' against Argentina in the 1998 World Cup in France. After he'd pulled off a clever, first time flick of the ball to get past the first defender and then raced away towards the goal with that terrific burst of lightning speed, there was a brief moment just on the edge of the box when, as he jinked to the right of a second defender, Paul Scholes looked as though he was thinking about taking the ball on himself. But no way was Michael Owen going to let that happen, not for anybody. He just powered in front of Scholes and smacked it back across the keeper into the far side of the net. Absolutely brilliant! The run was breathtaking and the finish was clinical. As described by the TV commentator at the time: 'Oh that's a wonderful goal. What an amazing moment in Michael Owen's young career. A fantastic run that cracked the Argentinians and a most unerring finish.' What a goal that was! And I'd seen that side of Michael's game so often when we were kids.

### Exciting Times From Under-12 to Under-14

From the under-12 year onwards, as well as still training for ninety minutes twice per week, the Centre of Excellence also introduced some scheduled games. We played on Sundays against other Centre of Excellence teams, such as Manchester United, Manchester City, Birmingham City, Wolves, Wigan, Crewe, Tranmere Rovers and as far away as Carlisle. Those games not only gave us the good exposure of playing against other kids but also allowed us to see the other clubs' facilities. We quite naturally compared them to Liverpool and quickly realized just how lucky we were to be with the club. We knew we were privileged to be able to pull on that famous red shirt and train and play in such top class conditions. The other thing that drove home the message about how fortunate we were to be with Liverpool was to experience first hand just how badly those other clubs wanted to beat our team – simply because of who we were. For every other team, when they played Liverpool that was the highlight of their year, that was their cup final! And all those lads, especially the ones playing for the likes of Tranmere and Carlisle, really wanted to be in our place: they wanted some of that for themselves. So they were desperate to beat us to try and show how good they were, at both the team and the individual level. No surprise then that those games used to be very intense, 100 mph stuff straight from the kick-off, non-stop running, a bite in every tackle and twenty-two young kids pushing themselves to their limit. That extra competitive edge was definitely good for us and kept us on our toes no matter who we were playing against.

To counteract that fired-up aggression from opposing teams, our own coaches never stopped reminding us that once we were wearing that Liverpool badge then we had a responsibility to protect its good name and nothing but our very best would be acceptable. They would tell us to first of all respect ourselves and then respect the opposition; start the game working hard enough to match their commitment and then gradually let

*Me upended, with Steven Gerrard about to win the ball in the background!*

*Versus Wigan under-14's*

*Me and Michael Owen versus Leeds under-12's*

*Me and my strike partner MO ... he wasn't bad!*

our football ability take over. The critical message the coaches were drilling into our young brains was that we couldn't just expect to turn up and win; we had to fight to earn the right to prove that we were a better team. As a rule, once we'd been playing a while and the match had settled into a proper rhythm, the extra talent and technical ability that we had on our team would inevitably take control and we'd come out on top. I can't remember us ever getting beaten by anybody between the under-11 and under-15 age groups, not once. It wasn't until we reached the under-16s and things started to level off that we might have been beaten a couple of times by teams like the England national squad and Manchester United. But, even against teams of that calibre, those losses were very rare.

As much as we all loved those early years at the Centre of Excellence, or over at Melwood in the holidays, I can remember that we all kept unusually quiet in the dressing room before the sessions started. I suspect that it was mainly because as well as being excited we were all a bit nervous. As soon as we arrived we were supposed to write our names on a sheet of paper on the notice board to show that we were there, plus make a note of our preferred position. The coaches would then use that list to pick two teams. And while we sat there waiting, there'd only be a couple of lads who'd actually be doing any talking; usually kids who knew each other from school or were old mates. Other than that, the only noise would be bags being dropped on the floor or the sound of studs clicking on the tiles. It was eerily quiet really. Steve Heighway used to walk in and try to crack some corny joke to break the tension: 'Hello lads, I didn't know there was a funeral here today.' On match days Steve would often ask if any of us were nervous and if anybody was brave enough to put their hand up he'd say: 'Well done son. Being nervous proves that you care and that it's important to you to do well. I like that!'

Don't get me wrong though, we had a great group of lads and it wasn't a bad dressing room. It was more that we were all so keen to do well that we found it hard to relax before we went out onto the pitch. It wasn't until we reached the age of about fourteen and felt much more settled and secure in the squad that all the laughing and joking started. But when the banter did eventually kick in it was absolutely brilliant. That same bunch of so-called quiet lads suddenly transformed into a bunch of mad pranksters, razor sharp comedians and ruthless piss-takers.

Nowadays the dressing rooms full of kids that age are completely different to our generation. The kids today are not shy in any way; in fact they are so lively we have a struggle to get them to calm down. To be honest, I don't think that this is because the kids themselves are any different to what we were. It's not that they are any more extroverted or confident or even badly behaved, I think it actually boils down to good old-fashioned respect. In our day, as kids at Liverpool, especially Melwood where the first team trained, we were simply in awe of the people around us, as well as the surroundings. We were at Liverpool Football Club and we were constantly reminded about what that meant. We were mere midgets in a land of giants and we knew our place; and our place was to keep quiet and be respectful to everybody and everything around us and to focus on the job at hand. Somehow, these days, that sense of natural respect seems to have been completely lost somewhere within the realms of the so-called progress of modern society. The natural behaviour and tendencies of the kids today are no different to our generation of schoolboy footballers; it is the acceptable standards within everyday life that have changed.

There again, the different attitudes of the lads today might also be a reflection of the fact that today's schoolboys and youth players are all based at the Academy and generally only come into contact with each other. Whereas when we had the chance to train at Melwood, even at the age of eleven, we were immediately immersed into the very real world of first team professional football at one of the game's most successful and iconic clubs. Believe me, it was very easy to feel respectful under those circumstances just by being privileged enough to be there in the first place; but when you add to the already potent mix the fact that quite regularly we came into contact with Graham Souness or Roy Evans, whoever was manager at the time, Sammy Lee the first team coach, as well as first team players who were our idols, then it is easy to understand why we all kept our heads down and worked hard to impress!

During the under-12 season Michael Owen and I played up front together in just about every game. Steven Gerrard missed quite a few matches that year because he had a lot of trouble with his knees, due to Osgood-Schlatter disease that is quite common in growing boys. Plus he had a bad accident when he stood on a rusty spike playing in a game by his house and that kept him out for a while. He nearly lost his toe because of that injury. What an absolute tragedy that could have been!

I can still vividly remember our first under-12 game, which we won 4 – 1 against Tranmere. Michael and Steven both scored a goal each and

I managed to get two. The reason that game really sticks out in my mind to this day is that we got a penalty early on, when we were 1- 0 down. I made sure that I grabbed the ball quickly so that I could take the penalty myself. Which is amazing really because I know that Michael would have wanted it for himself, so I must have been off the mark really fast to get to the ball before he did. Then I missed it. Shit! A bit later we got a second penalty and this time Jason Koumas came running over to take it because I'd missed the first one. But no way, I wasn't having any of that. I clung on to that ball and point blank refused to let him have it. It was precisely because I had missed the first one that I now absolutely had to take the second one, so I could put it in the back of the net and prove that the miss was a fluke. Jason still had other ideas though and he tried to rip the ball out of my hands, so we ended up in a bit of a tugging match. It only stopped because Steve Heighway shouted out from the line for Jason to leave me to take it. That obviously made me feel really good about myself, so I just planted the ball on the spot, took a few steps back and then ran up and blasted it into the roof of that lovely red net. Get in! Then, as we were all making our way back to the halfway line, I heard Steve Heighway shouting out again: 'Michael Yates. Well done son, great show of character.'

Incidentally, in those days all the goal nets at Anfield and Melwood were red. As a kid I really loved those red nets because Liverpool was the only team that had them. Apparently the tradition had first started back in the 1960s when Bill Shankly changed the nets from white to red in a superstitious attempt to improve the team's fortune after a long goal-less spell. The great man's wizardry worked and the goals flowed again, so the nets stayed red for many years before reverting to white some time ago. Perhaps it is a good omen for the club that our current manager, Brendan Rodgers, has once again switched back to red nets at Anfield.

Strangely enough, I don't have any records of how many goals I scored in total as a schoolboy for Liverpool because back then the club didn't bother keeping those statistics. Rather than emphasizing the number of goals scored, the main focus was on the overall development of the player; and that is how it should be. One season we did have to keep a diary and log in everything we had done in training and in matches but, for whatever reason, that was soon scrapped after just a couple of months. It could possibly be that was when the Football League first set a limit on the number of hours of football that schoolboys could play, as a way of trying

to reduce injury and general wear and tear on young bodies. At first the coaches asked us to monitor the hours ourselves but then soon realized that system would not work, so they took over the responsibility. All I know for sure is that I scored regularly, in fact most times we played, so that must have added up to quite a lot of goals over the years. Michael Owen might have scored more than me but I can't have been very far behind him each season.

Another very distinct memory from that first game is an incredible goal that Steven Gerrard scored. We had a throw-in over on the right wing and he made a really great run in the inside channel that created an opportunity for a quick throw. As the ball reached him he took it on his chest without changing pace, guided it a few yards forward and then absolutely smashed it from outside the box right into the top corner of the net. It was breathtaking. At the end of the game, during his team talk, Steve Heighway made the comment that he really wished that there had been a video camera there to record that goal because it had been so technically perfect; a mirror image of what he would expect even the first team players to try to achieve. From my perspective today, that goal was a classic illustration of just how technically gifted Steven Gerrard was, even at that very early age playing for an under-12 team.

There was another match that season that provided me with a nice personal lifetime memory. It was against Wigan Athletic, we won 4 – 1 and I scored all four. Just try to think what it felt like for me, a twelve-year old boy, to have just scored four goals for Liverpool. Then imagine me floating around on cloud nine. I was always a bit slow getting dressed after a game and usually the last out of the changing room, which used to drive my dad potty if he was waiting outside, and that day was probably worse than ever. Just as I was leaving, Steve Heighway called out to me: 'Michael. Well done again today. You played very well and to score four in a game is really fantastic.' So, by now, I'm about to walk through the door and feeling about twelve foot tall, when he calls me back: 'But Michael, just remember you won't score four every week. It won't always be that easy and there's still a lot of work to be done.' That was my first introduction to the Liverpool Way, an ethos first started by the legendary Bill Shankly and then passed down over the generations through other giants like Bob Paisley, Ronnie Moran and all the other Liverpool 'Boot Room' brigade.

*Opposite: Ian Rush and the famous red nets*

It was, and still is, a simple means to keep a player well grounded and constantly focused on doing even better in the future. Give out the praise when it has been rightfully earned but then temper that praise with a bit of a reality check.

Of course Steve Heighway was 100% right because it was never that easy and it did get tougher in the following years, both physically and mentally. Even though I trained as hard as anybody, kept myself in top condition, continued scoring goals on a regular basis and was openly considered a first choice player on the team, I soon had to learn how to deal with sitting on the bench for some games. And I found that very, very hard to handle. When it started, around about thirteen, it wasn't anything to do with my ability but rather I'd be asked to sit out a game, or part of a game, to give a player on trial a chance to fill my position; usually lads from Ireland or some faraway part of Britain who had to travel a long way to get to Liverpool. Even though the coaches would explain that I was only on the bench so that they could have a look at the lad on trial, and reassured me that they already knew how good I was, it was still tough to take. I really hated it. My dad was always encouraging me to 'have a polite word' with the coaches if ever I didn't like the way I was being treated, so that they knew how much I cared and how badly I wanted to play. Plus of course to find out for myself if there was anything wrong with my game that needed improving and that I should be working on. It was very sound advice and I always respected Dad's opinion - so I did make a habit of 'having a polite word!' As I say though, in those days whenever I did go knocking on the coaches' door about being left out, it was always the same story: 'Don't worry Yatesy, we already know how good you are. These lads have come a long way to get here and so we're just having a bit of a look at them.'

I suppose I learned how to bottle up my anger and not let my frustration get the better of me because I really had no choice. That was the name of the game and I had to play by the club's rules, so in the end I had no alternative but to accept the situation.

I'm really not so sure that my dad was so easily placated though. In those days the club didn't provide a bus to take us to our away matches so the fathers, or sometimes mothers as well, would drive us there in their own cars, occasionally to the other end of the country. So, apart from the obvious disappointment he felt whenever I wasn't picked to play, there was also the other huge negative for him that sometimes he would have driven a couple of hundred miles to take me to an away game, which was always a big sacrifice for him and indeed all the other parents, only to then discover when we got there that I wasn't even playing. Especially since, as a sub, we often never got off the bench because they wanted the trial player to have a full game. And, being a typical dad of course, he could never ever accept that I should be on the bench in the first place anyway.

So it wasn't just tough for me to handle, it was absolutely horrendous for my dad.

## Stop Playing for Other Teams and Focus on Liverpool Football Club

Around the time that we were moving up from the under-13s, just before signing Schoolboy Forms, Steve Heighway advised me to stop playing for St. Bede's, my school team; mainly because I'd be missing too much valuable coaching time at Liverpool. His basic approach was, 'Why miss important messages from your Liverpool coaches just to listen to people shouting rubbish at you on a school pitch?' Plus, if I ever got injured, it would have definitely slowed down my development and possibly could even have ruined my future chances of becoming a professional player.

Despite the obvious attraction of playing for Liverpool, that was still a very difficult choice for any young boy to make. Obviously I knew I was being told to do this for a very good reason, but it was still a tough situation for me. I really enjoyed playing for my school. Apart from the fact that the other players were my best mates, the lads who I saw every day, we were also a good team. The previous season I had captained the team and we had won two trophies, plus a 5-a-side competition, and I'd banged in loads of goals. And now I had to make myself walk away from all of that success, the fun, the fantastic team spirit and the bonding that I had shared with my school friends. So, in addition to feeling guilty about letting the lads down, no longer being part of the school footy team also made me feel like a real outsider. We'd all be in class together and my mates would start talking excitedly about the game they were due to play at the end of school later that day; but I wasn't involved, I wasn't one of them.

That was hard to live with and it had me a bit confused for a while, because at the time I didn't think it was fair. It was especially difficult to handle the situation when the teachers carried on asking me to play for

58

the team, even though they knew I had to keep saying no. Having said that, one of my teachers, Mr. Smith, was very supportive and often came to watch me play for Liverpool. Later on the school coaches tried to tempt me into playing a few particularly important games for them but I managed to avoid that situation. After I'd made the initial decision to not play, it was relatively easy to say no to those occasional offers because basically I was frightened that Steve Heighway might find out and it would spoil my good reputation at Liverpool.

Playing for Liverpool Football Club was my ultimate dream and I wasn't going to let anything get in the way of that ambition. In any event, I also knew that those same lads on the school team all desperately wished they were in my shoes, going off to train and play with Liverpool, rubbing shoulders with their football heroes. Every single one of them would have swapped places with me in a flash.

As far as I know, there was no written rule about Centre of Excellence players not representing their schools and the club didn't actually speak to my teachers to tell them that I couldn't play. It was really just a strong recommendation from Steve Heighway. He was convinced that it was just not worth interrupting my development at Liverpool and running the risk of getting injured, perhaps even as a result of something as simple as playing on a bad pitch and twisting an ankle. He also mentioned the fact that some opposition kids might be tempted to have a bit of a go at one of us because they knew we were on Liverpool's books. There is no doubt that Steve Heighway was only trying to protect us, even if it was partly for selfish reasons. I really didn't like having to stop representing my school but realistically I had no choice and deep down inside I knew it was the sensible thing to do.

On top of that, by the time I was playing at the under-14 level for Liverpool it would have been physically impossible to play for the school as well. It literally would have meant training or playing every day of the week and that simply could not have happened. As it was, I still found it to be too much of a challenge to effectively juggle my time between football and academics. Even though I always worked hard while I was at school, my homework was almost impossible to fit in. Many a night I would end up finishing off my course work way after midnight. And, to be honest, while I was in classes I still spent a lot of the time daydreaming

*Opposite above: St. Bede's before the School Cup Final*
*Opposite below: St. Bede's five a side*

about training with LFC, wondering what session we would be doing that night! But I somehow managed to maintain the required academic standard, mainly because I didn't want to let anybody down: not myself, not my parents and not Liverpool. The club kept a regular check on my progress by calling the Headmaster or sometimes somebody would personally visit the school, just to be 100% sure that I was working properly. Despite my limitations, I still managed to pass all of my GCSE exams with grades ranging from B to D. My results were OK, but I know for a fact that I could have done better with greater application.

As well as packing in representing my school, I also had to stop playing for my local youth team, Burscough Dynamo. Worse still, it was even frowned upon when I was later selected to play representative football for Lancashire and North West England Schools. Steve Heighway knew that the quality of the coaching was better than standard schoolboy level but he was afraid that I would be getting too many mixed messages from different coaches. He wanted me to focus on learning football the Liverpool Way. Nevertheless, the club tolerated this conflict of interest to some extent and allowed me to play in some of the matches, even though they were clearly not happy with the situation. In fact there were a number of occasions when I was selected to play for Lancashire on the same night that I was due to play for Liverpool and I had to pick one over the other. Having to make those kind of decisions really caused me a lot of anxiety. Every schoolboy player wants to play at the highest possible level, so it was always a bit of a heartbreaker for me to turn down those opportunities when there was a clash of fixtures. But, out of loyalty to Liverpool, I always did. In fairness to Steve Heighway, I have to say today that he was right. There are many young players who have represented their region at schoolboy level but very few who can proudly say, 'I played for Liverpool Football Club.'

Over the years my parents have helped me enormously by teaching me the kind of life skills that we all need to make any kind of success of ourselves, whatever job we do. One of the most valuable lessons that my dad taught me during those challenging episodes of 'should I or shouldn't I play for Liverpool or Lancashire' was how to take responsibility for my own decisions. In addition to making the final choice in the matter, I was also the one who had to call whoever I was turning down and let them know why. It was a nightmare for me to have to do that, especially the first few times. No matter how hard I tried to remain calm and no matter how much I rehearsed my lines, it was always a horrible, nerve-wracking experience for me. But, as Dad well knew, it forced me to think very carefully about the decisions I made because I was going to have to personally justify them to whoever I was declining. It was a powerful lesson that has stuck with me ever since.

In the end I think I was the one who figured out for myself that, as far as my budding football career was concerned, it was better for me to play for Liverpool than represent my county. It was clearly a big honour to be picked for Lancashire in my own age group, but being selected to play for the Liverpool B Team as a fifteen year-old boy, alongside older lads who were already on YTS apprenticeships or even professional contracts, was undoubtedly a much more meaningful step towards my long-term goal of playing Premier League Football for Liverpool.

I have to say that whenever I did manage to fit a representative game into my schedule, Steve Heighway was always very supportive and did whatever he could to help me out. An unusual example of that would be an occasion when one of my boots split during a training session with Liverpool and I was due to play for North West England the following day against the Midlands at Gresty Road, Crewe Alexandra's ground. So I knocked on Steve's door, explained the situation and asked if there were any spare club boots available that I could use. He told me no, that the delivery of new boots hadn't arrived yet. Seeing the disappointment on my face he immediately reached under his desk and gave me his own boots, adding: 'There you go son, you can use mine.' They were Adidas World Cups with his initials, SH, on the back of the heel. His offer surprised me but I was absolutely made up to have a chance to wear them. As I thanked him and turned to leave his office, he called me back: 'By the way Yatesy, I'm coming to watch that game with Hughie McAuley.'

So off I went and played for North West England Schools, wearing a Liverpool Legend's own boots; and he was on the sidelines watching! I felt like a giant and it must have all had a positive effect because I had a really good game. Stevie G played in that match as well, as did Michael Ball, also from Liverpool. Then of course there were some good players from other clubs, such as David Dunn, Mick O'Brien and Clarke Carlisle. The first half went well for me and I won a penalty when I was brought down from behind. Unfortunately I wasn't able to take it myself because I needed treatment after the bad tackle. But, fortunately, I did get my chance in the second half when I was able to get on the end of a clever flick-on. After a good first touch, I looked up and saw the keeper slightly off his line so I just instinctively smashed the ball with my left foot, then watched it whistle into the top corner. It was a good goal to score in any match but I was especially thrilled to have netted that one for North West England in front of my own coaches from Liverpool. At the next training session back at the club, Steve and Hughie came up to me and let me know, in the typically grounded Liverpool Way, that they thought I'd had an OK game. Only OK! Meanwhile, of course, I thought I'd had a brilliant game but knowing I had to avoid coming across as a big head I simply commented that I had enjoyed getting a goal. 'Yes,' piped up Steve, 'and you scored it with your left foot. It must have been because you were wearing my boots!'

I can remember playing in another game for Lancashire against a Merseyside team that included Steven Gerrard, Stephen Wright, Michael Ball, Ian Dunbavin and Lee Andrews, all in my group at Liverpool. Lancashire lost 3 – 1 but I did manage to grab the goal. The match was played on a school pitch in Skelmersdale and, without wanting to sound like a football snob, after playing at Melwood and on other good pitches, it really struck us that the conditions were quite poor. That negative experience helped me to better understand the reluctant attitude of the club towards us playing in these schoolboy fixtures.

Coincidentally, within 24-hours, another similar experience even more forcefully underlined how lucky we were to play on top class pitches at Melwood. The same six players were back in action the following day, but all playing on the same team this time, for Liverpool in an away match against Bury. It had poured with rain all through the night and into the day and we fully expected the game to be called off but, as was customary, we travelled anyway. Good job because the match was still on. When we arrived at the playing fields where the game was to be played we were disappointed to see the terrible state of the pitch – even worse than the night before! Then we were further shocked to discover that the changing rooms were nothing more than a scruffy, freezing cold, concrete block building. It was so small that both teams couldn't fit in there at the same time, so we took turns at getting changed.

When our lads were all ready, Steve Heighway got us together for one of his special pre-match talks. He made us look closely at the surroundings

*Opposite: Half-time at Melwood with Steve Heighway and Paul Lever discussing how we are playing before giving us feedback.*

63

Me and Steven Green, both local boys. I signed
for LFC and Steven signed for Reading.

Onto a through ball from Stevie G!

Seriously, what was I thinking - what a shirt! Me with Roy Evans, Jason Koumas and Andy Moran.

we were expected to play in and then told us to think carefully and compare that to what we were accustomed to getting at Liverpool. He was using this unsatisfactory situation as a convenient tool to drive home the message that we were privileged to be Liverpool players; and to remind us that all such privileges in life have to be earned.

Once he felt sure we'd fully understood that critical aspect, he then switched his focus to ensuring that we performed to the best of our ability under those poor conditions: 'Right, now then lads. That pitch is a disgrace and these changing rooms are a joke. I think they have done this on purpose. They are taking the piss out of us. So we have to go out there and prove that they can't mess with Liverpool Football Club. I want you to remember the badge on your shirt and still try to play good football but, because the playing surface is so atrocious, you've also got to roll up your sleeves and work harder than ever. Let's get this match over with and get out of here as soon as we can.' At no point did Steve Heighway tell us that we had to win, as that was simply not the Liverpool Way of developing young players, but we all instinctively knew what had to be done.

The team didn't let Steve down and we won 3 – 1. Unfortunately for me, although I scored, I also had my right ankle broken when a defender slid in from the side. That injury kept me out of the game for about six weeks. During the recovery process, even as a schoolboy, I was encouraged to go to Melwood to be treated by the club physiotherapist, just like a first team player. Liverpool took very good care of me, including a full rehabilitation programme. I wasn't allowed back to training until I'd successfully completed my rehab and passed a club fitness test.

When you think about it, being told by Liverpool that I shouldn't play for any other team was in fact a huge compliment. Here was one of the very top football clubs in the world telling me that they wanted me to only play for them. In its own subtle way it was a massive moment in my life and a big leap forward in my football journey. From that point on my entire focus was on training and playing for Liverpool FC. I instantly felt like I really belonged at the club.

I was no longer just another kid trying to become a footballer, I was now somebody who the Mighty Reds wanted to protect and keep for themselves.

# John Barnes

*Liverpool FC Legend 1987 -1997, England International 1983 – 1995*

Young footballers need to be mentally strong whether they get signed as a professional or not because life is tough! It's not just football. If you go for any kind of job there will be plenty of competition and somebody will be prepared to jump all over you to get it

Everybody aims high in football but the biggest question is 'What are you prepared to do to get to the top?' Parents and society tell young players that's where they need to be, but knowing how to actually get there is a completely different story.

The character of the individual plays a huge role because there will always be major challenges to face. And there is no standard way to give advice about the inevitable stumbling blocks ahead. When I am asked to talk about racism and give advice to young players, I reply that I can't give them any! It all depends on the person's own mental strength. When I got racially abused there was no issue with me whatsoever because I knew they were ignorant people, so it was just water off a duck's back for me. I never found it difficult to walk away. So, even though we must warn the kids about the possible pitfalls, they still need to have their own inner resolve to deal with whatever happens.

Handling hardships is a critical part of the game but these days England is bringing up players and mollycoddling them. The facilities are great, the pitches are superb and everything is first class. But what happens when young people have to step out of that comfort zone? When they have to play in 90-degree heat or minus-20, how do they respond? How can they cope in a foreign hotel where the food isn't right? If an opponent spits in their face out on the pitch what are they going to do?

People talk about coaches and managers having to inspire players but I don't buy into that. Inspiration must ultimately come from within each individual. A lot of young players automatically look to members of staff to inspire them but hey …. you're the one out there, so make a decision. Show some balls. When things aren't going well, what are you going to do?

I personally think it's important to get the right messages over in the most formative years, between the ages of eight and twelve, because by the time kids reach fifteen they are already who they are and it's much more difficult to change their mentality.

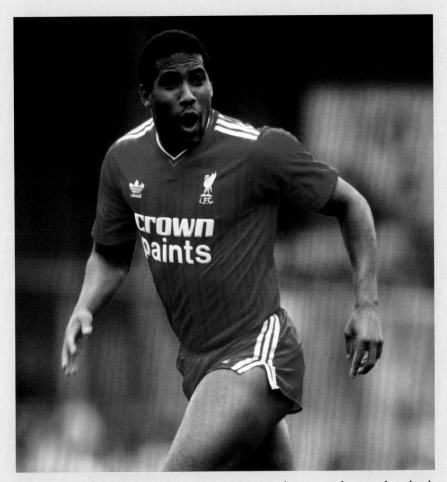

The best advice I could give to any young player is to have a close look at Jamie Carragher. He is the biggest role model in English Football. Steven Gerrard and Michael Owen were destined to be successful players because of their immense natural talent but Jamie Carragher was a good player who had to work harder than anybody else just to make it into the first team; and yet he has gone on to win the Champions League and lots of other cups and he played well over 700 games for Liverpool Football Club. That is truly outstanding.

The fact is that 99% of academy players are going to be more of a Jamie Carragher than a Steven Gerrard, so they should study Jamie's attitude, his mentality, his desire and his determination. If they can apply themselves like Jamie then they might have a chance.

## Ready to Sign Schoolboy Forms

As we approached the end of the under-13 season, I knew that I'd had a good couple of years and I was confident about moving up into the under-14s. So, when one Monday night after training the coaches gave me my regular pep talk that I'd done really well and not to worry about getting signed on for the following year, that my letter would soon be in the post, I actually believed them for the first time ever. It was the least nervous I'd ever been about getting signed back on. The real significance of this, quite ironically, is that this was by far the most important transition point I'd faced since I started training with Liverpool. Up to the age of fourteen a player is signed on each year for the next twelve months, but at fourteen you are invited, or not invited, to sign Schoolboy Forms for the next two years. It is a huge step. I think that I felt so positive this time mainly because we had settled down into a really good, well-established group, and there had been no signs at all of that squad getting broken up. We had a great side, including exceptional players like Steven and Michael, and I was an important part of it. I was flying!

True to form, my happy year finished with a fine flourish. At the end of each season, after Presentation Night had taken place, the club used to arrange an 11-a-side match for us on the actual Anfield pitch, made up of players from amongst our own squad and the coaching staff. The ground would be practically empty of course but it was still brilliant, especially if a couple of the first team squad had hung around and were watching the game. That particular year, 1995, Blackburn Rovers, ironically with Kenny Dalglish as manager, had needed a draw in their last match of the season at Anfield to be sure of winning the Premier League. They went one up through Alan Shearer but a good goal by John Barnes and a brilliant injury time free kick from Jamie Redknapp won the game for Liverpool. Luckily for Blackburn though, Manchester United didn't get the win they needed at West Ham, so Blackburn still won the title.

All of that high drama took place the day before our special annual treat on the Anfield pitch, so naturally we were all really buzzing during the presentation, even more so than normal. Later, when we all went to get changed for the match, my group was given the away team dressing room and the floor was still sticky with champagne from Blackburn's celebrations. Well, talk about a young boy's imagination running wild. Pulling on that red kit, smelling the champagne in the air, getting ready to walk through the players tunnel under the infamous 'This is Anfield' sign, it was impossible not to stand there fantasising about playing in the Premier League for Liverpool and winning trophies.

By the time we got started I was on such a high that I must have thought I was Roy of the Rovers. It apparently didn't do me any harm though because our team won 4 – 1 and I scored three, including a really good header from a trademark Gerrard cross. I had already scored two good ones and I was absolutely buzzing. The conditions were ideal, the pitch was perfect and the lads were really pinging the ball around sweetly. This was football at its very best, the way it should be played.

And I wanted that third goal.

As soon as the ball broke out of our defence and I saw Steven Gerrard moving into a wide position down the right, I knew I was going to get a chance. By the time his clever first touch had brought the long pass under control and helped him to ghost past his marker, I was already sprinting towards the penalty area. Close to the byline Stevie G whipped in a hard, flat cross that curled away from the keeper and rocketed towards a space on the edge of the six-yards box; a space that I was about to fill. Bursting past a defender at full pace, I met the ball square on and it thumped off my forehead, flew into the top corner of the net and thudded back off the stanchion. Get in!

A hat-trick at Anfield!

We were fourteen years old, signed on at Liverpool Football Club, and I was living every schoolboy's dream.

Life couldn't get any better than this.

Well, goodness me, by the time that day was finished, I had really started to believe that my dream of one day becoming a first team player at Liverpool Football Club was well and truly within my grasp. I even kept the bits of grass from the bottom of my boots after that game and put them in a clear plastic container next to my bed, to remind me about that day and what I had the potential to achieve. Obviously the grass eventually shrivelled away to nothing, but luckily my dad filmed that match so I was able to watch it whenever I felt like afterwards. I still have it on a DVD. Now that I'm getting a bit older, if I ever start thinking that it was nothing more than just a young boy's daydreaming I can pop it in the machine and relive it all over again.

All joking aside, when you watch that DVD it is easy to identify the great depth of talent and the really good technical quality that our group of players had developed by the age of fourteen. The staff playing in the game were all good footballers themselves and they are not backing off or taking things easy here, they are playing properly, playing for real if you like; including Steve Heighway himself who was enjoying a really good run around. Yet, all the young lads are more than holding their own and really looking as though they belong on that Anfield pitch. Michael didn't play that game for some reason but Steven is there buzzing in midfield and doing things with the ball that would make you think it was a video of him playing today.

After such a fantastic end to the season, I couldn't wait for the next one to start. Bring it all on!

Even though I was confident of being offered a Schoolboy Contract at Liverpool, the seemingly never-ending wait for that letter to arrive at our home was still a real fingernail-biting ordeal for me. Every day of praying and hoping seemed more like a whole week. It was like stretched out torture. I'd go to sleep thinking about the letter and I'd wake up thinking about the letter. Whatever time the postman arrived, I'd already be there on the step waiting for him, bubbling with eager anticipation. Day after day I was left disappointed and still feeling miserable. Then, one very special morning, I noticed that the postie was smiling as he walked towards our gate. He had it! Oh shit here we go! Ripping the envelope apart and speed-reading the first few lines typed on the official LFC paper I first spotted the word 'congratulations'. Relief flooded through me; quickly turning into laughing, screaming elation as I picked out the magical words that meant I was going to sign Associated Schoolboy Forms for Liverpool Football Club. Game on! My dream of one day playing for Liverpool was not only intact; it had now started to take on a genuine sense of reality.

From the time that I first started to train with Liverpool, my dad had regularly bought me all kinds of LFC videos and books, so that I could better understand what the club was all about and appreciate the amazing history, the traditions, the values and so on. He also did it as a way to help me respect the men who were coaching me, by letting me see how successful they themselves had been as players at Liverpool. When I first met Steve Heighway I didn't know anything about him, so dad went out and bought me some videos that showed him playing at his peak, scoring great goals and appearing in cup finals, so I could see for myself what a great player he had been and how much he had achieved. It also taught me that with Liverpool he had won five League Titles, two UEFA Cups, one FA Cup, three European Cups and two League Cups. Wow, what a player and what a record! That created instant respect.

So it was along those same lines of thinking that Dad gave me another new video as a gift on the morning that I had to go to Melwood to meet Steve Heighway to sign my Liverpool Schoolboy Forms. I watched the video before we left home and one of the best highlights was Heighway himself, scoring his famous, amazing goal against Everton, where he beat his full-back and then ran the ball right along the byline before somehow banging it past the keeper from an unbelievably tight angle. When we went into his office Dad told him: 'Mike's been watching you this morning on a video.' Steve's response was quick as a flash and typical of the man's humility and modesty: 'It must have been in black and white then!' He was quite shy about his own success as a player and he never mentioned it to us young lads. That wouldn't be his way or the Liverpool Way.

Shortly after signing my schoolboy contract, I got another letter from the club, this time from another Liverpool Legend, the Manager Graeme Souness. He started by saying he was happy that I had chosen to play for Liverpool and encouraged me to make the most of the opportunity I had been given. Then to finish off, once again true to the Liverpool Way, he reminded me about what would be expected of me from now onwards: 'I would like to point out that we expect the very highest standards, both on and off the pitch, from all the youngsters associated with this club.' My inner reaction to that gentle but clear warning was: 'No problem. No need to worry about me on that score. I'll do whatever it takes.'

## A Great Start to the Under-14 Season

After enjoying a very solid under-13 season and having formally signed my Schoolboy Forms for Liverpool Football Club, I was now totally up for the under-14 season. I was longing for it to begin and bursting to get started. Perhaps the rest of the squad felt the same way because we went to Wales to play in the pre-season Ian Rush Tournament, which was a big competition that attracted some top European clubs as well as British teams, and we won it! Steven ran the midfield, Michael and I played upfront together and we both scored goals, and the rest of the lads all played their own special part. Even though we had a very strong side, we still had to deliver an especially

Manager
GRAEME SOUNESS

Chief Executive/General Secretary
PETER ROBINSON

Registered Trade Mark

# LIVERPOOL
# FOOTBALL CLUB
## & ATHLETIC GROUNDS plc
Company Registration Number 35668, England

## ANFIELD ROAD, LIVERPOOL L4 0TH.

GS:SW

7 December 1993

Michael Yates

Burscough
Lancs

Dear Michael

I am absolutely delighted to hear that you have taken the
important step of signing Associated Schoolboy Forms for
Liverpool Football Club. I hope that your time with us will be
enjoyable and rewarding and that you will take full advantage of
all the opportunities that our Youth Department will offer you.

I would like to point out that we expect the very highest
standards both on and off the pitch, from all the youngsters
associated with this Club.

Congratulations and best wishes for the coming seasons.

Yours sincerely

G Souness
Manager

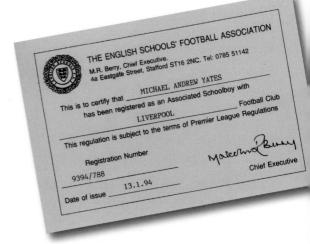

THE ENGLISH SCHOOLS' FOOTBALL ASSOCIATION

M.R. Berry, Chief Executive.
4a Eastgate Street, Stafford ST16 2NC. Tel: 0785 51142

This is to certify that _____ MICHAEL ANDREW YATES _____
has been registered as an Associated Schoolboy with _____ Football Club
_____ LIVERPOOL _____

This regulation is subject to the terms of Premier League Regulations

Registration Number

9394/788

Date of issue _____ 13.1.94

Malcolm Berry
Chief Executive

Administration                          051-263 2361/2
Match Information Service Only          051-260 9999 (24 Hours)
Match Ticket Office: Enquiries Only     051-260 8680
Fax Number                              051-260 8813
Telex Number                            627661 LFC G
Registered Office: 52 Mount Pleasant, Liverpool L3 5UN.

Official Sponsors

Banqueting & Conference Suite Bookings   051-263 7744
Souvenir Shop                            051-263 1760
Sales & Marketing                        051-263 9199
Public Relations & Museum Visits         051-263 2361
Development Association                   051-263 6391

good overall team performance to win that trophy.

It was a really hot summer that year and for most of us it was our first experience of playing tournament football, which involves one tough match after another in a short space of time. So, for the first time in my life, I was starting games already feeling achy and tired, having to play with stiff joints, sore muscles and even carrying little niggling injuries. Steve Heighway used that tournament as his first real opportunity to teach us how to distinguish the differences between an ache caused by hard work and an actual injury. That is another essential facet of a professional player's knowledge but as young lads we found it hard to recognize when we were really injured or when we could just run out the soreness, so Steve did his best to teach us that skill.

Our first match was against a Welsh Select side and we won that one 3 – 1. Then we went on to play Glasgow Rangers in the semi-final. They had a big, strong team that played a very physical game – especially against Liverpool – but we played really well and managed to win 3 – 1 again. I remember we went up 1 – 0 but they soon equalized. Then, at 1 – 1, we got a free kick wide on the right. Stevie G whipped it into the box and I got on the end of it for a good header to go into a 2 –1 lead. No surprises that it was Michael Owen who grabbed the third. At that time, whenever one of us scored a goal, Michael and I had a special celebration that we'd thought up during our free time. It sounds a bit cheesy talking about it now but basically we'd run over to each other, give a high-5 and then do this sort of wiggle at the knees. Just two young lads having a bit of fun really but I am sure that it also had a lot to do with the fact that we were both full of confidence and expected to score every time we played. It was kind of like, 'Well we are going to score later today, so let's plan our goal celebration now'. It was almost a natural thing to do.

That semi-final match also produced a truly classic Steven Gerrard moment, an unforgettable incident that underscored just how much further developed he was as a player at that age when compared to the rest of us. As we came off the pitch the whole team was in really great spirits. We'd just beaten Rangers and now we were in the final. The atmosphere amongst the lads was fantastic until the bubbly mood was suddenly deflated when somebody pointed to the next pitch and bawled out: 'Shite lads, just look at the size of those lot from Spartak Moscow. No wonder they've been battering everybody. I don't fancy playing against them in the final.' Quick as a flash, before anybody else could even react, Steven

*Shielding the ball against Welsh Select*

*Jason Koumas and Steven watch as I gain possession.*

Gerrard turned around and confronted the whole group, coaches and all: 'Don't you fucking mind about them, just leave the bastards to worry about us!'

He was still only thirteen but he'd taken instant command and immediately blown away any possible lingering doubts that later on might have festered into a lack of confidence amongst our team. With that one biting comment he'd dismissed the fact that Spartak was a physically imposing team and reminded all of us who we were – Liverpool Football Club! It was an incredible example of natural leadership and such a powerful moment that it is etched on my brain forever. It was also the first time I'd ever heard anybody my age swear like that in front of adults!

Bolstered by Steven's battle cry, and no doubt well motivated and guided by the coaches, we went into that final full of determination and brimming with confidence. It wasn't easy in any way whatsoever but we duly beat the mighty Spartak Moscow 3 – 0. True to form and reputation, they were a very physical side, dare I say dirty, and they used any tactics they could to try to knock us off our stride. I can remember being kicked a lot, stamped on, shirt pulled and all the other tricks all through the game, until at some point in the second half I was elbowed in the side of the head and had to be taken off. I was desperate not to be substituted, not in the final, but I was having dizzy spells and getting flashes across my eyes so there was no way I could continue.

Obviously I was very disappointed not to finish the game but, at the same time, I was absolutely delighted that we had won the Ian Rush Tournament and done so in style, including beating two big European clubs. Furthermore, I knew that I had played a significant part in the team's triumph and that was especially important to me. Strangely enough though, we never actually got to collect that trophy as a team because our bus was scheduled to go back to Liverpool before the presentation took place. The result of some bad planning by somebody I suppose. In the end Michael Owen was nominated to stay behind and collect the trophy on the team's behalf, presumably because he was closer to home than the rest of us and could go back in his dad's car.

After that first experience of playing in and winning a tournament, I knew that I had successfully climbed up another rung or two on the ladder towards my goal of playing for Liverpool Football Club. I was very excited about the prospects ahead.

The dream was rapidly gaining real momentum.

# Paul Lever

*Senior FA Youth Coach Educator, Former Coach at the Liverpool FC Academy*

My memories of working with the under-14 group at Liverpool FC that included Michael Owen, Steven Gerrard and Michael Yates are all very happy and very positive. It was a real pleasure to work with them. There were a lot of talented players in that squad, at least seven at International standard, including Michael Yates. My job was to support them with their learning and deliver practice sessions that made them think about the game. If I ever told any of those players 'this is how you should do it', they were the type of lads who would try to prove me wrong. Not because they were trying to be in any way clever, this was just their means of challenging themselves. They constantly wanted to be put to the test.

I took that group to the Ian Rush Tournament in Aberystwyth in 1994. The idea was to make sure the players were competitive. And they certainly were. I remember we played the Wales Under-15 National Team in the quarter-finals and we were 2-1 down with ten minutes to go. Then Michael Yates won a penalty, which Michael Owen took and scored. With just two minutes left on the clock we won a free kick on the halfway line. Without me saying anything to them, Steven Gerrard took the kick and put it right on their keeper. The two Michaels closed in on him and under the pressure he took it over his own goal line. I hadn't seen it happen but the whole team soon let me and the referee know that it was a goal! We eventually won that match 3-2 and the lads then went on to win the tournament.

Those players all had a natural desire to win football matches. They were also very disciplined as a group. We could tell them anything we required, such as when to meet as a team, what time to report for breakfast or maybe lights out, and whatever it was they always did it. There were never any issues.

In the end Michael Owen and Steven Gerrard got to the very top, but around the age fourteen there were several others, Mike Yates included, who were all showing the right signs. When we saw the two Michaels play together we all knew that they both had high potential. For the National School trials Michael Owen was always at the top of the pick list but Yatesy was prominent on the radar too. The whole country knew he had an opportunity of getting into Lilleshall. I can remember the final trial game was played in foggy, rainy and windy conditions. Yatesy got no service that night; in fact none of the strikers got any service. That caused a big problem for the selectors when they had to decide who went through and who didn't. Unfortunately Mike Yates just missed out.

*Paul Lever giving a team talk in Italy*

## Starting to Belong at Melwood

Many of my fondest recollections of being a schoolboy footballer at Liverpool all revolve around life at Melwood, especially starting from that period of our under-14 year. I suspect that was the age when it really sank into my mind just how truly blessed I was to be able to train and play football there. Even just driving into the facility in my dad's car gave me a full-on buzz! The pitches always looked immaculate: never more so than early in the morning when overnight rain or dew gave a silvery sheen to the perfectly flat surface. Magic in every way!

Everybody at Liverpool Football Club is devoted to maintaining the highest possible standards in every single aspect of the organisation, playing and non-playing, from the bottom to the top. Melwood was, and still is, the living epitome of that professional attitude. Although I was just a young teenager, it really struck me that the everyday operation was very well managed, even for us schoolboys.

Anybody who has ever played football at school or grass roots amateur level will have lasting memories of turning up to play, going into the changing rooms and having to scramble with your teammates to dig through an old kit bag trying to find a decent pair of team shorts and socks without holes in them. If you were lucky you might have had a manager who'd toss a shirt at you; otherwise you'd have to fight for that too. It's a classic amateur footy scene; one that I'd personally experienced many, many times prior to signing for Liverpool.

So, against that background, think about how I felt the very first time I walked into our under-14 dressing room for the opening game of the season at Melwood, not really knowing what to expect. As usual, I was early and the very first player to arrive for the match. To say I was shocked by what I discovered would be a complete understatement. In fact my first reaction was that I'd walked through the wrong door. The room was spotlessly clean, with brass clothes hooks, one for each player, lined up along a beautiful, wood panelled wall. But what really threw me off guard was the kit. There was a row of hangers, each one holding a Liverpool shirt with a number on the back. It was quite clearly first team gear! I could tell straight away because the badges and numbers were stitched on the shirts, not printed like the ones you could buy in a shop; plus I spotted the Premier League crest on the sleeves! On the bench below was a neatly folded pile of shorts, socks, underpants and a towel. Underpants! Oh my

God. I felt like a right idiot for going into the first team dressing room. Just as I was about to sneak back out, some of the other lads walked in, with a grinning Steve Heighway behind them. Blimey, it really was our changing room. I was gobsmacked! But .... what about the kit? Well, yes, that kit was first team gear but it was there for us to wear. Even the undies! And it had all been laid out there waiting for us, just like the first team. Incredible. Truly incredible!

No wonder Steve Heighway and the other coaches used to regularly make a point about how lucky we were to be at Liverpool. Where else would you get that kind of treatment? Why would any of you ever want to leave Liverpool for another club? That was the constant positive message drilled into our young heads – you are privileged to be here so make the most of it!

On one of the first occasions that I turned up for training I got out of Dad's car, walked into the dressing rooms and came face to face with the Liverpool Manager, Graeme Souness. As fate would have it that day, I was wearing a Glasgow Rangers training shirt, another team that Souness had both played for and managed. As soon as he saw my shirt he stopped and told me: 'Nice one son, I like that.' Well I liked that too! It's not every day that the club manager talks to a schoolboy player. So when I got home I asked my mum to wash that shirt for me straight away and I wore it again for the next session at Melwood. And, sure enough, he spotted me for the second time and couldn't help having a bit of a laugh with me: 'Oh OK then, I can see that you know how to play the game!'

Steve Heighway would occasionally mention to the schoolboy players that the doors at Melwood were always open to us if we ever wanted to come along in our spare time. Not many lads took up the invitation but I was always keen to go along whenever I had a chance, especially during the school holidays when I could spend whole days there.

It was on one of those occasions that I first got picked to make up the numbers in an 11-a-side staff match. I was blown away by the experience of playing alongside the likes of Graeme Souness, Steve Heighway, Ronnie Moran and Don Hutchinson, even if it was absolutely bucketing down with rain. Nigel Clough played in that game as well, presumably because he was recovering from an injury. The match was played on the shale pitch because of the wet conditions and I can remember that Cloughie's amazing movement and ball control, even on that difficult surface, was a complete eye-opener for me. I was still buzzing long after I'd got home. It

was a fantastic and inspiring experience for me, as a fourteen year-old, to witness that level of ability first hand and up-close. I probably learned more like that than I could have in a dozen coaching sessions.

On another one of those special days at Melwood, I got to meet Jason McAteer for the first time. He had just been signed from Bolton and, even though the first team had a day off, he came in anyway and trained with the YTS and Reserve Team players. At the end of training they arranged an 8-a-side game and I got picked on his team. As always, it was an absolute thrill for me as a young kid to be playing alongside Liverpool's latest acquisition: a player who all my mates at school had been reading about in the news headlines!

When I told those kind of stories to the other lads in our squad, that encouraged a few more of them to come into Melwood during breaks from school, especially Steven Gerrard and Michael Owen.

Another good example of how the schoolboys gained tremendous inspiration from working so closely to the first teamers at Melwood during the holidays was simply by overhearing their conversations. I particularly enjoyed jogging around the pitch with the first team squad, listening to all their chat. I can vividly recall John Barnes, who was just back from watching the 1994 World Cup in the USA, enthusing excitedly about the way Brazil played their football. He was going on about them playing a style that allowed them to periodically switch their pace from aerobic to anaerobic, so that they could keep control of the game. I spent the whole time running fast enough to keep up with Barnesy and trying to figure out what he actually meant. It was my first lesson in tactical strategy and I was in awe.

On another occasion, during an unusually hot summer spell, I went bounding across to one of the Lucozade stations that had been set up around the pitches to get myself a cold drink. Just as I arrived, so did Ian Rush. Even though he'd got there just before me and had his container ready to fill, he still stepped back and invited me to go first. It really amazed me that such a great player would do something like that for a kid like me. I'd always held Rushie in high esteem but after that display of humility my respect for him soared even more. What a top man.

With memories like those, it is little wonder that I just loved going to Melwood as often as I could. One time, when a player in our group was

*Opposite: Graeme Souness*

*Me and Stevie G leaving Melwood after one of our schoolboy days training with the youth team and mixing with the first team!*

not showing as much enthusiasm as he should have, Steve Heighway came out with the line: 'You need to be as dedicated as Michael Yates. He spends so much time at Melwood that he'd pitch a tent on the A Team pitch if we let him!'

## Trials for England and a Personal Statement from Stevie G

Liverpool had an extremely strong under-14 squad that year and we simply brushed aside most of our opponents. Playing on that particular team was truly a fantastic experience. Most of us had been together since Michael Owen joined us at the under-12 level and we had really gelled and made excellent, rapid progress in that two-year period. From day one we'd earned the nickname of the 'Dream Team' but now we were an even more formidable unit. Even back then, I think the players all knew we were playing an extraordinarily high level of football for our age group but what reinforces that opinion is when I meet people today who had watched our side perform. Former players, coaches and general fans consistently rave about the skill and technical prowess our team displayed. Paul Lever, a former Liverpool coach who was our team manager at the Ian Rush Tournament, often referred to 'Owen and Yates, the best pair of under-14 strikers in the country, absolutely unstoppable'.

The outstanding quality of that Liverpool under-14 team was recognised at the national level when more than half the side was selected for England trials: Steven Gerrard, Michael Owen, Stephen Wright, Jason Koumas and me; plus Layton Maxwell, though he actually ended up playing for Wales.

When we attended the trials we were of course mixing with the very best players from every club around the country, so we were totally surrounded by top quality. Everybody could play. That was when I first came across players of the calibre of Wes Brown, who went on to play at the highest level.

Just because it was England, and the fact that playing for your country is generally considered the ultimate accolade, I was very nervous when I went to those trials. Unfortunately it was made a lot worse for me because they were 3-day residential camps and that was literally the first time that I'd ever stayed anywhere away from home without my parents. That really was a very strange experience for me and, to be truthful, it proved to be quite an ordeal. We roomed on our own, the whole atmosphere was quite strict, the lights went out early and it was easy to feel very lonely when there was no football going on. Clearly it was a lot different to being with our Liverpool squad because we all knew each other well and there would be plenty of mixing and socialising. With the England group I always felt as though I was alone and isolated. Steven, Michael and I would still try to stick together but it just wasn't the same. Maybe that was because it was essentially a big group of strangers and everybody was competing with each other to get one of those very limited eleven slots on the team sheet. It really was a case of 'every man for himself', even amongst the Liverpool lads.

The first England trial had been for three days at Padgate and I can remember doing well at that one. That was where Michael first started using that line just before we kicked off, 'Alright partner, let's go to work.' My dad somehow managed to arrive early for the last day and watched the whole of that session. He actually parked next to the entry road to the complex and hopped over the fence to get a good view! Anyway, I must have done OK because I was then invited to the next level of trials at Lilleshall itself. I can remember putting in a good performance there as well and I got through to the last twenty-six; but it started going downhill from there and I didn't quite make it past that stage.

Nevertheless, the England coaches must have seen something in me because I was also invited to more trials for the actual England Schoolboys team later that season, as well as the following year at the under-15 level. However, as had happened on the previous occasions, I did well enough to progress to the last twenty-six but got no further than that. In retrospect, I don't think I was mature enough at fourteen and fifteen to cope with the dual challenge of living away from home on my own and still performing to the best of my ability in the trials.

Michael was duly selected to attend the England National School at Lilleshall as a full time resident, but none of the other lads from Liverpool made it into the final squad, not even Steven. After those trials, we never really saw that much of Michael because he spent most of his time down at Lilleshall. The most we ever saw of him was during the school holidays when he'd come back home and join us for those Melwood sessions that we all enjoyed so much. It was an indication of his passion for the game, as well as the fantastic set-up we had at Liverpool, that whenever Michael did have any free time away from Lilleshall he'd always come and join our

*England trials at Belfield*

*After trials for the National School at Lilleshall*

*LFC players selected for trials for England Schoolboys: (left to right) Layton Maxwell, Jason Koumas, Michael Owen, me, Andy Moran.*

*Playing against the National School and my toughest opponent since first playing against Stevie G at age 8, a certain Wes Brown.*

sessions rather than just relax back at home with his family.

While I was able to shrug off the disappointment of not making it into Lilleshall and actually looked forward to going back to train with Liverpool, Steven was totally pissed off and felt very bitter about the whole situation. Deep in his soul he knew he was way better than most of the lads who'd been selected, so he naturally assumed that he'd been unfairly treated. I have to say that, even now, I would agree with him because even though he'd suffered a lot with injuries he was still an awesome player and he outshone everybody he ever played with or against. It was against that background of intense disappointment and deep-seated resentment that Steven was so determined to drive his point home when Lilleshall came to play our Liverpool under-15 side at Melwood the following season.

I can remember playing in that match against Lilleshall as if it was yesterday. Before the game, Steven got himself really wound up because he was desperate to prove to everybody that he was better than any of the lads on their team. He wanted to show the England coaches that they had made a big mistake by not picking him to go to Lilleshall. He really wanted to embarrass them. He wanted to shove his anger and resentment right up their backsides.

The England players, including Michael Owen, all arrived wearing their full Lilleshall school uniform and that gave Steven his first bit of ammunition. He burst into our dressing room, almost snarling: 'Wait until you see the state of those absolute belters outside, all tarted up in their bleeding blazers, shirts and ties. Let's make sure we really stick it to them today lads.'

Then, out on the pitch, as soon as the game kicked off, the very first thing Steven did was to clatter into Kenny Lunt; who happened to be the lad who had got his place on the Lilleshall team. That was just Steven's way of making his mark straight away and saying, 'Here I am, so watch out for me.' And that message wasn't intended just for Lunt, but everybody else who was there: all the players on both sides, the England staff, the LFC coaches, the spectators, everybody. And that became his total focus for the rest of the match – watch out for me!

In my opinion, it wasn't really about all the people around him; it was all about Steven. He needed to prove himself to himself. But, at the same time, he knew he couldn't do it on his own, so he drove and dragged our team along with him. He made sure that the rest of us did our jobs properly and never slacked off at any moment. Stevie G was the ultimate leader that day – he commanded, he demanded and he delivered. Needless to say, Liverpool won, 2 -1.

That same game was the first time I actually played against Wes Brown and, no disrespect to the teams we'd played before, he was the first really top quality defender I'd ever played against. Wes was very strong but also skilful on the ball; he had plenty of pace but remained calm in possession; he was clearly a good reader of the game and he displayed intelligent tactical awareness. In other words, he was the full package. It was kind of similar to that first occasion when Steven was put to mark me one-on-one: a real eye-opener and a bit of an education for me. I got nothing out of him that day. Mind you, having said that, I did score in that game. And it was a good header at the far post, so I must have got away from Wes at some point. Unless of course he'd been substituted to give somebody else a run!

So anyway, there it was, our Liverpool under-15s had beaten the Lilleshall boys, the so-called cream of the crop of young English players. Following a great result like that it could have been very easy for the lads on our team to get a bit carried away about our own abilities and self-importance. But there was no way that was going to happen to us, not with all of our coaches making sure we kept both feet firmly planted on the ground. The staff went round each player individually in the dressing room, praising us for what we'd done well but also talking to us about the mistakes we'd made, what we should have done and how we could improve. So, at least in my case, instead of limiting myself to thinking how good a player I was, this made me reflect on the game and analyze my own performance. This definitely helped me to stay grounded and to become a better player.

After the game Steve Heighway just said something like: 'Well done lads, excellent performance today. Now start getting yourselves ready for your next match, away to Stockport.' Bang, just like that, straight back to the real world. And think about it .... that must have been very difficult for Steve and the other coaches to do, because the truth is they would have been feeling just as proud and elated as all the players. Their lads, their trainees, had just beaten the England national team. They must have been totally ecstatic deep inside but they forced themselves to hide it in public. Allowing yourself to get complacent because you happened to have enjoyed a very good result was simply not acceptable. It was not the Liverpool Way of doing things.

On the other hand, we did benefit from occasional confidence boosters and a few words of encouragement when we might have least been expecting them. Not long after I'd got my letter from England Schools informing me that I hadn't been accepted for Lilleshall, I was leaving the dressing room, last out as usual, when Steve Heighway called me over and surprised me with: 'I'm sorry that you're disappointed that you never made the England squad Yatesy, but keep your chin up because as far as I'm concerned this is where you'll learn your trade best, right here at Liverpool. In fact, if I can be honest, I'm delighted that you're not going away because now we can really get to work with you.'

Now I don't know whether he really meant what he said or he was just boosting my ego but, either way, it did the trick. With the great respect that I had for Steve Heighway in those days, I truly appreciated him taking the time to say that to me. It definitely lifted my spirits and helped drive me forward

I was getting closer and closer to my target of playing professional football for Liverpool.

**Geoff & Cheryl Yates:** 'As parents of a Centre of Excellence player we had to make ourselves endure a lot, particularly when the inter club games started. There were times when we drove half way across the country to watch Mike play, only to discover that he was on the bench! To make it happen for Mike, we gave up a lot of our own life. Spread over ten years, it all adds up to a big sacrifice. But we have no regrets and there are no sour grapes because we also loved every minute of it!'

# Gareth Southgate

*Current England Under-21 Manager; Former head of the Football Association's Elite Development; football analyst and writer; former England international and Manager of Middlesbrough FC.*

Photo courtesy of Liverpool FC via Getty Images

When I was about twelve, I signed as an associate schoolboy with Southampton, who had centres of excellence in Newcastle, Slough and Crawley, where I grew up. I used to train with them one evening a week and then we would be invited to play matches down in Southampton during the school holidays.

Looking back, I was never part of their 'elite group', which at the time included Alan Shearer, Neil Maddison and both Wallace twins, so it was no great surprise when they released me at age fourteen. But I didn't like the fact that they used the excuse that I was going to be too small. So, even though I was perhaps a late-developer physically and lacked a bit of self-belief, I still wanted to stay in the game. On top of that, the release letter was poorly written and very impersonal, so I kept it as motivation right throughout the rest of my career. For whatever reason, whilst some people would react negatively to being released or suffering any other setbacks, I

*Gareth Southgate battling with Liverpool's Danny Murphy and Emile Heskey*

somehow always managed to find extra incentive.

Crystal Palace were my nearest professional club and they immediately asked me to train with them one night a week. I soon got into their under-18s squad and they offered me a £28 per week YTS apprenticeship on leaving school at sixteen. I struggled initially with the change from football being 'for fun' to becoming my job. Fortunately I had an outstanding youth coach, Alan Smith, who believed in me. He helped me develop as a man as well as a player, something which I think is a crucial role for any youth coach. He was very demanding and our physical training was extreme, but it helped me a lot to toughen up both physically and mentally.

Although I was always involved in the reserve team and considered one of the club's bright prospects, I didn't get my first team debut until I was twenty-one. So I have seen first hand the importance of 'opportunity' for the development of young players and how difficult it is to accurately predict how far youngsters will progress.

The recent overhaul of the academy system in England provides far greater contact time for clubs to work with young players. This gives coaches a better opportunity to improve players technically but also to work with them socially. Bill Shankly once said that 'Coaches don't make players –parents do'. I would agree with the idea that the formation of a player's character takes place very early on in their life. However, even for highly motivated lads with positive attitudes, there is still a need for good role models and mentors to keep them on the right path. When I look back now at all the hurdles I had to overcome to end up representing my country over fifty times, it is a remarkable pathway. I'm convinced that mental strength and personal character are as important, if not more so, in the progression of players, as technical ability. I also consider myself lucky to have had a stable family background, without which that journey would have been even more difficult.

There is no definitive pathway for the development of players. We can and should put best practice into place, but every individual is exactly that – an individual. They will respond and mature in different ways and at different rates.

We have a responsibility to raise the standards of coaching and player support as high as we possibly can. But any boy starting out on this path needs to be fully prepared to ride a rollercoaster of emotions and experiences!

# Part Two
## Entering the World of Professional Football

## From Schoolboy Footballer to YTS Apprentice

The Youth Training Scheme, known by everybody simply as the YTS, was a 2-year on-the-job training course for school leavers aged 16 to 18, which was launched by the UK Government in 1983. As professional football was a career, just like any other job, it meant that clubs could sign sixteen year-old players as apprentices and they would be paid a small weekly allowance. This essentially enabled the clubs to closely monitor the progress of their young players on a full-time daily basis, prior to offering a professional contract at age eighteen. The huge significance of being signed onto the YTS scheme was therefore very obvious. Those young apprentices effectively had two years to perfect the skills of their trade sufficiently to convince their club to invest heavily in them. It was make or break time! Every single player in our under-16 squad wanted to be offered a YTS Apprenticeship; we all saw it as our passport to becoming a professional footballer.

I can remember that during the build up to our group's YTS decision time there was a lot of training and regular games taking place but not a sniff about who was going to be signed or not. Liverpool kept their cards very close to their chest. Naturally we all had a bit of an idea, based on our performances and comments from the staff, but we never really knew. You just couldn't be sure. The only real hint I ever got was one night walking off the pitch alongside Hughie McAuley when, out of the blue, he said something to me like: 'You're doing OK Yatesy. You'll be alright for the next couple of years.' It took me by surprise but it definitely came across as a nod of approval. Even though it made me feel good about my YTS prospects, I didn't tell anybody what he'd said just in case it didn't work out.

In a similar vein, Tommy Galvin, who was the scout that first recommended me to Liverpool and who played a huge part in my early development, had also given my dad a few subtle hints that everything would be OK. Tommy was very close to the Liverpool staff and he must have heard something positive from somebody. Nevertheless, as reassuring as it was to hear that news from Tommy, I was still not counting my chickens.

Overall, I truly believed that I'd performed well enough at schoolboy level to earn my chance at YTS but I was still taking nothing for granted. I suppose it was just me being my usual cautious self – I wanted it so badly

I was terrified in case it didn't happen!

When I did get my letter, it was almost unexpected. One night in late February 1996, I was about to leave Melwood when Steve Heighway handed me an envelope and told me I'd enjoy reading what was inside. I instinctively knew what the letter must be and what he had meant. Feeling confident about its contents, instead of tearing it open like I normally would, I decided to wait until I got home and share the moment with Mum and Dad. After all, they'd been almost as much a part of my Liverpool journey as I had.

Once I got home, I waited for a suitable moment and gave the letter to my dad. He took one look at it and gave it back to me:

'It's got your name on son, so you have to open it.'

'But I want you to open it Dad.'

'No, not me. You open it yourself Mike.'

Thankfully, Mum took charge:

'Here, give it to me you two. I'll open it!'

It was a relatively straightforward, official sounding letter, offering me a YTS Apprenticeship and inviting me to accept in writing within the next two weeks. At the very bottom of the page was a simple one-word message from Steve Heighway on behalf of the club: 'Congratulations'. Oh yes, there was also a PS, which stated that the offer was dependent on me passing a medical examination. But no danger there!

As part of our thorough medical check-up to confirm our YTS contract, we all had to undergo a special fitness test with Mark Leather, the club physio. Every player at the club had to do it, even the first team, who did their test the day before we did. One of the toughest drills we had to do was what they called the Bleep Test, which was essentially like doing shuttle runs against the clock. Most of the lads dreaded doing it. You had to get to the line before the bleep went off, and the more runs you did then the shorter the time between the bleeps became. So, as you became increasingly tired, then the test became increasingly difficult. In a way, it was as much a test of character as it was fitness. To make things even worse, it was ridiculously hot the day we did our test. So it was an absolute killer! We all started together and the idea was that everybody kept going as long as they could, while still beating the bleeps. Soon the lads around us started dropping like flies but Stephen Wright and myself kept going until almost the very end. When all the results were collated, only two first teamers had performed better than us and Steve

McManaman was one of them. So no shame there, especially since he was also a great cross-country runner and one of the fittest players in the game. That test, when I posted the third top time in the club, proved to everybody that there was no doubt about my fitness levels.

Obviously I was thrilled to get the confirmation that I was going to be a YTS at Liverpool, as were my parents, but I felt more content than ecstatic. Somehow, getting successfully over this big hurdle was less about celebration when compared to the other previous stages of advancement within the Liverpool system. If anything, this particular benchmark moment was more about maturing. I'd done well enough to progress all the way through the schoolboy ranks and now I was moving up into the adult world. Gone were my schooldays of play time and long holidays. I was now about to become a paid employee. I was growing up. It actually felt really good!

The following week, after we had passed our medicals, the club invited the new YTS players and our parents to attend a meeting at Melwood. Steve Heighway spoke at length about the many challenges of the big step up to the next level of YTS and the critical importance of the next two years. He emphasised the fact that this was when the hard work really began and underscored all the values of Liverpool Football Club. Steve made it clear that it was not going to be easy for any of the young lads who had been signed up and encouraged the parents to provide as much support as possible.

In the end, actually signing my YTS forms turned out to be a fairly low-key affair. Steve Heighway asked Dad and I to come and see him and Hughie McAuley at his office. My dad went in on his own first and they asked if he had any questions. Dad just said that he trusted them to look after me properly and he knew how important Liverpool Football Club was to me. So he had no questions. Later on though, Dad found out that some parents had asked there and then for a professional contract and other conditions. That made him regret that he had not done something similar for me but I always believed, and I still do, that he did the right thing.

When they finally called me into the office, Steve basically repeated his speech from the earlier parents meeting but now on a much more personal, face-to-face basis. Then they congratulated me, shook my hand and gave me the YTS forms to sign, which I did with a mixture of controlled delight and a great sense of relief. There was no pomp and

# THE LIVERPOOL FOOTBALL CLUB
## & ATHLETIC GROUNDS
## PUBLIC LIMITED COMPANY
Company Registration Number 35668, England

ANFIELD ROAD, LIVERPOOL L4 0TH.

SH:SW

22 February 1996

Michael Yates

Burscough
Ormskirk

Dear Michael

In accordance with Premier League Regulation 20.8, it gives me great pleasure to inform you that Liverpool Football Club are offering you a Y.T.S. Apprenticeship, to commence in July 1996.

Within the next two weeks you should let me know, in writing, whether you wish to accept your Apprenticeship. We will shortly be meeting with parents and boys.

Congratulations.

Yours sincerely

Steve Heighway
Director of Youth

P.S. As is customary, this offer is subject to your successfully passing a medical examination prior to signing the Y T Contract.

Administration               0151-263 2361/2
Match Information Service Only   0151-260 9999 (24 Hours)
Match Ticket Office: Enquiries Only  0151-260 8680
Development Association       0151-263 6391
Fax Number                   0151-260 8813
Registered Office: 52 Mount Pleasant, Liverpool L3 5UN.

Official Sponsors

Banqueting & Conference Suite Bookings  0151-263 7744
Souvenir Shop                0151-263 1760
Sales & Marketing            0151-263 2361
Sales & Marketing (Non Match Day)  0151-261 1166
Public Relations & Museum Visits  0151-263 2361
Public Relations/I.S.C.      0151-260 1433

97

ceremony, just a very down to earth, serious and businesslike approach. No doubt they were just keeping our feet on the ground and making us appreciate that this was not the end of the journey, it was in fact just the beginning.

Nevertheless, despite all the efforts of the staff to play down the significance of signing YTS forms, I knew that I had taken another huge step towards my aim of becoming a first team player at Liverpool Football Club.

Next season, I was going to start work as an apprentice professional footballer.

### Agonisingly Close to an Early Breakthrough

Around the same time that I signed my YTS forms, in May 1996, Liverpool won the prestigious FA Youth Cup for the very first time, beating West Ham 4 – 1 over a two-legged final. Other than the fact that I was there to watch on the big night, I wasn't involved. That was mainly because the team was made up of older lads, including a certain bright prospect by the name of Jamie Carragher, now of course a Liverpool Living Legend who is widely renowned and respected as one of the most dedicated servants the club has ever known. However, there was one player on that winning team who definitely wasn't affected by his young age .... Michael Owen. Aged just sixteen, Michael had scored two hat-tricks on the way to the final, including one against Manchester United. Then, having won the first leg 2–0 at Upton Park, the Reds won the second leg at Anfield 2–1, in front of over 20,000 fans, with Michael coming off the bench to score the first goal. Interestingly, it was Frank Lampard who scored for West Ham.

It was a fantastic night for the whole club. For me personally, it was particularly memorable and inspiring because I'd watched a group of lads who I knew well win the FA Youth Cup for Liverpool, playing on the hallowed turf of Anfield. And more to the point, I'd witnessed Michael Owen, somebody my own age who I'd played alongside for the last five years, score a goal in a cup final in front of thousands of cheering and applauding Liverpool supporters. And that was something that I'd been dreaming about achieving myself ever since I was eight!

Far from being jealous of Michael's success, I was absolutely delighted for him. By now it was so obvious that he was way ahead of the rest of our age group that it didn't even enter my mind that I was being left behind. On the contrary, he'd done so brilliantly that I just wanted to follow in his footsteps.

And that is exactly what I set out to do.

By the time my first YTS year officially kicked off, in July 1996, I had already played quite a number of games for the A and B Teams, including scoring on my B Team debut against Burnley, while I was still on Schoolboy Forms. So I was brimming with confidence and more than ready to make my mark at this higher grade. Formally signing my YTS contract had given me an added sense of security and I was coming off the back of two very successful years, including some very solid recent performances. I was on a good streak and thoroughly enjoying my new life in the exciting world of professional football.

That summer, for just about the whole of June, England had hosted Euro '96, with Germany beating the Czech Republic 2-1 in the final. Football was still the talk of the town when I reported to Melwood for my first pre-season training as an apprentice player and I was simply buzzing. My already upbeat mood then rocketed through the stratosphere when I discovered that our training squad would include a number of first team players. Me, officially training with first teamers! Now I knew that this was purely because a lot of the senior players had not yet returned from international duty or were still recovering from injury, and I think Michael Owen was away with England under-18s at the time, but this was still a huge opportunity for me to impress the coaches. It was a chance for me to pit my skills against senior pros. And I loved it!

The thought of taking that big step up did not overawe me in any way; in fact I relished the challenge. The reality was that I'd been accustomed to the first team environment ever since I was a kid of thirteen, from the days of spending most of my summer holidays at Melwood just hanging around, taking any chance I had to interact with the players. It's something that could never possibly happen today, not with modern Health and Safety requirements, but back then it was OK. So I was already familiar with the senior players and had in fact already played with or against most of them, including the regular five-a-sides or Friday afternoon games. So, far from being nervous, I actually felt at home amongst them and very comfortable out on the pitch with them.

Suitably inspired by my new status, I got stuck into my work straight away, pushed myself in training and did everything I could to make a good impression on the coaches and the boss, Roy Evans: especially when I heard a whisper that there might be a few additional spaces on the pre-season club tour to Norway! It's not unusual for the club to take a few up-and-coming young players with them on a tour like that, as it is a good way to give them some early exposure to the international game and accelerate their experience. Those overseas friendlies also provide an ideal opportunity to blood a youngster in a first team game and see how he handles himself. So now I had a realistic target to aim for. If one of those spaces on the tour was up for grabs then I wanted it. Badly!

At the end of the first week's training the coaches arranged a full 11-a-side practice match. Even though a few members of the squad were still missing, the line-ups that day still included top players and seasoned internationals such as John Barnes, David James, Phil Babb and Neil 'Razor' Ruddock. Things went well for me from the time we kicked off. I had a decent all-round game and managed to bang in two goals past David James. As we were walking off the pitch a couple of the lads told me I'd had a good game and then Ronnie Moran himself came up and told me well done. As per the Liverpool Way, I kept a lid on how happy I felt and said nothing to anybody about my performance. But inside I was bubbling.

The next morning I bumped into Doug Livermore in the car park, just as he was getting out of his car. He let on to me straight away: 'Alright Yatesy, I heard you scored two good goals in the match yesterday. Keep it up lad.' Dougie, who was Assistant Manager to Roy Evans, had been away from Melwood the previous day, so clearly the word had travelled overnight and they had been talking about me. Knowing that I had been noticed at the very top gave me a big boost and I was already looking forward to my next opportunity to prove myself.

With just a couple of weeks remaining before the club went to Norway, more of the regular first team squad returned to training and I was one of the younger players taken out of the group. But I wasn't sent back to the A or B Team as normally might have happened; instead, Sammy Lee moved me across to train with the Reserve Team with him. Determined to keep moving forward, I kept working hard in training, soaked up everything they told me and applied myself in the best possible way. My good form on the pitch continued and by the end of the week I was rewarded with a place in the Reserve Team Squad for the first time ever, away to Accrington Stanley. I was on the bench, alongside Paul Dalglish. Neither of us got called on to play but it was still a good start for a sixteen year-old.

Once again I put my head down in training and pushed myself even harder. The general consensus around the squad was that I'd be given my Reserve Team debut in the next match. Now that really had me buzzing! It was as if the gods had lined that one up for me because that next fixture was against Burscough, my local club, where I'd played a lot of schoolboy football. By now, with my adrenaline pumping, it had crossed my mind that if I did get selected and played well in that game, then it might earn me one of those spare slots on the tour to Norway. This was my chance to grab a huge opportunity. I couldn't stop myself thinking .... who knows what might happen if they give me a chance to play in Norway.

Suitably fired up, I was in great form at the last training session the day before the Burscough game and really striking the ball well. My confidence was sky high and I was at the peak of my game. During shooting practice I was pinging the ball as sweetly as I'd ever done, rifling in shots from all angles. After hitting one shot from just inside the box, I wheeled around to go back to my starting position and, completely unexpectedly, a ball cannoned into my arm. The force of the impact bent my wrist right back and sent excruciating pain searing through my arm. I was devastated because I knew straight away, without any doubt, that it was broken. Despite the terrible pain that was throbbing from my fingertips to my shoulder, the only thought on my mind was that I would miss my Reserves Team debut against Burscough. 'Why? Why now? Fuck!'

The lad who'd hit the ball, Jamie Cassidy, was horrified to see the state I was in. I don't think he realized that it was mental anguish that was killing me, not the pain in my arm. It was a complete accident and he kept apologizing but I knew it wasn't his fault. It was just a freak accident with a well-struck ball: with me on the receiving end!

Sammy Lee calmed me down, helped me get myself sorted out and then sent me off to see the club doctor. He took one look at my arm and immediately confirmed my own worst fears. Fractured. No debut for the Reserves, no match against Burscough and definitely no chance now of a pre-season trip to Norway.

That ball didn't only break my arm; it broke my heart.

Later that night, Sammy Lee called my parents after we'd got back

from the hospital to check on how I was feeling. He was really concerned about me and it was obvious that he was really disappointed about what had happened and just couldn't believe how desperately unlucky I'd been. Later in life Sammy told me personally: 'That was really bad timing when you broke your arm. We were going to have a good look at you against Burscough, with a view to taking you on the pre-season tour to Norway to see how well you coped.'

Life can be very cruel at times but you just have to get on with as best as you can. So I did.

My next step was to try to recover from the injury as soon as possible and get back out onto the pitch. About a week after the accident, the tour party left for Norway and I started doing my rehabilitation with the Liverpool physios. I began with light work in the gym as a way to maintain some level of fitness.

Luckily, my life was made a lot more interesting and bearable during those long, dark days of rehab because I was in the company of three other injured players: notably Jamie Redknapp, who'd broken his ankle playing for England against Scotland in the Euros: Patrick Berger, who got injured while playing for the Czech Republic in the final against Germany; and Rob Jones, the England right back who, after playing in Liverpool's 1996 FA Cup Final loss against Manchester United, had been advised to take a six-month break from the game in order to try to recover from persistent problems with a back injury.

That was really very fortunate for me because all three of them were ideal role models for me to work alongside during that very challenging period of my life. Keep in mind that I was still only sixteen and I'd just been dealt a very severe blow mentally, so it would have been easy for me to get depressed or let my mind wander to negative thoughts. As it was, with that trio of exemplary professionals recovering next to me, those days in the gym turned into private lessons in self-discipline, patience, commitment, perseverance, positivity and focus: delivered one-on-one by three top tutors. To quote those popular MasterCard advertisements - priceless!

My respect for Jamie Redknapp just grew and grew the more I learned from him and about him. Patrick Berger was a player that I loved to watch in action, especially from close quarters on the practice ground. He was

*Opposite: Patrick Berger is a great guy and a great player*

really good at making surging runs from midfield and he had a great left foot, with one of the most powerful shots in the game. Patrick also turned out to be a fantastic person and it was always a pleasure to chat with him. When I first met him his English was not too good but, typical of the man, he worked really hard to improve and by the end of our treatment period he was much more fluent. Rob also proved to be top pro and a very easy-going guy and we are still in touch to this day. I simply could not have chosen three better players to mentor me during that challenging spell of recovery. At least something had gone right for me!

When the medical staff finally gave Jamie and Patrick the go-ahead to return to training, I found it tough to watch them going back to the first team squad while I had to start all over again with the B Team. It was impossible for me not to think that if it had not been for that freak accident and the incredibly bad timing of my broken arm things might have been very, very different.

As things turned out, by the time I had passed my fitness test to resume playing the pre-season tours and training had all been completed, the new season had already started, and life at Melwood had returned to its regular routine. But it didn't seem so regular to me. Despite all the encouragement and reassurance I got from lots of good people around me, in my own mind I felt as if I'd taken a step backwards. While the reality was that my YTS contract had only just started and I still had two full years ahead of me to keep climbing the ladder, my own perception was that I'd got close to first team contention but now dropped back down to the bottom. So it seemed to me that I was way behind schedule. And, as the saying goes, perception can sometimes be stronger than reality. Nevertheless, true to the Liverpool Way, after limiting myself to a few brief moments of self-pity, I shook off those lingering regrets, rolled up my sleeves and got stuck into my work.

I was determined to get myself back into good form and resume my journey towards the top.


## My Daily Routine as a YTS Football Apprentice

From the day I started my YTS at Liverpool, I quickly settled into a regular daily routine. I'd get up early, usually at 6:30 am, eat a good breakfast, get all my kit ready and then my dad would drop me off at the railway station in Ormskirk. From there I'd catch a train to Maghull, where I used to meet Neil Murphy, another YTS lad at Liverpool. Neil and I would travel together by train to Old Roan, get off and catch a bus to the Black Bull, where we had to then get off again to catch another bus that took us close to Melwood; then, finally, we'd have a 5-minute walk to get to the actual training ground.

It really wasn't the easiest of journeys to deal with every morning of life, especially in the winter, but of course what made it bearable was that I wasn't just turning up for a practice session, I was now actually on my way to work. Football was now my job and Liverpool Football Club was my employer. It was all I'd ever wanted since I was a little boy, so that long trip to Melwood was in fact no problem at all. Especially because by that stage we were training at the same time as the first team, so we were constantly rubbing shoulders with the Liverpool players and having regular opportunities to interact with them in all different kinds of ways. Spending time playing football around all of those top players was literally a dream coming true for me. I loved every minute of it.

As soon as we arrived at Melwood, around 8:30 am, all of the YTS lads would have to straight away start doing whatever jobs had been allocated to us. For example, somebody would have to get all the kit ready in the players dressing room, others would be responsible for getting all the balls out, there might be some tidying up still to do from the day before. Anything really that needed to be done first thing in the morning before the training sessions got going.

My job was to get all the staff kit from the laundry and then line it up in their changing room, so that when the manager or the coaches arrived their gear was already waiting for them. It was quite a tough job because there were ten of them in total and, like most people, they all had their own little quirks about what they liked about their kit. I didn't like letting anybody down, so I'd be there as early as possible every morning, fussing over each individual's personal preferences. Imagine having to look after all the kit for Roy Evans, Dougie Livermore, Ronnie Moran, Steve Heighway, Sammy Lee, Joe Corrigan, Hughie McAuley, Dave Shannon, Mark Leather, Tom Saunders and even the club doctor! There are some big football names in that list and for any sixteen year-old lad it was a big challenge to keep them all happy, especially with the likes of Roy, Ronnie, Hughie and Sammy who often got to Melwood even earlier than me so that they could set up the sessions properly. But, as with everything, I truly loved doing that job because it constantly brought me into direct contact with the manager and the first team coaches. One of the most enjoyable perks of being in and around the staff changing room so often was that I regularly overheard snippets of conversation about first team players, opponents, matches, tactics and other bits of juicy news and information; things that ordinarily I never would have known about.

The morning jobs would finish about 9:20 am and by then we'd have already got through a lot of work. There was no time to relax though as we barely had a chance to come up for air before it'd be time to put on our own boots and get outside, ready for the training session to start. We didn't need a bell or anything to let us know when it was time to get going because Ronnie Moran always made a point of banging on all the dressing room doors and bellowing out, 'Away the noo, lads.' That was our clarion call to get into action and that's when the dressing room banter calmed down. The senior players and the reserves would start appearing first, the YTS lads would gradually join them, then everybody would assemble on the balcony before going down to the B Team pitch to wait for the day's instructions.

Ronnie Moran, aka Bugs, was absolutely manic about us all staying off the A Team pitch until we were invited to go on it. One bitterly cold winter's morning he sent one of our YTS lads to collect some cones and the poor sod forgot about not going on that particular pitch and ran straight across it. Ronnie spotted him immediately and yelled out some kind of expletive laced warning, but it was way too late. And what really made matters ten times worse was that it was a really frosty morning. As a result, the glaring evidence of that youthful indiscretion was a very clear trail of dark boot prints diagonally dissecting the otherwise perfectly pristine white surface of Mr. Moran's beloved, manicured pitch. It was a damning trail of guilt that would be there for a long time, since walking on a frozen pitch kills the grass underneath! Ronnie went absolutely mental. We were all absolutely dying to laugh but daren't let out even a snigger because we would have ended up on the receiving end of a major bollocking as well.

One of the more enjoyable and beneficial aspects of the quiet period the players all spent together just before training started was that all of us young lads got the chance to talk with the senior players or even just listen to their conversations. Ronnie Moran used to jokingly refer to the first teamers as 'the big-heads', but in reality they weren't like that at all. On the contrary, living legends like John Barnes, Jamie Redknapp and Steve McManaman would happily talk to us about games, ask us how we were getting on and generally chat with us. It was a terrific experience for any young footballer and I just lapped it all up as much as I could. In many ways it was like a surreal experience really, even more so because when I went home my mates would be asking me all kinds of questions about the players and anything they had done or said. To all my friends, these Liverpool players were heroes who they worshipped from afar, but for me they were real people who I interacted with every day at work.

Rubbing shoulders with great players like that also had the very positive dual effect of keeping us youngsters grounded while still providing inspiration. For example, if I scored two goals for the A Team it would be difficult to get too big-headed about that when I am bumping into Robbie Fowler who has scored a hat-trick in the Premier League. But, at the same time, if Robbie Fowler bumps into me and says, 'Well done Yatesy, I hear you scored a couple on Saturday,' then that provides an enormous boost. I was definitely aware at the time that I was fortunate to be at Melwood amongst those legends, and to be part of a club with such a rich heritage, but when I look back on it now I can truly appreciate the full extent of the privilege that had been bestowed upon me.

When training actually started around 9:30 am, the three different groups, first team, reserves and youth team, would all be called in together by Ronnie Moran, Sammy Lee, Steve Heighway and Hughie McAuley. We'd start with some gentle stretching, warm-up drills and light exercise. At this point the jokes would still be flying around, especially amongst the first teamers, often talking about their social adventures or the last match, next opponents and such like. Then we'd all do two laps together walking around the perimeter of Melwood, stopping at each of the four corners for more stretching. Next would be some easy paced jogging, followed by a last full lap at a quicker pace. Once that first session was finished we'd split up into our three respective groups and go off to carry on doing some more intense warm-up routines in our own areas. In the case of the first team that was usually 5-a-side matches or passing drills; the reserves would continue their warm-up, start a practice session or sometimes look at team shape for an upcoming match; while most days our YTS group usually started off with some technical training, working on skills like passing or possession, and then we'd later play some form of a match to finish.

As a YTS Apprentice, my jobs around Melwood weren't only limited to the mornings. The minute that training finished, I then had to start looking after the staff kit, including collecting and cleaning all of their boots. I can still picture myself walking along the corridor, through the first team dressing room and then into the boot room, with ten pairs of boots hanging around my neck, all tied together by their laces so they didn't get mixed up. Ten pairs of boots to clean! Luckily for me, it was something I actually enjoyed doing. The first challenge was to get all the mud and grass off with a wire brush, wipe them down with a damp cloth and then give them a really good polishing; including the soles, which also had to be spotless. And if the boots were ever a bit hard from having been used in wet conditions the previous day, then before I even started to clean them I'd have to smack them on the floor a few times until they softened up.

Ronnie Moran had a habit of regularly popping his head into the boot room while I was in there to constantly remind me to put a ring of dubbin around the soles of the boots, so they wouldn't crack. He wasn't just making sure I did a good job; he was also emphasizing the high standards that existed at the club. It was another example of the Liverpool Way being filtered down through the club. All of our coaches would find subtle ways to teach us simple lessons in life whenever the chance cropped up; like Hughie McAuley frequently looking under pipes to see if we'd cleaned them properly, while repeating his favourite football mantra, 'If you're lazy off the pitch, then you'll be lazy on it!'

After I'd finished the staff boots, once they were all in spanking clean condition, I'd take them all back to their dressing room and place them carefully next to each person's own speck, ready for the next day. As soon as all that was done then I'd leg back to the first team dressing room and get Jamie Redknapp's boots to clean them too, as I'd been assigned to look after his kit. I used to clean his boots the same way as I did my own, including really buffing them up by using my shirt to get a brilliant shine. He was always happy with the end result.

At the same time that I was doing my jobs every day after training, some of the other lads would have their own things to do as well, such as tidying up the dressing rooms and the medical room. I was much happier doing the kit and boots!

*Opposite above: Jason McAteer wearing a pair of boots similar to the ones I had to break in for him!*
*Opposite below: Left to right - Ronnie Moran: 'Standards!....'Watch the Harry Limes!'*
*with Roy Evans, Joe Fagan & Tom Saunders*

Although Jamie Redknapp was my main responsibility, I'd occasionally have to look after the boots of other players as well, particularly Jason McAteer. To give you an idea of just how demanding but fun the life of a YTS player could be back then, there is an interesting story about a time that Jason asked me to break in a pair of new boots for him at very short notice. Late one Friday afternoon, after training at Melwood, he walked right past me in the corridor carrying three boxes of boots. Then, almost as an afterthought, he suddenly turned back and tossed a box of Reeboks to me: 'Heh Yatesy, do me a favour mate and get them ready for me for tomorrow's game.' Well, OK, no problem; except that I had an away game to play at 11 o'clock in the morning for the A Team at Manchester United and he was playing at Anfield at 3 o'clock in the afternoon against Middlesborough! In the end I had to wear his boots to play in my game against United. Then, as soon as our team coach got back to Melwood, I had to dive off and rush to the boot room, clean the boots to the normal high standard, write the initials JM on the back in marker pen and then somehow get them across to Anfield in time for the kick-off. I didn't drive in those days and I couldn't get a lift from anybody, so the only way I could travel was on the public bus. It was sheer madness really. In the end I sprinted to the bus stop, shoved myself onto the first bus that came along, jumped off at the nearest stop to Anfield and then made a frantic dash to the ground. To the shock of the security guard, who fortunately knew me, I burst through the Players Entrance, ran to the Home Dressing Room and slid inside just in time to place Jason's sparkling new, but now supple, boots neatly in his speck before he walked through the door. The joke is I never actually got to see him, so he had no idea whatsoever of the trauma I'd had to survive to get those boots to him on time. I didn't even get a tip! But the only reward I really needed was to go up to my seat in the stands and later watch Jason McAteer play a good game for Liverpool in the same boots that I'd played in that morning.

As apprentices, we were paid a YTS allowance of around £42 per week. Compare that to everything that the kids are paid and given today! It sounds totally ridiculous to say this now, and I am literally laughing as I write it, but we were also rewarded with a bonus for good results in the A and B teams: we got £1.50 for a win and 50p for a draw! Unbelievable in this day and age!

One day, quite early on in our YTS, we were all in the middle of a team meeting when Hughie McAuley made some casual comment about it being Pay Day. Quick as a flash, Stevie G came out with a cracker: 'Pay Day? Yeah, good one! I'll nip into town, buy a new pair of trainers, have enough left for a Big Mac and then I'm skint again!'

### Learning Our Trade Amongst Legends

While the regimented routine at Melwood and all the jobs we had been assigned were designed to build our character and help us to develop positive attitudes and self-discipline, it was out on the pitches that we really learned our trade. No matter whether it was a training session, a full-scale practice game, a 5-a-side match or a fixture against another club, we were constantly monitored, guided, educated, motivated and encouraged to do the right thing.

Even though I have always enjoyed fitness work and been a keen student of tactics, like most players, I was always at my happiest with a ball at my feet and a goal in my sights. I loved to play whenever I could, so I particularly looked forward to any kind of game that came along as part of our training programme.

On Monday afternoons there would always be a regular staff match. The first teamers who'd just played that weekend would leave at that point, and so would the reserves if they were playing that night or on Tuesday, which would leave the staff, the YTS lads, plus any senior players who were recovering from injury or on the fringe of the squad. The coaches would pick two teams, including whatever youth team players were performing well at the time. They were good competitive games and I was thrilled every time I got picked to play.

The same applied to the 5-a-side matches we used to play on Friday mornings at the end of training. Even though they were loads of fun they also had a bit of bite to them as well, which made them great games to play in, especially with that same mix of staff, senior players, youth team lads and the occasional first teamer having a bit of a run out as a fitness test. We all knew that we had to tone things down a bit because we had to play the next day, but nobody wanted to lose those 'fiveos' so they were genuinely very competitive. Arguments and little spats were par for the course, with the occasional minor bout of fisticuffs not being uncommon. It was one of those Friday games that threw up what has since become something of a famous incident at Liverpool and a legendary episode in the Steven Gerrard story. Rather than holding back in the tackle out of respect for the senior players, Steven drove himself into a crunching tackle on Paul Ince, who was club captain at the time. Incey, as befits a man with his own rightfully earned reputation as a hard player with a no-nonsense attitude, took great exception to this YTS lad clattering into him and let him know so in very direct and easy to understand terminology. However, far from being intimidated, the sixteen year-old Gerrard stood his ground and told his club captain, a seasoned international footballer, to watch out because he was after his place in the team. The tackle itself had been a shock but when Steven came out with that line I was totally gobsmacked, literally speechless. I think everybody was.

Quite incredibly, we'd just witnessed a young YTS lad upend Paul Ince, the Guv'nor of all people, and then tell him to his face that he was challenging him for his position. Wow! If we hadn't seen it with our own eyes it would have been a hard story to believe.

After the bust-up the game was stopped to calm things down and take the heat out of the situation. I can remember Steven just walked off the pitch in his usual characteristic manner, as if nothing had happened. Knowing how he operated, I am sure that he never actually planned to take out Paul Ince and definitely didn't intend to hurt him; it was just that he was really up for the challenge. That was the way he always played because he wanted to win every battle in every game, regardless of who he was up against. If there was anything more to it, it was probably just his way of saying, 'Here I am, look at me', trying to impress the manager and coaches. Steven was always desperate to win because he had such a burning and passionate desire to play for Liverpool Football Club.

Of course the club's coaches recognised that Steven needed to learn to restrain himself in the tackle, more to protect himself from injury and getting booked or sent off than anything else. So, without killing his determination to win, they started encouraging him to be more controlled with his aggression. The biggest problem was that he would occasionally fly into tackles that there was no way he could ever possibly win, often with bad consequences.

One particular tackle he made against Everton's youth team at Melwood really sticks in my mind. I couldn't begin to try to explain why Steven even went in for that tackle, because he was never ever going to get to the ball first, so the inevitable end result was that he just completely obliterated his opposite number. He didn't even bother to look at the referee, just stood up, pulled his shirt off and walked towards the dressing rooms. Nobody needed to send him off; he already knew he was gone. Even though this was possibly Steven Gerrard at his worst, sent off for a reckless tackle and reducing his own team to ten men in a big match, I still have to say that I think this was just another example of his extraordinary drive to succeed as opposed to any kind of bad intentions or lack of football intelligence.

Ever since the time I first came across him as a kid, Steven has been a great ball winner and a great match winner. He has been a huge asset to every team he ever played for and no manager or coach would ever want to drill that aggression out of him, but Liverpool did have to try to educate him how to best use it. I think that Liverpool and Steven himself have together done a good job in that regard. When you look back over his career, from the time he broke into the Liverpool first team right up to today, you can see that the number of bone crunching tackles he has made have reduced significantly as he has matured more as a player; but he still has that fantastic will to win and never-say-die attitude.

I have a particularly fond memory of the first occasion when one of those Friday morning 'fiveos' sessions was cut short because Roy Evans and Ronnie Moran wanted the youth team players to line up on a full size pitch in the same formation that they were expecting Liverpool's opposition to line up on the Saturday in the Premier League. I couldn't believe my ears when they told us what to do. Then they picked the first team starting eleven to play against us for about twenty-five minutes, to give them a run out together and see how they held their shape. Can you imagine how it felt to be 'playing' against Liverpool first team, under the watchful eye of the manager and all of his top coaches. It was absolutely amazing! Anyway, that first experiment must have worked well because it then became a regular routine. For the rest of our time as youth players, we lined up every Friday afternoon against the Liverpool first team selected to play that weekend. It was every boy's dream come true!

To put that in perspective, it is worth noting that Liverpool's squad for that 1996/97 season included players like John Barnes, Steve McManaman, Robbie Fowler, Jamie Redknapp, Patrick Berger, David James, Michael Thomas, Stan Collymore, Rob Jones, Mark Wright, Phil Babb, Neil Ruddock, Jason McAteer, Dominic Matteo, Jamie Carragher, Steve Harkness, Mark Kennedy and Stig-Inge Bjornbye. Not a bad line-up for a sixteen year-old apprentice to face every week!

Needless to say, we never really got much of a kick in those games and it was essentially just a bit of an exercise for the first team; but I do remember one match when I tried a bit of cheek to try and take them by surprise to give us an early advantage. One of my regular party pieces when we were playing amongst ourselves was to hit the ball from the halfway line and clear the keeper, so on this occasion I decided to give it a go right from the kick-off against the first team. None of their players or the coaches would have been expecting that from me, so I am sure that it took all of them by surprise. It could have been an embarrassing disaster for me if it had gone wrong but luckily I didn't make a fool of myself because I struck it really well and accurately. In fact it would have gone in but at the last second big David James was able to jump up and catch it over his head. As he landed with the ball he just looked up, glared at me, shook his head and then burst out laughing. Even though I hadn't scored, it was still a very special moment.

Generally speaking, even though we were a bit like extras on a film set, mainly there to make up the numbers and provide a bit of a crowd scene for the real stars, those short games against the first team still provided incredible experiences for a group of youngsters who were all eager to learn. There can be no doubt that they would have helped us enormously in our development as players. Our coaches would play alongside us in the game and be constantly shouting out advice to us. I can vouch from personal experience that it is a lot easier to remember the lessons you have been taught under those kind of fast-paced, real-life match conditions, especially when you end up being embarrassed in front of a bunch of top players as well as your mates. Trust me, you never forget it when you knock a sloppy pass to somebody like Steve Heighway and he screams back, 'Fire it into me, fire it into me! I'm an international for God's sake!'

Just playing against, or should I say playing on the same pitch as, those great players was truly inspirational. Being so close to Robbie Fowler in action and watching how he moved around the pitch, used the space, timed his runs, controlled the ball, completed the finish and so on, was an immensely valuable first-hand education for me.

John Barnes would regularly give out good advice, often by telling us little sayings that we could remember easily. One of his favourites was: 'Remember who you are, what you are and who you represent.'

Sometimes those games took on an extra dimension when we were given special instructions to play in a particular way, to try and mimic the style and tactics of some upcoming opposition. One good example that sticks in my mind is when Liverpool was due to play a team that loved to hit long diagonal balls into the box. So the coaches told us to forget our normal way of thinking about how we could best distribute the ball and instead to just concentrate entirely on pinging balls into the box from every angle. I especially enjoyed that session because I could knock in a cross as well as anybody and I also liked getting on the end of them. Best of both worlds that morning!

One session that really opened my eyes to the monumental gap between our YTS level and the top first team players was when I was given the job of man-to-man marking Steve McManaman. I think it was before a match against Aston Villa and the coaches thought that Villa would aim to stifle the creativity of Macca's free role by trying to mark him out of the game. So, it was up to me to try and replicate that match day situation, but I didn't stand a chance! Even now, I still have a crystal clear vision in my head of Steve picking up the ball and running straight towards me at terrific pace, moving incredibly smoothly with the ball under complete control, and me not having any clue whatsoever which direction he was going to go. Then, before I could make any kind of decision, with a quick drop of a shoulder or a shift of his feet, he was gliding past me, gone and racing off towards the goal. What a player he was. What a privilege it was to be roasted by him that day!

Whenever I get asked about who were my role models in football when I was working my way through the Centre of Excellence and the YTS years, I always have to stop and think about it carefully. The reality is that, apart from admiring Eric Cantona's playing style, I can never get past the great Liverpool players of the day. Instead of having a single role model, I had an entire squad of them all around me. Even the coaches and managers at Liverpool were living legends! If I was put under serious pressure to name a few individual players then I would have to choose Steve McManaman and Robbie Fowler, since they were local lads who'd reached the top; along with Ian Rush, John Barnes and Patrick Berger, who were truly exceptional players; plus Jamie Carragher, who we all looked up to as a young local player like us who'd made into the first team. Steve Heighway used to make a point of stopping YTS training sessions at Melwood and tell us all to listen. Inevitably we'd be able to hear Jamie screaming out instructions to the first teamers, even though he'd only just broken into the squad. He was the epitome of passion and confidence.

Jamie Redknapp also features at the very top of any list of my favourite players. Jamie was the ultimate professional and he gave me a lot of personal guidance and encouragement. As I was the apprentice assigned to clean Jamie's boots then obviously I came into contact with him more than any of the other first team players. He always seemed to have time to talk to me about my own progress and he'd often give me bits of spare kit he'd picked up at England camps or let me have his old boots whenever he got new ones. He was just an all-round top man. Not surprisingly, I also admired the way he played the game. In the end I started copying him; not just how he handled himself on the pitch, but other small things like how he tied his bootlaces or rolled up his socks. I even grew my hair long in the same style that he preferred. Needless to say, that gave the rest of the lads a readymade excuse for taking the piss out of me. The next thing I knew I had a new nickname – Redders!

My favourite player in the game today is undoubtedly Steven Gerrard.

## Bring on the Banter

Put a bunch of healthy young men together in any environment, anywhere in the world, and at some point the banter will start. It is almost like a law of nature! Footballers are no different; in fact some experts might argue that they are the biggest culprits. Our squad had enjoyed its own fair share of schoolboy antics ever since we came together as kids, but it was during those two years of YTS that the dressing room really started to come alive with wicked piss-taking, stupid but hilarious practical jokes and endless ways of fooling about.

We all had to learn to be very thick-skinned and to always expect the unexpected. Apart from the obvious ribbings that lads would regularly give each other about choice of clothes, a recent haircut or rumours of a new girlfriend, our dressing room got quite creative when it came to other ways of winding people up. Hiding shoes, undies, bags and so on were merely par for the course. The more innovative tricks of the trade involved ploys like cutting the laces on somebody's trainers, so that when they went to tie them they literally came away in their hands; or cutting the ends off socks, so the lad's toes popped out the end when he put them on. One of

*Opposite: Steve McManaman, 'Macca' ... glided like the wind and was unstoppable in full flight.*

the more destructive but undeniably comical tricks was to cut through the bottom of the handles on somebody's kit bag; so when the unsuspecting owner tried to pick up the bag all he was left holding was a pair of handles. Some of those episodes were so funny we literally wet ourselves laughing. But the poor victim then had to go to his parents and try to explain why he needed a new pair of footy socks or even a new bag. And if anybody ever made the mistake of confessing to the lads that they got into trouble for it when they went home then they earned themselves even more grief. Better to keep quiet and get on with it.

A regular event that always provided plenty of entertainment and lots of laughs and kicks – both figuratively and literally - was the post-training game of 'sock-ball'. We used the bench legs at one end of the dressing room as one goal and put down coats for the goal at the other end. Then we'd stuff about five pairs of socks together as the ball. The matches would be played one versus one, with each player only allowed two touches of the ball, one to control and one to shoot. The first two lads to finish their jobs would start the first game and then it would just carry on as the rest of us got back to the dressing room and sat in a line to show who was the next man up. We always had a winner-stays-on rule and, no great surprise I suppose, Michael Owen seemed to be on forever. He was even the top scorer in 'sock-ball'!

One of the most cruel, but equally most popular, pranks was to mercilessly wind-up Don, the Melwood janitor. The lads actually liked Don and generally treated him well; but he had a really short fuse and the piss-taking ringleaders were ruthless with anybody like that. There were no windows in the changing rooms so, every now and then, when he walked in somebody would quickly flip off the lights to plunge the room into pitch-black darkness. At that precise second a barrage of shoes, bags, rolled up socks, cups and other sundry missiles would immediately be flung at him from all corners. Every time it happened, Don would just explode and start swinging his fists in every direction, trying to connect with anybody he could get his hands on in the dark. Other times we'd knock off the lights and then all start flicking at him with the ends of rolled up towels. He'd go absolutely ballistic and try to fight back but he was totally outnumbered. I think that's what kept making us do those things; Don was too easy to wind-up. He just kept taking the bait. On a couple of occasions we got a bit of a bollocking from the staff, telling us to back off, but I have to be honest and say that never really stopped us.

We all got such a buzz and a great laugh out of it. Even though it might sound like a bit of a miserable torment for Don, I somehow think he actually enjoyed it too. I am sure he could have put a complete stop to it if he really wanted.

We were all on the receiving end of the banter at some point and occasionally it did get out of hand, but it was an unavoidable part of our development and we had to learn to cope with it as best as we could.

My worst personal ordeal happened one day when I was in the boot room, peacefully doing my regular job. I was focused on polishing when the door suddenly exploded open behind me. Before I could even turn around to see who it was, a gang of the lads jumped on me, held my head down on the ground and started cutting off chunks of my hair. Goodness knows what they used to do it! Within twenty painful seconds it was all over and they were gone; and I didn't have a clue who had done it. When I looked in the mirror I was horrified to see the mess they'd made. There were whole clumps of hair missing and my head was literally in tatters. But what could I do? I carried on cleaning the boots of course. Despite feeling devastated, I made up my mind there and then that I wouldn't let them beat me. I'd just get my hair cut to tidy it up and then start all over again.

I was just about managing to hold on to my emotions when Jamie Redknapp and Steve McManaman arrived to collect their boots. As soon as they saw the terrible state I was in, they wanted to know who had done it and why. It was then, when I tried to give them an answer, that I finally lost the battle to control my feelings and my eyes welled up with tears. In the end I explained that Steve Heighway had been telling me to get a haircut for a couple of weeks and at the last squad meeting he'd casually said: 'Well if you don't get it done yourself then I'll have to ask the lads to do it won't I!' As far as the lads were concerned that would have seemed like an open invitation. So they took it!

Macca and Jamie weren't happy with the sound of that background story so they mentioned it to Sammy Lee, to be sure that he knew what had gone on.

When I got home later that evening, my dad went absolutely ballistic. He was livid and I had to really plead and beg him not to go and see Steve Heighway right there and then. I didn't even want him to talk to Heighway on the phone. But, apparently, he did call him later that night. For my part, the next day I got my haircut properly at the barber, in a new, shorter style, and I carried on playing my football.

# Jamie Redknapp

*Liverpool FC 1991 – 2001 and Former England International*

My time as a schoolboy and apprentice at Bournemouth gave me some of my happiest days in football. Even though my dad was the manager, I still had to do all the usual jobs around the ground: mopping the dressing rooms, sweeping the stands, painting the lines on the pitch, cleaning the toilets and any other odd-jobs that needed doing. The club didn't have much cash so to save money the apprentices did a lot of the maintenance work. It might sound a bit harsh now but we actually enjoyed doing it.

I used to have to clean Luther Blisset's boots, even though I was playing for the Bournemouth first team same as him. He always wanted his boots to be nice and shiny but he also wanted them to be a bit damp, so they were soft. It's almost impossible to shine damp boots so I had to work really hard to get it done. I'd be there, with all my kit on ready to play, but having to polish away at Luther's boots like a mad man. Many a time I'd hand them over to him and he'd give them straight back: 'Not shiny enough yet Jamie, keep it going son'. It looked like he was giving me a hard time but really he was trying to take my mind off the game, making sure my nerves didn't get the better of me. I was only sixteen in my debut season, so that was a good way to keep me grounded. And of course I loved it whenever Luther told me 'well done' or gave me a twenty quid tip at Christmas. It helped shape my character.

Cleaning Luther Blisset's boots didn't teach me how to pass the ball, but what it did do was to give me a sense of perspective and remind me that I hadn't made it yet. I might have been playing for the first team but I still had a lot to learn. It helped me keep my head down, do my jobs and have respect for the senior players. Sadly I am not sure that respect for seniority and authority exists today.

Some of the young players today are already being paid big money and driving fancy cars by the time they are eighteen. While that might look like a very attractive situation for young lads, it can also cause serious problems for some of them. If you've already got more money than you really need, then it can be very tough to motivate yourself to work even harder. And the only way to succeed in football is to have a very deep desire, some special fire burning in your belly, to make you keep pushing yourself to a higher standard. Sadly, a lot of talented players today don't

*I took great pride in cleaning Jamie's boots...*

kick on and reach the next level because they are given too much too soon. The youngsters who'll carry on fighting all the way to the top are the ones who've got that desperate hunger to be a footballer, regardless of the size of their pay packet.

I was fortunate in that I was able to survive that incident and the general banter of the dressing room but I do know young players who couldn't handle it and dropped out of the game; and that of course should never happen. On the positive side though, when dished out within the realms of reason, that same dressing room banter can help to forge strong bonds in any team unit. Kind of like, 'I can take the piss out of my best mate but don't you dare say a single word against him!'

All footballers, young and old, enjoy a good laugh; so if you can tell a funny joke or pull off some humorous trick or other, then you'll always be popular in the dressing room. My special talent, and I honestly can't remember when or how I started it, is that I can do good impressions of people. For some reason I can mimic people's voices, especially if they've got a strong accent. My two all-time favourite impersonations that I do well are John Barnes and Alan Hansen. I had Digger's voice down to perfection and the first team used to love asking me to do that one. Other times I would be called into their dressing room to put on an Alan Hansen Match of the Day Show, complete with comments about the day's game or training, and they'd all end up falling over laughing. It was certainly an unusual but very effective way of getting to know the senior players.

One time Jamie Redknapp was driving out of Melwood and he stopped to ask me who else I had in my impersonation locker: so I told him that he was in there too and immediately started mimicking his voice. Jamie cracked up and shouted out to Neil Ruddock who was still out on the pitch: 'Heh Razor, Yatesy's only got me in his locker too!' Quite soon after that first bit of banter, another afternoon after training, Jamie keyed a number into his mobile phone and just shoved it into my hand: 'Here, that's my wife Louise. Tell her to put the pasta on because I'll be home soon.' So I did. And she did! What a laugh.

After that early success Jamie made a few other 'special requests'. One of the best ones was when he asked me to call his dad, Harry Redknapp, and pretend to be Alan Hansen, wanting to arrange a game of golf for the following week. I had Harry convinced it was Hansen and we were chatting away for ages about all kinds of things, until he suddenly asked me where I was calling from. When I said I was at Melwood with Jamie, the line went dead for a few seconds. Then a confused Harry blurted out:

'No you're not. You're at the Masters in Augusta!'

## A Bizarre Incident with Joe Corrigan

During my first YTS year, and still only sixteen, I had to deal with an unfortunate and bizarre incident that dropped me in a deep pile of the proverbial – a freak accident that had all the lads killing themselves laughing and smiling for days on end but one that got me into serious trouble.

At the end of training Joe Corrigan asked a few of us to stay behind and do some extra shooting at the three keepers, David James, Tony Warner and Ian Dunbavin, because the first team was scheduled to play Arsenal at Anfield that same night in the Coca Cola Cup. When the session ended, even though it was drizzling quite heavily, a few of us stayed out on the pitch, doing some passing, shooting or chatting with the boss, Roy Evans, and first team coach Ronnie Moran. I was banging a few balls into the net when I heard Jamie Carragher shout me to knock one over to him. When I looked up I saw that he was about 60-yards away. There was a shiny, new Mitre Delta right in front of me, so I just touched it out of my feet with the outside of my right boot and then absolutely pinged it. I really caught it sweet and it flew like a rocket towards Jamie. As I was admiring the ball's trajectory, I suddenly realized that big Joe Corrigan was heading back to the dressing room and he'd walked straight into the line of the ball's flight path. Oh no, oh shit! Before I could shout any kind of warning it clocked him right on the back of the head, sending him sprawling forward across the A Team pitch. The gloves he was carrying flew out of his hands and into the air before landing next to his prostrate body! Everyone saw it happen and of course they immediately burst out laughing.

With Joe being the unit he is, I went straight over and apologised profusely but he wasn't too happy at all, he just didn't want to know, so I kept out of harm's way for as long as I could!

Back in the changing rooms the players and the staff, even the boss, all still thought it was totally hilarious and they had plenty of banter flying round: 'Heh Yatesy, you'd better watch out for Big Joe. He's after yer lad. I'd go home now if I was you!'

The thing is, that ball would have been pumped up to the full 12psi air pressure that Ronnie Moran demanded. He wanted the balls to zing and ping at all times. If not there was trouble! Any time that a ball had not been pumped up properly Ronnie would hunt down whoever was supposed to have done it and he'd make sure that they never made the same mistake again! Ronnie Moran was always a stickler for maintaining standards. So that ball, from that distance, at that speed, would have really smacked very hard into the back of Joe's head.

Later on I had to go into the staff dressing room to do my job of collecting their kit, so there was just no way I could try to avoid the big man. Before I could apologize again, he collared me: 'What the fuck were you playing at? Think before you ping balls like that! And why didn't you fucking shout me?'

Anyway, when he'd stopped ranting, I somehow managed to get in another apology. He was still groggy and just mumbled, 'Alright, no problem, apology accepted.'

At that point, as far as I was concerned, he'd got his message across, I'd apologized for my mistake and I had learned my lesson. OK, let's move on now. But it wasn't going to be that easy! That night I went to the game against Arsenal and, as I always did, I got there in time to watch the teams warm-up. To my horror, there was no sign of Joe. He would normally be out on the pitch warming up the keepers, but I could only see Jamo and Bonus (Tony Warner) working together in front of the Kop. What was going on?

Liverpool beat Arsenal 4-2 that night (Fowler 2, McManaman and Berger) and I went to training as usual the next day at Melwood. As soon as I walked into the staff room Joe was already there, waiting to pounce on me: 'You twat! I couldn't do my job last night 'cos of you!'

It turned out that the Club Doctor, Mark Waller, had advised him to stay at home because he had concussion!!! Whoops.

That bizarre incident happened over sixteen years ago but I am still living with it to this day. In the Anfield match programme for an FA Cup game against Manchester United on Saturday 28th January 2012 (which we won 2-1 by the way), Steven Gerrard was interviewed and asked, 'What's the funniest thing you've ever witnessed in training?' Part of his answer included: 'I remember when Michael Yates, a striker I played with when I was a kid coming through, struck a ball and it hit Joe Corrigan on the head. It knocked him out.'

More recently, I got this Linkedin message from Layton Maxwell, a former YTS team mate who I hadn't heard from for over twelve years: 'Yatesy, the hardest, most accurate pass in the Vernon Sangster and the only man to knock out big Joe Corrigan on a footy field!'

Even all these many years later, it's still a really funny memory for everybody; except maybe for Joe and me. Thank goodness it had a happy ending.

## Climbing Up the Ladder

During my time as an apprentice the A and B Teams played in the Lancashire League Divisions 1 and 2, and the Reserves competed in the Central League, against sides like Everton, the two Manchester teams, Notts Forest, Sheffield Wednesday, Newcastle and other clubs from Northern England and North Wales; plus there were a few knockout competitions. Very often in the Lancashire League our Liverpool A and B Teams would be playing against the reserve teams of clubs like Rochdale, Morecambe and so on, because the quality of our young players was so good.

The ultimate goal of all the young players was to try to work their way from the B Team to the A Team, up into the Reserves and then, the biggest prize of all, to win a place in the First Team squad. At the same time though, the coaches had a very open policy of rotating players between all the teams. So it was not unusual for somebody to play for the Reserves in one game, to be picked to play next for the B Team and then be put back into the A Team. It was really all about the development of the player, so selection was based on individual needs and team requirements at the particular time, rather than sticking to a very rigid squad system. In my own case, I can recall being on the bench for the A Team in an away game in the morning, where I went on for about 10 minutes, then going straight to Melwood to play a full game for the B Team in the afternoon.

In fact, while I have been doing interviews for this book and looking back over the years, it has really impacted on me that I can remember a lot more about training than I can about all the many matches I played. To me, this is a clear indication of just how much our coaches focused on developing us as players, rather than just trying to grind out results. There was no great significance attached to what team you were playing for, it was what was best for the players that really mattered. While there was an obvious pathway of progression, from B Team to First Team, the overriding emphasis at Liverpool was on overall development.

It was also quite common for first team players, who perhaps needed a game to help them recover from injury, to turn out for the A Team or even the B Team, not just the reserves. I can remember playing once against Crewe at Melwood, in a behind-closed-doors friendly that was arranged especially to give John Barnes a start to his comeback after a series of hamstring injuries. Digger wore black cycle shorts under his kit and a pair of black knitted gloves and I learned so much from him in that game. He was unbelievable. I don't think he gave the ball away once and he was always talking to the players around him. He told me to hold up whenever he got the ball and stop running through the space. 'Stand still Yatesy, I'll find you!' And he did! I think we won the game 3 – 1 and I scored one of the goals. So when you had the likes of John Barnes happily playing for the B Team, there was definitely no shame attached to any of the younger players being asked to do the same job.

The first time I ever played with Jamie Redknapp was when he dropped down into the B Team for a match against Everton because he needed a bit of a run after a knee injury and there was no other fixture available. He didn't object to that at all. His positive attitude was that a game is a game! We played at Melwood and because Jamie was playing we used the first team dressing rooms and played on the A Team pitch. I also later played alongside him for the A Team and the Reserves. There was one occasion when were both due to play for the A Team and he decided to go for a bit of a run in the morning, to loosen up before the game later in the day. When he'd finished, as was his habit, he sent his boots to be cleaned. And that of course was my job! So, as well as polishing my own boots for the game, I ended up cleaning his pair as well and putting them on the bench next to his speck. An hour or so later we were both getting changed and going out to play on the same team. It was bizarre and brilliant at the same time! In no way did I feel that I shouldn't have been asked to clean his boots for that match. Quite the opposite, I was really proud to have the opportunity to clean Jamie Redknapp's boots and then go out and play alongside him. In fact it was a privilege. Happily for me, that scenario was repeated on several other occasions after that game.

One of the really interesting aspects of playing at the YTS level was that our coaches would often use the same tactics as whatever the first team planned to adopt in their next match. Our line-up would always mirror the first team. So, for example, if they were playing three at the back, then we would also play three at the back. That was another big reason why those Friday afternoon games with the senior players were so

**B**OTH the A and B teams were in action at Melwood a week ago and they had mixed results.

The A team won 2-0 against Preston North End with two goals by Michael Yates. Overall it was a good performance. We competed well and passed the ball around well at times.

If anything we needed to get at them a bit more and close down quicker but we tended to let them have too much ball at times. We could have won the game more convincingly.

The first goal was created by Ritchie Partridge, who delivered a good cross from the right wing. Michael Yates got away from his marker and had a shot saved by the goalkeeper before tucking away the rebound. Sean Friars and Gareth Roberts combined down the left for the second goal and Michael, at the far post,

## HUGH McAULEY
### Youth Team Coach

headed into the roof of the net. They were two well worked goals. The quality of our crossing has been really good, but we are still searching for that extra cutting edge in all areas of the field. There were signs that we are getting there.

■ The B-team went down 6-3 defeat against Manchester United. We fielded six schoolboys and with ten minutes to go were only trailing 3-2. Conceding six goals is obviously a concern but Dave Shannon, the team manager, felt that there were a lot of good things to come out of the game.

Three or four of their goals came about from counter-attacks, which we must learn to defend against. And a couple were down to individual errors.

From an attacking point of view, John Boggan and Matthew McManus had their

# Another Michael among the goals

## LANCASHIRE LEAGUE FIXTURES

| DIVISION 1 | DIVISION 2 |
|---|---|
| Aug | |
| Aug | |
| Aug | |
| Sep | |
| Sep | |
| Sep | |
| Sep | |
| Oct | |
| Oct | |
| Oct | |
| Oct | |

*Versus Man UTD 'A' team at the Cliff...I'm breaking Jason McAteers boots in here!*

beneficial, as it helped us to better understand the system by actually experiencing it. This flexible policy also resulted in the young lads being given the chance to play in a number of different positions. Over the course of a season, I'd end up playing upfront, out wide and even as a wingback. I am sure that it was no coincidence that just after the training session when I'd been instructed to man-mark Steve McManaman, to try to stop his creativity, I was picked to play the same, free roaming role as Macca in our next Youth Team match against Manchester City.

It was in that same game against Manchester City that Steven Gerrard gave another unforgettable demonstration of his outstanding quality. We had won a free kick on the right, just outside the box, in the sort of position where I'd normally take it and whip the ball into a danger area. Anyway, I was going about my business as usual, placing the ball, when Steven came bouncing over, unceremoniously moved me out of the way and told me: 'I'll have this one Yatesy. I can score here.' No debate; no problem. I jogged off and took up my position. Thing is, instead of just pinging the ball at the goal, Steven cut across it powerfully with the inside of his boot and put enough spin on it that it bent right to left around the wall, flew across the keeper, and thudded against the stanchion in the far corner of the net. It was an incredible strike and once again Steven had pulled off the extraordinary. It was the kind of free kick that later became David Beckham's trademark, but at that point we'd never seen anybody do it before. The amazing thing that really struck me at the time was that Steven had obviously seen that opportunity the split second we won the free kick and that's why he came flying over the way he did. It blew me away that he had the vision to imagine what he could do with the ball from that difficult angle, the sheer audacity to have a go and the technical ability to execute it successfully. Only Steven Gerrard!

During the period while I'd been recovering from my broken arm and working hard to earn a place in the Reserves Team, Michael Owen had already broken into the First Team squad. Michael eventually made his full debut at the end of the 1996/97 Premier League season, away to Wimbledon at Selhurst Park. And, in keeping with his prolific goal scoring record as a junior, he netted on his first outing with the senior team. Was I jealous? Absolutely! Was I resentful? Not at all! At the tender age of seventeen, Michael had turned his football dream into a reality and

*Opposite: Michael Owen, a model of poise and balance*

it gave hope to the rest of us who all aspired to join him.

Before Michael had been promoted permanently to the First Team squad, I did get one more chance to enjoy playing alongside him as his strike partner. As part of our development programme, the Liverpool Youth Team entered a tournament in Dusseldorf, Germany. It was a high quality competition and we played really well to win all of our qualifying matches, against strong sides like Borussia Dortmund, FC Bruges, 1860 Munich and Kaiserslautern. I can remember having a decent tournament, scoring a few goals and linking well with Michael; especially against Kaiserslautern when I set one up for him, then he returned the compliment by setting me up for one, in an eventual 4-1 win. In the end we were knocked out 1-0 at the semi-final stage by Shizuoka, which was some form of Japanese representative team. We were really disappointed not to have gone all the way to the final and won, but it had still been a very constructive learning experience. We all benefitted from undergoing the particularly demanding tests that only tournament play can provide and, consequently, we went back home as better players.

Following that Dusseldorf tournament, during the second half of the season, I was training regularly with the Reserves squad. I felt as though I was getting closer and closer to my debut, especially when Sammy Lee picked me on the bench for a few games to get me back amongst the mix. One of those matches was away to Sheffield Wednesday; and when I found myself warming up at the Leppings Lane end, I couldn't help thinking about 'The 96' – those ill-fated, innocent Liverpool supporters who'd tragically lost their life during the catastrophic Hillsborough Disaster in 1989. What an unnecessary waste of good lives. May they all rest in peace.

For several very different reasons, I can especially remember an away game against Nottingham Forest Reserves at the City Ground. Our team that night included quite a few first team regulars like Jamie Redknapp, Neil Ruddock, Danny Murphy, David Thompson and Dominic Matteo, and the journey to the game on the team coach was a blast. Apart from the fact that the banter from those characters was top-drawer quality, we also watched Quadrophenia on the TVs. And that was a big thing for me and the other young lads who had never experienced this before.

For the match itself, I started on the bench but got called on with about 25 minutes to go. I went on to replace Thommo who'd got a knock and I played left side of midfield. I can remember immediately getting a pass off Jamie Redknapp. As I received it, he shouted, 'Keep it Yatesy!' So I controlled the ball, then played it into Paul Dalglish's feet and we kept possession. Jamie gave me a thumbs up and I got a 'well done' off Dominic and Razor. That settled me quickly. I soon got another pass from Jamie and this time he yelled, 'Be positive! Get at him!' So I did. Being right footed out on the left wing meant that I could drop my shoulder and cut inside. After I'd done that I was about 25-yards out, with the goal in my sights, so I hit it. Even though it went just wide of the far post my decent effort still earned me another round of 'well done' from the experienced players. We lost 2-1 but I felt as though I had done OK in the time I was on the pitch.

Later that night, on the coach going home after the game, I was in the middle of doing a few of my favourite impersonations for the lads when Paul Dalglish came up with the bright idea that I should telephone his dad, Kenny Dalglish, the idolised former Liverpool player and manager. Paul wanted me to pretend to be Alan Hansen, another Liverpool legend, and one of Kenny's best mates from his playing days at Anfield. That one sounded a bit too dodgy in my opinion but there was simply no escape for me once the senior players heard about the idea. So there I was, surrounded by a bunch of giggling Liverpool players, dialling the immortal Kenny Dalglish. Luckily the phone went to voice mail so I took a deep breath and just launched into a message: 'Hello Kenny, it's Alan here. How are you doing?' Despite my initial, uneasy apprehension, it went well and I suggested we - as in Kenny and Alan – should meet the next day for a round of golf. I don't know how I managed to keep a straight face and a steady voice because all the big idiots around me were creased up laughing, with their hands shoved in their mouths to stifle their sniggering. After I hung up, the lads just erupted in laughter. I was smiling myself because it was really hilarious and it's always good to make people laugh; but I was also a bit worried about how Kenny would react. To this day I still don't know if the great man saw the funny side of it too. I hope so. Especially if he reads this book and finds out it was me!

Other than pre-season training with the First Team squad before the disappointing calamity of my broken arm, the absolute highlight of my first YTS year was making my debut for Liverpool Reserves. And that long awaited moment was all the sweeter since it was in a really good game against Everton Reserves, in the semi-final of the Liverpool Senior Cup. It was played at Widnes and because it was a 'mini-derby' it attracted over

9,000 spectators. There were so many people trying to get into the small ground they had to delay the kick-off by about half an hour. Sammy Lee picked me to play right side midfield and I played the full 90-minutes. It was fast and furious right from the start, with all the blood and thunder you would expect from a derby match. We went 1-0 down but equalised through Paul Dalglish and held on for a very creditable 1-1 draw. We had a fairly young side out that night and Sammy was really pleased with us at full-time. My brother Geoff and my dad were at the game and it was a great feeling to know that they were somewhere in the crowd. Especially for my debut, especially for that game and especially because they were Everton supporters! We won the replay 1-0 and later went on to win the cup, also 1-0, against Tranmere Rovers. I was disappointed to miss out on a place in the team for the final but the reality was that a number of first team players were drafted in; so I had no chance.

In my opinion, breaking into the Reserve Team squad and playing matches for the Reserves was a lot tougher back then than it is now. In our day it was a regular occurrence to have First Team players turning out for the Reserves: not just to get a game when recovering from an injury, but also anybody who hadn't played at the weekend.

As we approached the end of that first YTS year, our B Team, with just three matches left to play, was running second in the Lancashire League Division 2 and in a perfect position to win it. After having enjoyed a really great season, we only needed four points from the last three games to guarantee the title.

Much to our own disappointment and our coaches' disgust, we lost away to Wigan, so no points from that one. But our next match was at home against Marine, when a win or a draw would set us up nicely for the title, and we were confident of getting a good result in that one. It was a mid-week fixture under the floodlights at Melwood. That night there was a howling wind and it battered down with rain. Marine managed the conditions better than we did and they beat us 1-0. We'd blown the title! After the game, Steve Heighway was furious and he ripped into us about not showing enough character and mental strength.

Steve also hammered us for allowing the weather to affect our performance. He reminded us: 'One day some of you lads might be lucky enough to represent this great club in some hostile place like Russia, in the middle of a freezing winter, when it's minus-20, and you'll still have to perform to the best of your ability. Or you might have to go and play an FA Cup match at some shitty little ground with a mud bath for a pitch, but you'll still have to stand up and be counted and get a result. That is what this club is all about. So remember that lesson from tonight and don't ever forget it!'

We won our last match but by then it was all too late. We'd thrown away a league championship. It was a very chastening experience and a bitter pill for all of us to swallow.

As that 1996/97 season came to a close, I was acutely aware that my first YTS year had been a very eventful period, with a real roller-coaster ride of extreme highs and lows. So, even though overall I thought that I had come through the experience in good shape, I was still quite relieved to get that episode of my life behind me.

It was time to take a break during the summer, regroup my thoughts, recharge the batteries and return for a fresh start the following season.

It was time to get into that First Team squad.

## Steve Heighway Picks Me Out for Something Special

Very early in my second year as a YTS Apprentice, in August 1997, I made my home debut for Liverpool Reserves against Aston Villa at Anfield. I still have a copy of the team sheet from that match and a quick glance at the two sides that lined up against each other that day gives an instant indication of the calibre of the teams. No less than eight of Liverpool's starting eleven went on to represent their country of birth, either as a full international or at the under-21 level. And in the case of Dominic Matteo, he represented both England and Scotland!

The full list reads: Dominic Matteo (Scotland and England under-21s), Jason McAteer (Republic of Ireland), Bjorn Kvarme (Norway), David Thompson (England under-21s), Sean Friars (Northern Ireland), Paul Dalglish (Scotland under-21s), Nicky Rizzo (Australia) and Tony Warner (Trinidad & Tobago). As you can see, I was in good company that day!

The season continued to tick along nicely and I was generally happy with my progress on and off the pitch. I was training well and, in addition to playing for the A Team and occasional matches for the Youth Team, I was now getting more games for the Reserves. Then, just when I was confident of moving another rung up the ladder, my comfort zone was suddenly disrupted.

# LIVERPOOL FOOTBALL CLUB

## PONTINS LEAGUE MATCH
## LIVERPOOL V ASTON VILLA
## SATURDAY, 16TH AUGUST 1997

## TEAMS

| | LIVERPOOL<br>(Red shirts) | | ASTON VILLA<br>(Blue/White shirts) |
|---|---|---|---|
| 1. | TONY WARNER | 1. | PAUL CHRICHTON |
| 2. | PHIL BRAZIER | 2. | GARY CHARLES |
| 3. | EDDIE TURKINGTON | 3. | LESLIE HINES |
| 4. | BJORN KVARME | 4. | BEN PETTY |
| 5. | DOMINIC MATTEO | 5. | LEE COLLINS |
| 6. | DAVID THOMPSON | 6. | RICCARDO SCIMECA |
| 7. | NICKY RIZZO | 7. | SCOTT MURRAY |
| 8. | JASON McATEER | 8. | LEE HENDRIE |
| 9. | PAUL DALGLISH | 9. | RICHARD WALKER |
| 10. | MICHAEL YATES | 10. | DARREN BYFIELD |
| 11. | SEAN FRIARS | 11. | NEIL DAVIES |

| SUBS: | | SUBS: | |
|---|---|---|---|
| 12. | STEPHEN WRIGHT | 12. | ALAN KIRBY |
| 13. | DANNY WILLIAMS | 13. | TOMMY JASZCZUM |
| 14. | JOHN NEWBY | 14. | AARON LESCOTT |

REFEREE: B. BELLO
ASSISTANT REFEREES: A.N. BUNDENBERG, P.J. HOWARD

NEXT MATCH HERE:
F.A. Premier League
Liverpool v Newcastle United
Sunday, 31st August, 1997
Kick-off 4.00 p.m.

In late November 1997 we were due to play Leicester City at Filbert Street in the FA Youth Cup. Our squad had travelled down for the game and Hughie McAuley called a team meeting in the hotel about two hours before kick-off. Based on recent performances I fully expected to be playing, so when Hughie read out the team and I wasn't even on the bench I just couldn't understand what was going on. Apart from feeling totally dejected, I was also very confused. To make matters worse, Hughie didn't say anything to me. No explanation, nothing. My next thought was about my dad. He was driving all the way down from Liverpool on his own, just to watch me play in the game. Back then he didn't have a mobile phone, so I couldn't even call him to let him know not to bother. So to dejection and confusion you could now add embarrassment!

I went to the ground with the rest of the squad but spent the whole time just sat there wondering what had gone wrong, rather than watching the game. It wasn't until the final whistle that Steve Heighway finally came up to me in the players tunnel to say something. 'You're disappointed aren't you Yatesy?' I thought to myself, 'Well, what do you think soft arse! Dead right I am,' but just politely mumbled, 'Yes I am.'

Steve Heighway then explained that he wanted to come round to our house the next night and have a talk with me and my parents about 'something special' he had in mind for me. The idea of something special sounded interesting but I still had no idea what it was all about. It all seemed a bit strange and I can remember thinking to myself, well what does he need to come to the house for? Why not meet in his office?

Anyway, that next day I went to work at Melwood as usual, did my normal jobs and our regular training sessions. The only thing that was noteworthy is that I picked up a leaflet that I found in the first team dressing room that encouraged players to work for coaching qualifications. It immediately struck me that I'd be interested in that kind of opportunity as I'd already completed my first coaching badge as part of the YTS, and I'd thoroughly enjoyed the experience. In addition, the club and my parents had always preached to me that all young players, no matter how good they might appear to be, should have some form of career to fall back on if they got injured or things didn't work out as a professional player. And coaching was something that appealed to me. So I took the leaflet home and put it on the mantelpiece, ready to give it some more consideration after the meeting with Steve Heighway that same night.

After he arrived at our house and went through the standard hellos and small talk with my parents, we all settled down in our living room with the customary cup of tea. Steve had been round to our home a number of times and we were all very comfortable in each other's company. So I didn't feel nervous at all, just excited to find out what all this intrigue was actually about. Especially because when he had used those words, 'I've got something special in mind for you', I had started to think that the club might be offering me a professional contract. I was really looking forward to hearing what he had to say.

Then, out of the blue, with very little preamble, Steve dropped the totally unexpected bombshell that Liverpool were not going to retain me as a player. Bang! Just like that. My earlier comfortable sense of security was instantly shattered into smithereens. They were letting me go!

My lifelong ambition of playing for Liverpool had been destroyed in seconds. At age seventeen my football dream was over. Just like that! Annihilated in my own living room, in front of my mum and dad. With just a few simple words, everything I had worked so hard for at Liverpool from the age of eight had been destroyed. Gone. Finished. Wiped out.

Probably because I held Steve Heighway in such high esteem and basically trusted him a lot, it had never even entered my mind that he might possibly be delivering some kind of bad news that night. For that reason, his words hit me particularly hard, as if I'd been physically pounded in the head with a hammer. When people use that word 'bombshell' to describe hearing sudden bad news, they are not joking. It really did feel to me as though some kind of explosion had erupted inside my skull. My eyes welled up, my ears were ringing, my head was banging, my throat went dry and my brain felt numb. I can't remember what conversation then immediately took place between Steve and Mum and Dad. In fact I honestly don't know if I was even aware of them being there in the room for quite a while. All I do know is that once my brain started working again I couldn't stop thinking about the recurring vision that I had always cherished of me running out onto the pitch at Anfield in front of 45,000 roaring Liverpool fans and banging the ball into the back of the net at the Kop end. Except that vision had now suddenly been brutally switched from a dream into a living nightmare.

I was in a crushed and desperate daze. I just couldn't get my head around the devastating news I'd just heard. How could they reject me now? After all that time! After all that work! After I'd done so well and got so close to the first team! It wasn't fair! It just wasn't right!

The next part of the conversation that I was truly conscious of was when Steve Heighway was talking directly to me, letting me know what it was that he had planned for me. I was probably snapped back awake because by an amazing coincidence, and a completely bizarre twist of fate, he explained how he wanted me to pursue my coaching qualifications with a view to becoming one of the first five full-time coaches at the new Liverpool Football Club Academy, which was due to open in time for the 1998/99 season.

Steve went on to say that based on what he had seen of the coaching work I had already done for my badge, he thought that I had all the right attributes to become a successful coach; as well as a good opportunity to make a rewarding career for myself in professional football and a real chance to play an important role in the further development of Liverpool Football Club.

Clearly those very positive words had something of a soothing effect on me and, even though I still felt very aggrieved that my dream of playing for Liverpool had been ripped away from me, it definitely helped to know that I at least might still have a future at the club.

He went on to add that while I was coaching professionally I would still have the opportunity to continue playing football, but at the non-league level. At this point my dad raised the question about what would happen if a club came after me while I was playing non-league and wanted to sign me on professional terms. Steve's immediate response was that if that happened then Liverpool would not stand in my way if I wanted to go that route. After telling me to take my time to think about it all and get back to him when I was ready, he said his goodbyes and stood up to leave.

As Steve Heighway slipped swiftly out through the front door, he left behind a stunned and shattered family.

It was like we were in mourning. And it was my career as a footballer that was dead. It had just been murdered.

I was in shock and hurting badly deep down inside. With barely another word to my parents, I picked up the coaching leaflet from the mantelpiece and, like a deadman walking, I trudged slowly upstairs to the sanctuary of my bedroom.

As soon as I was alone, I dropped my guard and let all the festering anger explode out of me.

'Fuck that! I didn't work my arse off for ten years just to be a coach.

I'm a player! And I'm a good player!'

The leaflet didn't last long, ending up strewn all over the floor, ripped into shreds by the venom in my broken heart. I wanted to scream. The tears poured freely as I slumped on my bed, buried my head in the pillow and spewed out a long list of expletive laden complaints. It was like the broken arm all over again. But this time it was worse. A broken arm can heal. Rejection is permanent.

Later on my mum and dad wanted to check on me but I couldn't face them. There was just no way that I could talk about it all. And there was no point in them trying to comfort me. I was way too far gone for that. Instead, I sobbed quietly for a while before sinking into a fitful sleep. No dreams of Anfield glory that night; just a shit-filled nightmare that wouldn't go away. Because it was my reality!

The next morning I felt terrible. My head was throbbing, my chest ached and I felt sick in the pit of my stomach. But I was still expected to go into training that day, just as if nothing had happened the night before. So, when Dad gave me my wake-up knock on the door, I forced myself out of bed and got ready to go to Melwood.

The anger had subsided by then, replaced by a sense of confusion and a feeling of betrayal. By the time I'd dressed, eaten my breakfast and left the house I was overcome with a new emotion. Embarrassment!

How the hell was I going to face my teammates and tell them that I'd been released?

It was almost cruel that the club had officially released me as a player but still wanted me to train with the lads and play for the A and B Teams for the last few months of the season. No wonder I felt confused! But true to character, I swallowed my pride, masked my disappointment and got on with it.

The spring had been knocked out of my step but I somehow replaced that with grim determination and went to work as usual.

Nobody was going to see how I really felt inside.


## Picking up the Pieces and Starting Work as an LFC Coach

At the meeting with my parents, Steve Heighway had snatched my dreams away from me with one hand but then used the other to give me a different vision for the future. He had softened his hammer blow by suggesting this new idea of becoming a professional coach at one of the world's biggest football clubs.

At least I wasn't being shown the door, as happens to so many young players at that stage of their career. I can't even begin to imagine how I might have reacted if I'd simply been rejected without that coaching lifeline to cling onto. There is no doubt in my mind today that knowing I had an opportunity to carry on at Liverpool certainly helped enormously to protect my sanity and preserve my self-worth.

In that regard, I was one of the lucky ones.

So, even though I still felt very heavy hearted and cheated that my chance to play professional football for Liverpool had been so clinically snuffed out, when I went to talk to Steve Heighway about his ideas for me as a coach, I did so with an open mind. I don't think that was a case of me displaying any kind of maturity beyond my years, I actually think it was driven by total fear. To me, at that point in time, any chance to remain at Liverpool Football Club seemed better than nothing.

At the meeting, Steve Heighway explained that he had a clear plan mapped out for my future in the game; and the way he presented it made it all sound highly appealing. I had the chance to go to Crewe and Alsager College to study for a degree in Sports Science, which was becoming really big at that time. His vision was for me to become the most highly qualified, young coach in Britain, if not in Europe, by the time I was twenty-four. When he pitched his idea like that, it was easy for me to buy into it. Though, to be honest, by now there probably wasn't any need for too much selling of it simply because it involved Liverpool, the club where I had literally grown up.

On reflection, I suppose I was also quite comfortable with the idea of becoming a coach because I'd had such a good, positive experience while doing my coaching badges during the YTS years. Thinking about tactics and analyzing games was something I'd always enjoyed, even as a kid just listening to former players giving their post-match views after televised games. I can remember often taking my dad by surprise when I'd make a comment about a period of play during a game on TV, like suggesting what a player could have done better, and then the ex-pro commentator would say exactly the same thing. There was many a time that my dad raised his eyebrows when I offered the same analysis as the pundit – but a split second before he did.

Plus of course I'd been surrounded by incredible role models during my entire time at Liverpool. When you've personally seen coaches like Ronnie Moran, Roy Evans, Steve Heighway, Sammy Lee, Hughie McAuley and Dave Shannon in action then you've seen the best. Even listening to the first teamers at Melwood provided a wonderful football education and encouraged me, as a young player, to learn more about the game. I just found it all to be really fascinating. Based on that very solid foundation that I'd been given by those living legends, I already knew that I could coach and I also knew that I actually enjoyed it, even including planning the sessions.

In the end I thought to myself, well I am still here at Liverpool, in the best possible hands, so yes, I can definitely have a go at becoming a coach instead of a player. On that premise, I stifled my desire to be a professional footballer and agreed to Steve Heighway's proposal.

My first coaching role with the Academy was as a Community Coach, which mainly involved us going into the schools during the day to coach local children. Then of an evening we would work with the Academy players, who were the equivalent of the Centre of Excellence boys in my day. Interestingly, the very first set of kids that I worked with was an under-10 group that included Jay Spearing, who went on to become a first team player at Liverpool. Coincidentally, that particular group of players also later became labelled the 'Dream Team', just like ours had in an earlier generation.

When I first started I was mainly responsible for the warm-up sessions and worked as an assistant to a senior coach during the actual drills, which gave me plenty of opportunity to observe and learn on the job. It was essential to understand how to structure the sessions and manage them properly; plus how to interact with the kids effectively. I'd work part of the time with the under-10s and the rest with the under-14s, who were then managed by Paul Lever, the same coach who'd been in charge of the under-14 team that I played on the year we won the Ian Rush Tournament.

It was a bit tricky working with those fourteen year-olds because I was only just going on eighteen myself, so there wasn't much difference in age between us. Teenagers can be a handful to manage at the best of times and I did find that a challenge at first, so I was always grateful to get any help and guidance that was offered to me. Having said that, one of the lads from that first under-14 group, Adam Flynn, is now a colleague of mine and he can still remember things I told him and coaching tips I gave him, so I can't have done too badly!

The whole set-up of my early coaching schedule was designed to give me as much exposure as possible in as short a time as possible. Strangely enough, or at least it seemed strange to me at the time, that also included working with my old YTS teammates. During the summer holidays all the schools were of course closed and we couldn't do our Community Coaching, so to keep us busy Steve Heighway asked us to help with the pre-season training for the Youth Team. By then the YTS lads had moved out of Melwood but the Academy was still not ready to open, so those sessions were held at the Liverpool University grounds. All my mates were there, including Stevie G, Stephen Wright, Richie Partridge, Tommy Culshaw, Neil Murphy, Ian Dunbavin and so on. Michael Owen was the only one missing as he'd already graduated to the first team squad by then. Even though my role was limited to overseeing the warm-up sessions and sometimes knocking balls in for certain drills, and although I never actually got involved with them on the pitch, it still all felt very weird. At that point, especially amongst that group that I knew so well, I still felt more like a player than a coach.

I never let it phase me while I was working, and I always got the job done and done well, but I knew deep down inside that I still wanted to be a professional footballer.

When the Liverpool FC Academy officially opened in 1998, with Steve Heighway as Director, the staff did indeed include the five coaches that had been referred to in our living room that fateful night when my playing career at Liverpool came to an abrupt halt. The first coaches were Frank MacParland, who is now the Academy Director, and Iain Brunskill, plus Stewart Gelling, Steve Hollis and myself, who had all played for the club.

Quite soon after I'd started working at the Academy I was thrilled to hear the exciting news that we were going across to Holland – not as coaches but as players! Mark Leather, the Liverpool physio, had some connections with Ajax and between them they came up with the idea of the coaching staff from the two clubs playing against each other in an annual fixture; partly for relationship-building reasons but mainly just for a bit of R&R fun. So off we went to Amsterdam to play for the Steve McManaman Trophy, which Macca had kindly donated to give the occasion a bit of edge. I can pinpoint the exact date of that game, May 16th 1998, because it was the same day as the FA Cup Final when Arsenal beat Newcastle 2 – 0, with one of the goals coincidentally being scored by Dutchman Marc Overmars, a former Ajax player. We won our match

Photo courtesy of Liverpool FC via Getty Images

3 – 1 and I was happy to get on the score sheet. What a great way to spend a weekend with your work mates!

The new excitement in my life continued when, not long after we got back to Liverpool, I was given a rare chance to have a first-hand look at an aspect of life that was completely unknown to me – the inside of a jail! As part of our community programme we were asked by the police to run a series of coaching sessions in Walton Prison. We all went together, Frank, Iain, Stewart, Steve and myself, and even though the banter was flowing as usual, I definitely felt a bit nervous about it all. Probably because I just didn't know what to expect.

After arriving for the first session, we went through a series of security checks before being escorted through the prison by one of the wardens. As I'd feared, lots of the inmates started shouting and catcalling us as we crossed the open courtyard while making our way to the sports facility and gym. Even though I didn't think they really meant what they were suggesting, and I knew we were completely safe, it still made me feel uncomfortable.

The convicts who we were asked to work with were the ones who had qualified for the session by being well behaved during the week, so they didn't give us any trouble. Plus the wardens were always on their toes and ready to step in just in case anything kicked off. I was very grateful for that because one thing that really struck me was the size of some of them. Since they had nothing else to do they had been pumping iron in the gym every day, so they were huge!

In the end everything went very smoothly and there were no incidents at all. To finish off the block of coaching, we arranged a 5-a-side tournament inside the prison. Despite the potential for 'payback', we played our best and eventually won the final. It was like having a starring role in Mean Machine!

For me, an eighteen year-old lad who had been training alongside Liverpool FC's first team just a month or so earlier, that revealing visit inside Walton Prison was a huge eye-opener. It reminded me just how fortunate I was with my own life.

There was no way I was going to end up in one of these places!

*Opposite: Steve McManaman*

# Gordon Taylor, OBE

*Chief Executive, Professional Footballers Association*

I have very vivid memories of the day I was to find out whether Bolton Wanderers wanted to sign me as a professional or release me. It was a nerve-racking ordeal as we all had to queue up outside the manager's office and go in one by one. Things went from bad to worse when the lad in front of me came out in tears and told us they were letting him go because he was too small. And I was the same size as him! So I was terrified when I walked in for my turn. But I needn't have worried, as they wanted to sign me.

Incidentally, that lad was none other than Alan Ball; and he went on to enjoy a fantastic career in top-flight football and won a World Cup Winners Medal with England. He was a great example of a young player having the mental strength to fight on after rejection and prove that he was good enough after all.

From my perspective, as an individual as well as head of the PFA, a good education for our young players is essential. It's right at the top of my list of priorities. As a young player myself, I was fortunate to benefit from a grammar school education. Plus my parents were wise enough to insist that I continued my studies while working as a football apprentice. So, every afternoon, I'd be allowed to leave early enough to go to Bolton Technical College. In the end I passed 'A Levels' in Geography, History and Economics. That was unusual for those days and I am grateful that I had that kind of opportunity. Even when I made it into the Bolton first team, I carried on studying and took an external degree in Economics with London University.

So, because I can appreciate the value of a good education, I completely understand why we must help all of our players, young and old, to attain as many qualifications as they can.

It is an important part of our PFA mandate to gently inform young players and their parents about the potential pitfalls and high drop out ratio in the game.

And just in case they have to leave football and enter some other form of employment, we work hard to help them improve themselves off the pitch as well as on it.

## Armenia Removes the Blinkers from My Young Footballer's Eyes

Towards the end of May 1998, still quite early on during my first year in the LFC Community Coaching Department, I volunteered to join a team of Liverpool coaches and staff who were going to work with underprivileged children in various parts of war-torn Armenia. The club had been approached for assistance by a charity called Operation Christmas Child and our Chaplain, Bill Bygroves, thought it would be good for us to get involved. The general idea was to use football coaching as a way to give support to children who had fallen victim to poverty, earthquake or war in remote regions of the world. Or, as was the case in Armenia, all three at the same time!

Despite the fact that we were advised upfront that we would encounter some harrowing circumstances, I was still determined to make the trip and do my best to help in any way possible. The reality is that at just eighteen years of age, having been blessed with a very comfortable and carefree life so far, I was very naïve. There was simply no way that I could have ever envisioned the stark reality of the woeful levels of abject human misery that I was going to witness in Armenia.

The most immediately obvious thing that struck me when we first arrived in Armenia was that the roads were full of holes and lots of cars were being driven with shattered windscreens and bits of bodywork missing. Many of the buildings were badly damaged and it was common for windows to be completely smashed, with people just hanging up bits of sack or a sheet of cardboard for a little basic privacy and protection from the weather. Wherever we went, the whole miserable scene just smacked of poverty.

One of our very first commitments was to visit a village in the Shahumian region. No amount of words, photos or film could have ever prepared me for what I saw when we got there. Most of the inhabitants of the village were women and children, because so many men had been killed during the war. Instead of living in houses, these people were holed up in rows of converted water tanks. Whole families, as many as six to eight people, were squeezed into these tiny, dark, round spaces and having to exist without proper furniture or any basic household equipment. From what we could see, these poor, destitute refugees did whatever little they could to keep their surroundings clean and tidy; but without any form of toilet facility, other than a simple bucket, every one of those dismal hovels gave off a terrible stench.

It was all very disturbing but we did our best to hide our feelings and made a point of going into several of the tanks to meet the families. And each time we did, we were given an embarrassingly warm reception. They were so happy to welcome us into their 'home' that their faces lit up with huge smiles, they hugged us and laughed, they even offered us bits to eat or drink. One old lady grabbed my hand and forced me to accept a tiny cup of some dark, thick, warm liquid; then she used sign language to encourage me to drink it. I really didn't fancy that at all. But, equally, there was just no way I could refuse her humble but heartfelt hospitality. So I clenched my stomach, held my breath and took a tiny sip. It didn't taste like anything I was familiar with but I assumed it was some kind of strong coffee that is popular in that part of the world. Trying hard not to take too much notice of the state of the cup, I swallowed a few more sips, smiled and nodded appreciatively. She was thrilled!

It absolutely amazed me that these incredibly unfortunate human beings were still able to cling on to their pride. Even though they might have lost all of their material possessions, they still retained their dignity. So much of what we saw that day was extremely emotional for everybody in our group. One particular moment that really sticks in my mind, and can still bring a teardrop to my eye, is when a thin, little boy of about thirteen latched on to me and pulled me inside his own tank. He looked so fragile and vulnerable that I couldn't help wondering how he'd even managed to survive. So I asked the translator to tell him that I hoped he was doing OK and that things would soon get better for him. When the lad replied, although I couldn't understand the words he was saying, his facial expression made me think that there was some kind of inner peace going on in his mind. That's why it totally shattered me when I was then told that he was the oldest person left in his family and he was entirely responsible for looking after his younger brother and sister. It was just way too much to bear and I had to get out of there fast and gather myself. So I gave the youngster a big poster of the Liverpool team, shook his hand and hurried outside to escape the awkwardness of the situation.

To finish off the visit, our group got together and sang a few songs with the kids. Bill Bygroves took his guitar with him wherever we went and a bit of a singalong was always a good way to raise peoples' spirits – ours included! Not surprisingly, 'You'll Never Walk Alone' was always a popular request.

As we returned to the vehicle to get ready to leave the village, a swarm of kids followed us, holding onto our hands, tugging our shirts and begging for anything we could give them. We willingly and happily emptied all of our pockets and bags, desperately looking for little gifts to hand over: coins, sweets, chewing gum, pens, pencils and whatever else we could find. In the end, we literally took the shirts off our backs and gave them away too. My mind was spinning as our vehicle drove off in a cloud of dust. How could that type of destitution be allowed to exist in the world today?

It really frustrated me that I had been unable to do any more for that poor little boy. I felt terrible, utterly useless. Though, looking back to that moment, I might have felt slightly better about myself had I been able to somehow see into the future. In a happy twist of fate, Bill Bygroves went back to that same village in Armenia quite recently and he was pleasantly surprised to discover that the boy, now a man, and his brother and sister, were all doing fine. And he still had his Liverpool poster proudly displayed above his bed!

Our next task on the trip introduced the additional element of danger, as we had to travel to a village called Shushi, located in the war zone of Nagorno Karabagh. We conducted a two-day training course for the local kids, albeit on a poor quality pitch. Straight away one kid in particular made a big impression on me. He was about eight or nine and he looked like a very decent player. Despite the fact that his old, beaten, hand-me-down boots were clearly way too big for him, his skill still shone through. He had a bit of personality about him as well. I am not sure how to spell it, but his name was Artu. As I watched him on the ball, I couldn't help thinking that if he'd been born in England like me, then he might have had a chance to make it in the game. But here in Armenia, he had no such hope. Instead of trying to become a footballer, his life was going to be all about fighting to survive war and poverty.

Anyway, I worked closely with him in the sessions and communicated as best as we could. A day or so later, our group of coaches was scheduled to play an exhibition match in another nearby village against a local team. Just before kick-off, much to my surprise, Artu came bouncing up to me with a man who I assumed was his dad. He shook my hand firmly, presented me with an Armenian pin badge and then said something I couldn't understand. One of our translators overheard and explained to me that the father had said that he knew it wasn't much but he'd wanted

*Me and Artu after training.*

to give me something to express his appreciation for what I'd done for his son over the last couple of days. It was another emotional experience; another shining example of how these people who had nothing, still retained a terrific pride and sense of honour. At the end of the match, I walked around the pitch looking for Artu and his dad and I handed them the Liverpool shirt I had been wearing. You would have thought that I'd just given them a million pounds! I was pleased to have been able to make them happy like that, but once again I found myself struggling to escape a deep feeling of guilt. Why did they have so little and I had so much?

The next part of our Armenia adventure involved a long, difficult, four-hour journey in a cramped and battered mini-bus that took us through the desolate area of Agdam, where the town had been completely obliterated during the fighting. Much to our horror, as we were passing through this war-ravaged landscape in the middle of the night, the bus broke down. Even though it was a scary situation, Iain Brunskill and I also saw it as a good opportunity to stretch our legs and answer an urgent call of nature. Without giving it a moment's thought we started to walk inland from the road, only to be immediately screamed at by the driver. He then proceeded to explain to us, and everybody else, that the area we were in was still riddled with live landmines. In fact, two members of the local group who had planned our project had been killed when they drove over an explosive device just six weeks before. Needless to say, after hearing that, we stuck very close to the van when we eventually went to relieve ourselves. If that was not enough of a fright, just as we were about to go back to the road, we spotted a red glow just above us in the trees. The second time we saw the glow we both knew for sure that it was a cigarette end burning. Somebody was there watching us. When we told the driver about what we'd seen he blew us away by saying that it was probably a sniper! He assured us that the guy wouldn't do anything to us, but we'd better play safe anyway and stay in the vehicle. Damn right! It was a very nerve wracking situation, sitting there thinking about being in the middle of nowhere in Armenia, surrounded by landmines and being monitored by a sniper. Bill's prayers must have been answered on behalf of all of us because, by chance, a Red Cross Land Rover came along the road and the crew helped to get the van started again.

When we did eventually reach our final destination we were dismayed to discover that there was no hotel. Our so-called accommodation was just the gutted shell of a bombed out building with nothing but rusty bedsprings for us to sleep on. To get in and out the building we had to ease our way up and down a steep, wooden plank that had been propped high against the wall to replace the steps that had once graced the entrance. Every morning, inevitably after an uncomfortable night's sleep, we'd trundle into an empty room where rough planks had been laid across a couple of trestles to serve as a table; and every morning we'd be given bread and salami for breakfast. To make matters even worse, by about the second day, the latrines in the building started to overflow and the whole place absolutely stank. It all became increasingly tough to handle and, even though we all gave it our best shot, after a couple of days we were really struggling to cope. My young brain was full of confused questions, like: 'How come it only seems like yesterday that I was on tour with Liverpool in Germany and staying in top class hotels and now I'm here with Liverpool slumming it in a broken down building in a war zone?'

Of course, as would be expected of any group of self-respecting Liverpool lads, we eventually found a local guy just down the road who could 'acquire' crates of rationed beer. He loved our money and we loved his beer: not to mention the fact that going to his house for a few hours every night allowed us to enjoy a temporary escape from our Hotel from Hell. We had a ball every time we went there and the jokes were always flying fast and furious. That combination of suffering together and sharing laughter in the face of adversity was the perfect recipe for developing a fantastic sense of camaraderie amongst the group and building very strong bonds between colleagues. In fact, in a perverse kind of way, it was the ideal way for me to start my coaching career.

Wherever we went in Armenia, our regular routine would be to do some coaching with the kids and then play an exhibition game against one of the local teams. To add a bit of spice to the matches, we'd play in the actual Liverpool kit, which always gave our opponents an extra buzz. A lot of the pitches we played on didn't have any grass on them, many were covered in stones and some were even pocked with bomb craters; very few were covered in grass. After every game we'd mix with the locals and Bill would pull out his guitar for the traditional singalong.

At the end of the tour we actually played against an Armenia XI in their national stadium. That was definitely our toughest match as they fielded a very strong side with plenty of international experience. Our makeshift team of young and not-so-young Liverpool coaches, plus a few other members of our party, had to really dig deep to salvage a hard-fought 1 – 1 draw.

But for me by far the most bizarre, and therefore most memorable, of our matches was when we played a game in the war zone. With rows of armed soldiers packing the sidelines, and other troops watching from on top of tanks and armoured cars, it was like a dramatic scene straight out of the movie 'Escape to Victory'! Despite the presence of an abundance of guns and heavy weapons the atmosphere was really good, with lots of singing and chanting during the game and plenty of banter going on after it finished. Just before the kick-off, both teams had lined up next to each other and the Armenians presented us with a variety of small gifts, as tokens of their appreciation for what we had done for them. My opposite number gave me a small, hand-carved wooden cross. I thanked him, asked one of the lads to pop it safely in into my bag for me and then kind of forgot about it. But, after the game, our ever-helpful translator explained to me that the guy had presented me with that particular cross because it was something he personally cherished. He didn't have anything of material value to give to me so, as a mark of respect and a way to say a special thank you for giving so much joy to the people of Armenia, he had offered me something that had tremendous personal value for him. Wow! The amazing people of Armenia had provided with me yet another benchmark moment in my development as a person.

Leaving Armenia was a surreal experience for me, with wildly fluctuating emotions of huge relief on the one hand for getting away from all of that human misery, but also an overriding sense of embarrassed guilt for not staying longer to help more. The journey back to Liverpool was a long and tedious one. With so much downtime on my hands, it was impossible to stop the cogs in my brain from spinning wildly in all kinds of directions, re-living all the many life-changing incidents I had been exposed to in that short period away from home.

The first thing I did when I walked into my parents' house was to dig into my hand luggage and give the wooden cross to my mum and dad. I was going to tell them the whole story behind it there and then, but decided it would be better to wait a while and let my emotions settle. By the time I'd had a quick shower and come back downstairs, my parents were already sitting at the dining table, happily waiting for me. Like all good mothers do when their sons come back after being away from home, Mum had made my favourite meal. As Mum and Dad watched me expectantly, I took one look at the plate of lovingly prepared lasagne and promptly burst into inconsolable floods of tears. There was no screaming or hysterics involved, but I simply could not stop crying. The tears poured and poured. Once the emotional floodgates had burst open, a torrent of pent-up mental turmoil from the Armenia trip came gushing to the surface. All of the fear, sadness and guilt that I had worked so hard to bury in my inner-being while we were on tour, now erupted out of me. My poor mum and dad were shell-shocked.

Instead of feeling happy and blessed to be back in my comfortable home, with both of my loving parents sitting there, and a delicious feast of a meal right in front of me, all I could see was Artu, those little, orphaned kids in the water tanks and all the other disadvantaged Armenians I had met.

Time is a natural healer, so in due course I was able to put those dark thoughts to the back of my mind. But I will never forget those proud people and I will forever live by the valuable lessons they taught me. From that day onwards I have always had a much greater appreciation for what I do have and I am much less concerned about anything I don't have. My perspective on life changed considerably after Armenia and today I constantly give thanks for my many blessings; especially the everyday luxury of being able to live in a healthy and peaceful part of the world, surrounded by the love of my wife, my daughter, my parents, my wider family and my friends.

Despite the many difficult challenges we faced, the Armenia tour gave me a powerful insight into the massive influence of the LFC badge and the wonderful community work that can be done around the world in the name of Liverpool Football Club. I truly think it would be good for our current generation of young players to experience something similar, but I am not sure that could ever happen again with the many legal restrictions of this day and age. That is a pity, because my Armenia experience undoubtedly removed the blinkers from my young footballer's eyes, revealed the harsh realities of the outside world and made me a better person.

To this day, every time I walk into my parents' home I look up at that simple, wooden, Armenian cross hanging on their wall.

And I remember.

# Dave McDonough

*Former LFC Academy Coach and First Team Analyst under Rafa Benitez; former First Team Analyst at Inter Milan; current First Team Analyst at West Bromwich Albion*

I first worked for Liverpool FC as a part-time coach at the Academy from 1997 onwards, and later, under Gerrard Houllier, I worked as a scout for the first team and the Academy. So, by the time Rafa Benitez arrived, I was already accustomed to writing detailed reports on players and opponents. Because of my own interest in the game, I had read a number of coaching books in Spanish and Portuguese, so my way of thinking was more in line with European ideas than perhaps the average English coach. In any event, it meant that I fitted quite neatly into the picture with Rafa and his assistant Pako Ayestaran. Shortly after their arrival I was appointed as First Team and Opposition Analyst.

I learned a lot from Rafa and Pako, and they definitely helped change the way I analysed the game. From English football's perspective, analysis is looked upon more as a sports science, whereas the Europeans consider it to be a coaching tool. They use the science to collect the data, but then they use that information to reach a coaching conclusion, either for fitness or tactical planning. I helped with both but specialized in tactical analysis.

Steven Gerrard and Michael Owen were just moving up into the first team when I arrived, so I never got to coach them, but I did watch them a great deal at Melwood. The two of them were clearly exceptional talents, but they had also been well prepared by Steve Heighway and his staff at the Centre of Excellence. I can remember the senior players being really impressed when they first came across these two young lads in training. I remember Patrick Berger, in particular, telling me he was amazed by Michael Owen's pace and finishing ability.

One of the big advantages of the old YTS days at Melwood was that it provided lots of good educational benefits for young players off the pitch. In a nutshell, while they were cleaning the first team players boots, they were also aiming to fill them. That provided fantastic motivation for all the trainees. While it was very unusual for two players so young to make such a seamless transition from academy level to the first team, it was not really a surprise. Thanks to the 3Ts – Talent, Training and Tournament - they were both ready.

One of Steven Gerrard's first games for the senior team was away to Celta Vigo in Spain. As fate would have it, his name was picked out to do a

*Dave McDonough, far left middle row, with Rafa Benitez holding the World Club Championship trophy which they won when they were at Inter Milan*

random urine drugs test. I went along with him and he impressed me with the way he managed himself throughout what would be a real ordeal for any young lad. He demonstrated his maturity that night. It was another indication that he was ready mentally to step up to the higher level.

I saw Mike Yates play a lot at that age as well, and later on I played alongside him in staff matches at the Academy. There is no doubt that he was a good player. He had lots of ability, a good touch and a sound understanding of the game. In terms of talent, he was as good as anybody in his age group. It's possible he wasn't as disappointed as he should have been when he was released.

Young players should definitely read this book, but so should their parents. They need to know what it really takes to be successful in football so that they can help their kids maximise their potential.

It's a tough, competitive business and everybody needs to know what to expect and the hard work it requires.

## Doing the Unimaginable - Leaving Liverpool

Even though I was enjoying coaching at Liverpool and making good progress, over the course of time I started to realize more and more that I wasn't entirely happy within myself. The inescapable truth was that I still couldn't shake off my lifelong dream of being a professional footballer. I was missing playing for Liverpool and I still had a burning ambition to play at the highest level. Almost inevitably, I kept asking myself the same question of 'what if, what if?' Wisely, with the helpful advice of my family and all the other good people around me, I made sure that I took my time and didn't rush into any decision. But, in the end, it became abundantly clear that I had to have another go at playing, even if it meant leaving my beloved Liverpool. I'd already climbed quite high in my quest to become a professional player and, especially after getting so close, I found it impossible to just walk away from that dream. My head was still full of visions of me running out onto the pitch in front of thousands of cheering fans. The whole exciting experience of being a player was what I really wanted.

When I first got the dreaded news from Steve Heighway that Liverpool were letting me go I didn't seriously consider the idea of playing for another team because the offer he made to me about becoming a coach immediately allowed me to stay at the club. I suppose that staying at Liverpool was my number one goal at the time, so my mind was a bit closed off to the idea of playing for somebody else. That all changed after a few months though, especially when I signed up to play non-league football with my local team, Burscough FC, and instantly started to enjoy all kinds of success as a player. The deal I agreed with Burscough turned out to be the best piece of paper I'd ever signed. On top of my basic wage of fifty pounds per week, which was already more than the YTS allowance, I was also offered a ten pounds bonus for each goal I scored. And I scored plenty! Within the first couple of months I scored in ten consecutive games, including several hat-tricks. The goals flowed and so did the money!

In addition to being in a better financial position because I was playing so well and scoring so heavily, I also ended up getting lots of headlines in the press. There is no doubt that seeing my name splashed across the papers definitely reignited my passion for playing the game. In our day at Liverpool, other than a few lines in the Anfield match day programme,

# Burscough look to Reds youngster Micha[e]

A TEENAGE striker who played in the same youth team at Anfield as Liverpool sensation Michael Owen has joined Unibond League newcomers Burscough.

Michael Yates, a YTS youngster, has been released by the Reds, and assistant Burscough boss Peter King said: "He looks quite sharp and he could put a bit of pressure on the other two strikers here, Robbie Cowley and Mark Wilde.

"Hopefully, it will make them realise that they haven't got things all their own way and there will be some good competition for places."

Another arrival at Victoria Park is experienced non-league defender Robbie Armstrong, who has joined from Lancaster City.

Armstrong's previous clubs include Knowsley United, Southport and Morecambe, and King said: "I am sure he will be an acquisition to us, with his experience and his strength."

The arrival of Armstrong further boosts the Linnets' defence following the recent signing of Prescot Cables defender Andy McMullen.

And competition for the goalkeeper's

shirt has been stepped up with the a[rrival] of one-time Southport keeper Paul [...] who has returned to the North West [...] a couple of seasons playing for Wor[...] City.

Moore played for Burscough the [...] night in place of the injured Paul [...] berry as the Linnets continued thei[r] season build-up.

And King said: "That was the one [...]tion where we were looking for co[mpeti]tion, and hopefully now we have it.

Burscough's final pre-season matc[h...] home to Mari[...]

---

# All eyes on Yates the hat-trick hero

YOUNG Michael Yates rocketed into the limelight with a hat-trick, including a wonder goal.

They are still talking about the 30 yarder he lashed in as Burscough hammered Flixton at Victoria Park.

Now all eyes are on the one time strike partner of Liverpool's Michael Owen as he makes his mark in the Unibond League.

Cup competition with a long trek to take on Morpeth Town.

Full reports plus action pictures you will find in this week's Ormskirk Advertiser.

There's news too of Burscough Liverpool Senior Cup final to be played next Wednesday September 30.

That was originally sch[eduled] to take place at Anfield [but] revised plans mean that the [...]

---

# Owen partner Yates shocks Bridge

By DAVID BASSETT

TEENAGER Michael Yates grabbed his fifth goal in three games to give Burscough a shock 2-1 win over premier division Bamber Bridge in their UniBond Cup first round replay at Victoria Park.

The former Liverpool youngster, who was a strike partner of Michael Owen in the Anfield youth teams, scored from the penalty spot in the first minute of extra time to complete a Burscough fightback.

Nigel Greenwood had given Bamber Bridge a 19th minute lead, the first goal scored by a visiting team in five games at Victoria Park, but the Linnets drew level through Darren

---

## Yates spot on with help from Saint

**Burscough 2 Bamber Bridge 1 (after extra time)**

BURSCOUGH claimed their biggest Unibond scalp to date with this victory over Premier Division opposition.

A Michael Yates penalty in the first minute of extra time, his fifth goal in three games, settled it.

That came after Simon Jennings had been floored by a charge from behind in this League Challenge Cup 1st round replay.

Burscough had fallen behind to a 19th minute strike by Nigel Greenwood from Ian Vickers' cross after Mike Clandon had lost possession in midfield.

But on the half hour Darren Saint's perseverance paid off

when he chased a 50-50 through ball and made first contact as keeper Martin Jones came out, for the equaliser.

Saint, along with Wilde and Nolan, was one of three Burscough players booked for dissent, but it was Bamber Bridge who paid the biggest penalty with Stuart Cliff sent off after 44 minutes for his second bookable offence.

Burscough deserved to go through on the strength of their second half showing.

Yates headed just over from Clandon's cross, a Jennings overhead was well taken and Saint was unlucky with a free kick just wide and a close range attempt hooked over the top as the ball bounced awkwardly.

---

# Yates on target for the top award

LEADING marksman Michael Yates signed off the old year with official recognition for services rendered.

He was voted Player of the Month for December, and received a plaque presented by award sponsors LB Plastics.

Guest of honour at Victoria Park to make the presentation was Brian Pilkington, the former Burnley and England winger.

Yates scored three goals in the month, including the winner against Farsley Celtic and a double in the 2-1 success at Harrogate Town.

Burscough played seven league games in December winning three, drawing one and losing three.

Yates (pictured left PH0199 with Pilkington), has scored 16 goals for Burscough this season.

Earlier in the season he found the target in seven consecutive matches.

● Pilkington is now the third [...]

---

## Teen ace Yates' Scottish mission

TEENAGE striker Michael Yates could be heading for a new career in the Scottish Premier League.

The Burscough starlet, who played in the same Liverpool youth team as Michael Owen, is currently having his second trial with Dundee after impressing the Dens Park club in an initial spell a fortnight ago.

"Apparently, he did well the last time he went up there and he played in the reserves and scored," said Burscough boss John Davison. "So presumably they will make some sort of decision about him after the next few days."

And Davison added: "Yatesie was always going to be a player who had the potential to play at league level, so we are keeping our fingers crossed that things work out for him."

Yates joined the Linnets last summer after being released by Liverpool and scored 11 goals in an explosive nine-game spell in [...]

---

## Yates too hot to handle from 30 yards

**Whitley Bay 1 Burscough 1**

WHITLEY BAY had the best of the first half, taking the lead after 18 minutes when Paul Blasbery failed to hold a shot from Priest with Mick Barkas on hand to score.

Three minutes later Phil Hildreth saw a tremendous 25-yard volley come back off the crossbar.

McMullen had a great chance to equalise for Burscough after 24 minutes, but his header from a Michael Yates corner was off

chances were proving elusive against the home side's determined defence.

With 20 minutes remaining, Howard's run into the penalty area seemed to result in a clear trip, but referee Rawcliffe waved the appeals aside. A minute later Graeme Blackett almost headed into his own goal as he attempted to clear a ferocious Yates cross.

Despite all their second half pressure, it appeared that Burscough were destined to leave Hillheads Park without a point. But they were awarded a free [...]

---

# Yates saves the day

## WHITLEY BAY 1
## BURSCOUGH 1

match official Mr Rawcliffe wa[ved]
the appeals aside and a minute l[ater]
Graeme Blackett almost hea[ded]
through his own goal as he atten[...]

IT was Whitley Bay who had the [...]

everything was kept very low key and youth players never really got any publicity, no matter how well we played. We were sheltered by the coaches and protected from exposure, so it was a lot different to today when all the young players even have their own profile page on the club website and appear on LFC TV. Anyway, I can't deny that moving from that kind of restrained culture at Liverpool to a completely different situation where I was regularly reading positive headlines about myself, often heralded as 'Michael Owen's Former Strike Partner', was definitely very exciting for me. It didn't seem to matter that it was non-league football; the buzz was still there anyway.

That sense of excitement and a growing reputation as a goal scorer even followed me back to Liverpool. Whenever I turned in for work at the Academy on the Monday morning after a game, the coaching staff and some of the players would usually make some comment to me, especially of course if I'd scored a good one. Interestingly, the kids I was coaching, and many of their dads, would also monitor my performances every weekend with Burscough. Some of them even came to watch me playing. Boys like the young Jay Spearing would be delighted if I'd scored or been mentioned in the press for having a good game. It was a very positive feeling for me as a coach to know that the boys I was coaching were able to follow my own progress as a player and see that I was 'practicing what I was preaching'.

Being publicly recognised for my own success on the field as a player undoubtedly gave me an extra degree of credibility as a coach, a kind of proven status as a football person if you like. Clearly you don't have to have been a good player to become a good coach, but it sure helps. The classic example of that at the highest level of football today is our own Jamie Carragher. Jamie has proven himself to be one of the greatest ever Liverpool players and he is widely renowned as a student of the game. He is also an excellent coach and always looks comfortable and completely in control, whether he is working with schoolboys or senior pros. Perhaps most importantly of all, Jamie Carragher is highly respected as a man. I am confident that, with all of his many attributes, Jamie could go on one day to become one of the very best coaches in the game.

Ironically, at the peak of that scoring streak for Burscough, I found myself playing against Liverpool FC in the Final of the Liverpool Senior Cup. The day of the match I was coaching at the Academy as usual, but it felt really odd to know that I would be playing that night against my former teammates; including Steven Gerrard and all the other lads who I still rubbed shoulders with every day. I suppose that put me in something of a unique position, as I can't think of any other Liverpool employee who ever had to play against Liverpool!

Everybody at the club knew about the game, and that I would be playing, but nobody said a word. There were no conversations and no banter at all; nobody tried to give me a hard time. That was the Liverpool Way. The only indirect acknowledgement of the match came when we finished work for the day and a couple of the coaches simply said 'see you later'. The atmosphere around Burscough was totally the opposite. For days prior to the game, I couldn't go anywhere without being reminded about the big match against Liverpool and how I had to score against my former club – which, as far as I was concerned, was still my current club!

As might be expected, my emotions were a bit confused when I drove into the ground. I was really excited to be playing against Liverpool and having a chance to prove myself, but it all felt very weird at the same time. That strange feeling intensified when I saw our Burscough kit hanging on pegs, ready for us in the home dressing room; and then I spotted the Liverpool kit, also ready and hanging up in the visitors' changing room. That was the first time that I'd ever seen the away team's gear put out at Victoria Park before they had even arrived. Their kit man had obviously travelled ahead of the team bus, which would never have happened with another non-league team. It reminded me of the high standards at Liverpool.

Later on, when the Liverpool squad arrived, some of the players did say hello and people like Hughie McAuley shook my hand and wished me well. Lining up in the tunnel before kick-off was particularly surreal, as I glanced across at all my mates wearing the famous red strip that I had always been so proud to put on. We didn't talk to each other at all. That was not for any bad reasons, it was more of a mutually respectful silence. We were all there to do a job and that was that.

Once the game got underway we managed to keep them at bay and, even though we didn't create many chance for ourselves, we held on until half-time. But early on in the second half Liverpool went 1–0 up. Then, in the 74th minute, I found myself in a good position just outside the box, ready to meet a great cross from Simon Jennings out on the right wing. In a bit of a twist of fate, it was the same end of the pitch where I'd enjoyed that marathon penalty competition as a seven year-old kid! Anyway, I kept my cool, hit the ball in my stride and bent it around Liverpool's Danish keeper, Jorgen Nielsen, safely into the far corner of the net. The big Burscough crowd roared their approval and started cheering as if we'd won the FA Cup, and so did the rest of our team. Obviously I was just as thrilled as all of them, but as I wheeled away after scoring I found myself right alongside the Liverpool dugout, where Hughie McAuley was standing with his hands on his hips. We didn't make eye contact but the old Liverpool Way instinctively kicked in and I stifled my urge to celebrate the goal, choosing instead to just walk calmly back to the halfway line. At first the Burscough lads were still trying to jump all over me but they soon realized what I was doing – or not doing! Inside I was absolutely bursting with pride and thinking 'get in there you beauty', but I kept a lid on it all. Considering the overall circumstances, and the fact that I was still only eighteen at the time, that was actually a major achievement as it would have been very easy for the occasion to get the better of me. It was also a clear indication of the enormous respect that I had developed for Liverpool Football Club.

After our goal, as the match went on, our players grew more and more tired and Liverpool's fitness and better quality started to dominate the game. In the same way that I had been taught by the Liverpool coaches as a Schoolboy and YTS player, they first of all matched our work rate and commitment and then gradually earned themselves the right to win the match with their superior technical ability. I could see it happening all around me. Nowadays, whenever the lads who played for Burscough that night get together and reminisce about the game, they always make the same comment about Steven Gerrard, how he eventually started to boss the game, to the extent that towards the end he was pulling all the strings and creating lots of chances for Liverpool. He was just a slimly built, eighteen year-old playing against grown men, but he was in control of them. In the end, Liverpool broke us down and scored a second goal for a narrow 2-1 win. Burscough had been beaten but not disgraced. It was a great game to have been involved in for all of us; and for me personally it was an experience that I will never forget.

After the match some people asked me the inevitable question about whether I wished I'd been on the other side that night, still playing for Liverpool. Clearly I occasionally had my moments of thinking 'what if', and I would have jumped at the chance to wear that red shirt again, but at the same time I can honestly say that I was quite content with life. After my Armenia experience, I found it much easier to accept whatever I had and not fret about what I didn't have. Even if deep down I did still want to be a Liverpool player, they had turned me down and that was that. Fortunately I had the ability to put that massive disappointment behind me and move on. I knew it was time for me to try something different.

As I would have expected, none of the Liverpool staff made any fuss of me after the game, other than the standard chat in the corridor and a bit of a casual analysis of how the game had gone. I don't think anybody even mentioned the fact that I had scored. But the local press gave me plenty of publicity, highlighting my connections with Liverpool and the fact that I'd got a goal against my former team and kept my recent scoring spree going.

The frequent news headlines soon started to attract interest in me from other teams, including several league clubs. Things especially started to heat up after a home fixture against Flixton. Just before we went out onto the pitch, Paul Lodge, a talented midfield player who'd been on Everton's books, pulled me to one side: 'This is your night tonight Yatesy. This is the night we get you back to where you belong.'

I can't be sure that Paul was a visionary but I do know for a fact that he created a lot of my chances during my time at Burscough, and that night was no different. I'd already scored two when, following a corner for Frixton, he collected a loose ball, hit it into space ahead of me and yelled at me to turn. As I peeled off my marker and sped away, I looked up to see the keeper back-pedalling towards his line. With my confidence sky high, and not hesitating for a split second, I just let rip from about 30-yards. The ball screamed into the top corner of the net and the crowd went absolutely wild. Nobody more so than my own brother! To say he got a bit over-excited would be a massive understatement. To my absolute amazement, and huge amusement, Geoff leapt over the barriers, stormed onto the pitch and started hugging me and jumping up and down like a mad man. After a bit of encouragement from a couple of burly stewards, he finally let go and scampered back off the pitch.

As I made my way slowly back to the centre circle, still soaking up the crowd's warm applause, a vision of Tommy Galvin sprung to life in my mind. The dedicated Burscough man, who'd played such a huge part in my football career, had recently passed away and I felt really sorry that he had not been there to witness that hat-trick, which I know he would have loved. Just before I reached the halfway line I pretended to doff an

Photo courtesy of Ormskirk Advertiser

imaginary flat cap, Tommy's trademark, to the stands. After the game the media asked me lots of questions about why I'd used that gesture to celebrate my hat-trick. I happily explained the reason to them but lots of the local fans knew exactly what that tribute was all about.

Future events would prove that Paul Lodge had been right, because my performance that night undoubtedly propelled me forward in my pursuit of becoming a professional footballer.

When the match had finished and the crowds were emptying out of the ground, two strangers approached Geoff, who by now was very easy to identify after his solo pitch invasion. They asked him if he knew how to get in touch with me. At first he was a bit hesitant, but the second they identified themselves as representatives of Oldham Athletic he was happy to reveal himself as my brother. The scouts asked for our phone number and in due course they called home to let my dad know that Oldham was interested in having a look at me. We were very willing to follow up but it quickly fizzled out as soon as Burscough found out about the phone call and labelled it an illegal approach, even though my dad had informed the club straight away. Around that same time, Manchester City made an offer for me but Burscough turned it down, apparently because they were hoping to get more money.

Eventually, the growing interest in me that had been simmering for quite a while finally came to a head when Burscough played an away game at Gretna in Scotland. I can remember being told that a good number of scouts had turned up again that night to watch. We won 2 -1 and I scored the winner. After the match our manager, John Davidson, pulled me to one side and told me that Burscough had been officially approached by a Premier League club who wanted to sign me; but that it was a team from the Scottish Premier League, not the English. He wanted to know how I felt about that idea. I said I felt brilliant about that! When he told me it was Dundee, I said that I'd definitely give it some thought but I'd like to talk to my advisors first – which really meant my dad! As usual, Dad's approach was calm and simple. He asked me what had I always wanted to do ever since I was a little kid running around the park. Play football! There you go then, he said, that's your answer.

So, the next day I informed Burscough that I was interested in the move to Dundee. Meanwhile I carried on coaching at the Academy. The

*Opposite: Me in action for Burscough in the FA CUP versus Jarrow FC*

next step was when I got a phone call from George Norrie, the scout who had recommended me to Dundee, asking me if I would go up there for a trial. By then I knew that I definitely wanted to give it a go in Scotland but the big challenge was that I was still employed at Liverpool, which meant that I had to tell them what was happening because I'd need to request time off to go to Dundee. Both my dad and I explained this to George Norrie and asked him to allow me a bit more time to get things sorted with Liverpool. It's probably true to say that I also needed some breathing space because I was very nervous about even talking to Liverpool about the possibility of me leaving the club. I couldn't get off my mind the thought of what if it all went wrong with Dundee and then Liverpool said, 'Well, as you want to leave us, off you go then.' That possibility absolutely terrified me. Luckily George Norrie was a very reasonable man and he completely understood why I was being cautious, so he promised to make sure that Dundee would wait until I was ready. Dad and I both instantly liked George and as time went by he became a genuine friend of the family. I still consider him to be a good mate to this day.

When the time was right I went to Steve Heighway and told him that I wanted time off work to go for the trial at Dundee. I explained that it was something I simply had to do. I couldn't spend the rest of my life wondering 'what if', so I had to at least give it a try. His response was OK, no problem, because that was what we had agreed when I started coaching. But, just as I was walking out of his office, he called after me: 'I bet your dad is happy now.' I really didn't appreciate his comment because it seemed to suggest that it was my dad who had got what he wanted, not me; and that was not the case at all. Dad only ever gave me advice and left me to make all of my own decisions. The truth was that I was the one who was determined to put myself to the test at Dundee. I needed to find out if I was good enough to play for them. My approach was based on the fact that if I failed at Dundee, there could still be a coaching job for me back at Liverpool. And at least I could then be satisfied that I had given it my best shot and wouldn't spend the rest of my life regretting a missed opportunity.

When I first went up to Scotland for the trials I was fortunate to hook up with Dave Rogers, a lad from Liverpool, who was already on Dundee's books. When I went back the second time, apart from letting me stay at his house rather than having to move into digs, Dave helped me a lot by showing me around and filling me in with useful inside information about the club. He even got two seats in the executive box for us to watch a home game against Dundee United. Dave really looked after me and made me feel very welcome; and that was very important for a young lad like me. After a couple of sessions on the training ground I was picked to play for Dundee in a friendly game against St. Johnstone. That first match went well for me and I scored a decent goal. They watched me a few more times in trial games and then picked me again for a second friendly match, this time against Dundee United. We drew 1 – 1 and, even though I didn't grab a goal, my general performance was pretty good. It was after that game that the Manager, Jocky Scott, let me know that he wanted to offer me a professional contract but that we'd have to wait until the end of the season before we could discuss the actual terms; presumably because he needed to know what their financial situation was like and that would partly depend on what position they finished in the league.

In any event, I soon got a call from Jocky Scott giving me a date to report to Dundee for pre-season training. It was game on.

I was going to become a professional footballer after all!

When the time came to formally hand in my notice at Liverpool I felt remarkably calm. Ironically, we had always been prepared for this situation by the club itself. Steve Heighway was forever reminding us as young players that we would all leave Liverpool at some point, whether we'd played 200 Premier League games or just one match for the reserves. In this particular instance I had made my own decision. I had chosen to move on and I was incredibly excited at the prospect of playing professional football, albeit away from home and not for the club I had loved since I was eight.

My last day at the Academy was fairly uneventful in that nothing out of the ordinary took place and nobody made any kind of fuss of me. I do remember coming off the pitch after my last session and thinking that I wouldn't be training with the lads again and that this particular part of my journey was now over. I said goodbye to as many of my mates as possible, thanked the coaches for all the help they'd given me over the last ten years and shook hands with the boss.

Later that same day I went to Anfield for the traditional end-of-season Certificate Night, where I was due to look after my under-10s and under-14s groups. Michael Owen presented the young players with their certificates and I couldn't help thinking about how much had happened since we first met as eleven year-olds and how our paths had differed so drastically: he was now a Liverpool first team player and I was about to leave the club. It was all hard to swallow.

At one point I was shaken out of my reminiscing when I heard my name mentioned. Steve Heighway was on the microphone and he had announced that I was moving on to become a professional player at Dundee. He congratulated me, thanked me for everything I'd done at Liverpool and wished me well in the future. It was a real struggle to hold back the tears during the applause from the parents and the kids, especially when I glanced over at Michael. Fortunately I managed to maintain my composure for the rest of the ceremony.

My mood brightened later on when I thoroughly enjoyed playing alongside the under-14s in their 'special treat' match out on the pitch, with the happy memories of my own under-14 Certificate Night experience vivid in my mind. But as soon as that game finished I had a long, lingering look around the stands and the Kop, left the pitch and went straight to the dressing rooms. I needed to get away as soon as possible.

After getting changed, I said a few last goodbyes and made my way quickly to the exit. As I went out through the players' entrance I glanced back over my shoulder for a brief moment.

Then, with a heavy heart, I walked away from my childhood and my youth.

The only certainty that I carried away with me from Anfield that night was that wherever I went in the world, the Liverpool Way would always be there to guide me.

I would never walk alone.

**Geoff Yates:** 'I think Steve Heighway had identified Mike as a future coach early on, at age fifteen. So, even though I was shattered when I heard that Liverpool was not retaining Mike as a player, it wasn't a complete shock. My bitter disappointment was also softened when I realized just how much Steve thought of my son. He reassured us that Mike was not a failure; he was just going to be a success in a different kind of way. I'm tempted to think that Steve felt that Mike, with his solid character and thoughtful approach, could add a different quality to the Liverpool coaching set-up.'

# Hughie McAuley

*Former youth coach and reserve team manager at Liverpool Football Club,*
*Director of the Hughie McCauley Football Academy*

I first spotted Mike Yates playing for Burscough Juniors, when he was about seven. He was always sharp and quick and showed excellent football ability and game understanding from an early age. He also had a real eye for goal and scored heavily throughout his schoolboy years.

When he joined us at the then LFC Centre of Excellence, Mike continued to make good progress and worked exceptionally hard at all aspects of his game. He was the kind of player who could add something extra to the team in every game and he maintained his high tally of goals. As a result of all of this, he was offered a two-year YTS contract when he left school. His attitude to training and playing games was first class.

Once again, now as a young trainee, Mike's commitment to his personal development was never in doubt. He also had a strong family structure and his dad was always there to support him as and when required.

During Mike's developmental years at Liverpool, the first team had players of the calibre of Kenny Dalglish, Ian Rush and John Aldridge; so the bar was already set at an exceptional height for any other striker, whether young or bought, to even get close to matching them.

At the same time, the club also had an excellent crop of outstanding, young local players with massive potential for the future. Lads like Steve McManaman and Robbie Fowler had already progressed to the first team, soon to be followed by Jamie Carragher, Michael Owen and Steven Gerrard. All five destined to become great players.

Mike Yates belonged in that group of very talented youngsters; but the bottom line was that, in the long term, he was competing against potential world-class players. And of course, over the course of time, that potential has been delivered.

It was always difficult having to release young players. My own son was a YTS trainee and I can clearly remember even having to tell him that he wouldn't be offered a professional contract. The reality was that most young players would eventually have to build their future somewhere else. But we always knew that our youngsters had been given a very solid foundation in professional football and we were confident they could go

*Hughie McAuley with a young Jamie Carragher*

on to play for other clubs.

Mike didn't reach the same level of consistency in his games and development that some of the others did. And maybe they had more X-factor assets in their lockers. But he followed the route of so many and played professionally for other clubs in his career; and he has since returned to the club he loves, to use all that experience in his present position.

Mike Yates will always be successful in his life because he has a great love and respect for his family, his friends and his football club.

# Part Three
# Rebuilding My Life
# Away from Liverpool

## Adapting to My New Life at Dundee Football Club

After leaving Liverpool my new life developed very rapidly, so fortunately I had no time whatsoever to reflect or ponder over my decision. I went straight up to Dundee during the closed season to negotiate my contract and sign on the dotted line; as well as to start dealing with other new responsibilities, including the major issue of where I was going to live. Unfortunately, by then, Dave Rogers had left Dundee for another club, so I wasn't able to benefit from his hospitality this time. The first accommodation the club offered me was to share digs with eight other lads. I didn't fancy that idea at all, so I killed it off very quickly. By chance a friend of mine owned a flat in Dundee and he offered it to me at a fair price per month, so I decided to rent it from him. Apart from wanting to live in the peace and quiet of my own space, I was also keen to try looking after myself rather than have to depend on anybody. This was going to be my first time living away from my parents' home and I wanted to become truly independent.

The extra cost of living in my own place must have been on my mind when Jocky Scott sat me down to go through my contract; because even though my wages were quite good for a new, young signing, I still asked for an extra fifty pounds per week – just for shopping! When I popped the big question about getting more money, Jocky was stunned speechless. He just stared at me open-mouthed and then burst out laughing: 'You cheeky Scouse bugger!' Luckily the bold approach must have worked because he agreed to give me the extra fifty quid!

My career with Dundee officially kicked off in July 1999 when I started pre-season training with the under-21 side, a few days before the first team reported back for duty. There were some very good young players in that squad; especially Lee Wilkie, a local lad who later played for Scotland, as well as Lee Mair, Graham Bayne, Steven Milne and our goalkeeper Jamie Langfield, who is still playing for Aberdeen. And once the senior players started training, I was left in no doubt at all that I was surrounded by quality footballers. I can remember being particularly impressed by the likes of Willie Falconer who was a seasoned professional, Rob Douglas and Tommy Coyne who both also played for Celtic, Gavin Rae who went to Rangers, and Barry Smith who became the Dundee manager.

It was blatantly obvious to me that it would be tough to break into

# YATES SIGNS IN A CLUB RECORD

Victoria Park to Scottish Premier League Dundee

# Teen ace Yates' Scottish mission

TEENAGE striker Michael Yates could be heading for a new career in the Scottish Premier League.

The Burscough starlet, who played in the same Liverpool youth team as Michael Owen, is currently having his second trial with Dundee after impressing the Dens Park club in an initial spell a fortnight ago.

"Apparently, he did well the last time he went up there and he played in the reserves and scored," said Burscough boss John Davison. "So presumably they will make some sort of decision about him after the next few days."

And Davison added: "Yatesie was always going to be a player who had the potential to play at league level, so we are keeping our fingers crossed that things work out for him."

Yates joined the Linnets last summer after being released by Liverpool and scored 11 goals in an explosive nine-game spell in September and October.

Meanwhile, Davison is delighted at Burscough's progress to their second successive Liverpool Senior Cup Final.

## Yates all set for a Dundee Den

ONE of Burscough's rising young players returns north of the border this weekend for a second trial with a Scottish Premier League club.

Michael Yates has been invited to join up again with the staff and players at Dundee.

And if all goes well, it could see the 19-year-old marksman sign professional forms with the Dens Park side.

Yates, on contract at Victoria Park, has attracted the attention of a number of football league scouts throughout his debut season.

A former strike partner of Michael Owen in Liverpool's youth team, the teenager has bagged 19 goals for the Linnets including a spell in September and October

when he hit ten in seven matches.

Speaking on the eve of his second trip to Tayshire, Yates said: "The first trial went really well.

"I trained with the youth team and was picked for the reserves' game at St Johnstone where I scored after three minutes.

"The people were great up there. Their manager, Jocky Scott, called me in and said he would like to offer me a two-year contract which I thought was fantastic.

"At the moment I'm coaching the young kids with Liverpool and I love doing that.

"But if I moved it would be a dream come true.

"I've had great support from my mum and dad and from Thomas Galvin before he died last year.

"When I was at Burscough Dynamo he kept encouraging me and that has kept me going."

Commented Burscough secretary, Stan Strickland: "We have had inquiries about Michael from a number of clubs during the season and this has been coming for a while."

Yates's link with the Scottish club began at the start of the season when Burscough drew 1-1 at Gretna, a game which attracted a scout from Dundee.

The spy was back in January for the return fixture and saw Yates net once in a 2-0 win.

● DUNDEE CAKEWALK? Michael Yates (right) heading for the Scottish Premier League club.

## Yates isn't Dun just yet

By RONNIE MACKAY

**MICHAEL YATES is hoping to use Dundee as a springboard back to the Premiership — so he can resurrect his partnership with England star Michael Owen.**

The hit kid came through the ranks at Liverpool with Owen before their respective careers took very different paths.

As Owen broke into the Liverpool first-team and became an England superstar, Yates ended up at Unibond League side Burscough before his £15,000 move to Dens Park.

But he hopes that a good season in the Premier League will earn him a quickfire return south.

Yates said: "It would be a dream come true if I could team up with Michael again. If I can get the breaks, who knows what could happen.

"One of my main goals is to try

and get into the English Premiership, but I have to take things one step at a time and breaking into the Dundee first-team is my main priority. It is up to me to prove myself."

Yates recalled how, the first time he played with Owen at the age of 11, they ripped the opposition apart.

He added: "It was when I was with Liverpool Under-11's, I played alongside Michael up front when we beat a Welsh Select team 10-2.

"This was a team which hadn't been beaten for 10 years, but Michael scored four while I scored twice — we were fantastic together.

"I know him quite well, though I haven't seen him that much lately, but his is a talent you won't see very often and I certainly don't begrudge him any of his success." Yates was

with Liverpool since he was just eight and admitted that he was gutted when they released him.

*He said: "I knew Liverpool were the club for me and thought that if I carried on playing for them, one day I would make the first-team and play for England.*

### Divide

"I ended up on a YTS scheme on a two-year contract and was training with the first-team every day.

"But I was released one year ago and was bitterly disappointed."

After hitting 19 goals for Burscough last season, Dens Park boss Jocky Scott beat Oldham and Manchester City to land the striker. Yates added:

"What has impressed me most about Dundee is everyone is so friendly and there is no divide between the top players and the kids.

"I have no problems coming to Scotland. I just want to play football and this is a big step for me."

Dundee gaffer Jocky Scott hopes that Yates will become a first-team regular before long.

He said: "Michael has a lot of potential and we hope things work out.

"He is quite capable of scoring goals and, although he isn't that tall, he has got some pace about him."

# I HELPED PUT MICHAEL IN CLASS OF HIS OWEN

173

that group of established first team players but I was still excited at the prospect. I was eighteen, hungry for success and ready to work hard to achieve it. There was also a bit of extra pressure on me to perform well because quite a fuss had been made about me in the Scottish papers. As had happened before, particularly when I was doing well at Burscough, the headlines often referred to me as 'the former strike partner of Michael Owen at Liverpool', which of course was a massive title to live up to!

To add to that pressure, the early days of transition from Liverpool to Dundee really tested me in more ways than I had expected. I knew from day one that living on my own wouldn't be easy but what I didn't fully anticipate was just how difficult it would be for me to switch from life at Liverpool Football Club to Dundee FC. No disrespect whatsoever to Dundee, because they were a very organised and well managed football club, but it was a real culture shock for me when I went there from Liverpool. That's obviously not surprising, since Liverpool is one of the greatest clubs in the world, but I hadn't been mentally prepared for the many significant, everyday differences. After being at Liverpool since I was eight, where we had access to superb facilities and were so well looked after, almost everything at Dundee seemed disappointing. The ground, the training conditions, the changing rooms, the pitch, the kit, the boots, the food and lots of other things, were all a bit of a shock to the system for me. It might seem unfair and harsh for me to say that now but I have to be honest about it. After growing up with the Liverpool Way and thriving on my football life at Melwood, it was tough to handle getting on a mini-bus to be dropped off at a school playing field to train with Dundee. Having looked after the staff boots and training equipment during my YTS years at Liverpool, it truly shocked me that the first team players at Dundee had to look after their own kit. I'd be the first one to admit that we were probably spoiled at Liverpool but that knowledge didn't do anything to make it any easier for me to accept those lower standards. It was difficult to adapt to the conditions at Dundee, especially when I first arrived, and that undoubtedly must have drained me of some of my enthusiasm.

There were other challenging issues too. Thinking back to an under-21 game I played for Dundee against Rangers, with Jimmy Bone as our manager, I can remember they were playing five in midfield and causing total chaos in our defence. Ian Durrant in particular, who was a regular first team player at Rangers and a Scottish international, was doing loads of damage. So I automatically did what I'd always been taught to do in those circumstances, which was to drop back and add some extra cover. Next thing I know, Jimmy is really yelling, moaning at me for switching position and ordering me to push back up. Anyway at half-time, when we were all sat in the dressing room, he carried on having a real go at me, wagging his finger and everything, screaming what did I think I was doing. The room went silent. So I just calmly explained what I thought was going on in the game, with them outnumbering us in the middle, and described why I'd dropped back to help out. The manager told me I was wrong to make that decision for myself and that I had to stay up front no matter what I thought. Well I couldn't agree with that, so I politely said that I'd still have to carry on dropping back in the second half otherwise they'd just run riot around us and we'd get slaughtered. Needless to say, he wasn't happy at all with that comment and he let me know so in no uncertain terms. Twenty-five minutes into the second half he pulled me off and that was the start of the two of us never really seeing eye-to-eye ever again.

I was fine with the first team manager, Jocky Scott, but never again felt comfortable with Jimmy. I think this standoff had actually been brewing for a while before, probably since another incident in a game against St. Johnstone. We had a throw-in at the bottom corner and, again based on what I'd been taught at Liverpool, I instinctively took up a covering position in case we lost possession. Jimmy on the other hand was shouting at me to push up the field as far as I could and forget about any defensive responsibilities. Rightly or wrongly, I tried to explain to him what I was doing and why. But he wouldn't have any of it and insisted that I did what he was telling me. Unfortunately, I couldn't respect a coach who wanted me to play like that and I started to have my doubts about his ability. It wasn't that I was a troublemaker or rude to him in any way, it was just that I found it very difficult to accept poor standards.

But I was at Dundee to be a professional footballer and so I had to act like a professional.

It was essential that I pushed any misgivings to one side, never complained, got my head down and performed my job to the very best of my ability, regardless of the circumstances.

And that is exactly what I set out to accomplish.

*Me signing for Dundee with manager Jocky Scott*

# George Norrie
*Dundee F.C. Scout*

When I first went to evaluate Mike Yates he was playing at Burscough. Straight away, I could see that he had been coached at a high level. I saw an intelligent footballer who could spot a pass and produce good deliveries when crossing the ball, who showed a willingness to run behind defences, had the ability to make superb runs and who would always show to receive the ball. Mike had a great work ethic and he always made sure that he performed his defensive duties. Very importantly, he also had the desire to progress in football. That is why we signed him for Dundee F.C.

Mike did well at Dundee but his good progress was disrupted when there was a change of manager and the new man wanted to bring in his own players. Young players sometimes just need to get a good break at the right time and unfortunately that didn't happen for him. In my eyes, Mike Yates has not failed football; it has failed him. But he has stored up so much information from all the players and managers that he has worked with that it will all stand him in good stead in furthering his quest within the game.

Mike Yates still has a great deal to offer football.

## Ten Years of Hard Work Finally Rewarded

Just before the start of the season, after a couple of weeks of putting maximum effort into training, I was rewarded with my first special moment at Dundee when we all lined up for the club's Official First Team Photograph. This gave me a bit of a buzz because it was something that I had often imagined myself doing and now it was actually happening. Things got even better though when we were all sent to get individual photos taken. When I asked why we were doing this, the photographer told me they were for Panini Stickers. Panini Stickers! Yeeeeessssssss!! That really, really thrilled me because I'd been an avid collector my whole life; and now I'd have my own Mike Yates Panini Sticker. It seems a bit embarrassing to admit it today but I was so excited about it all that I rushed off to phone my dad and tell him. He must have been just as excited as me though because he ended up buying loads of the stickers!

By now I had my own squad number, 25, (which later became 16 after that first season) and Yates written on the back of my shirt, complete with Scottish Premier League badges. I had my own boot boy, John Thompson, so my life as an apprentice and a player had gone a full cycle. Fans were even asking me to sign autographs! The lads at the club were great company on and off the pitch. I was doing well and enjoying training, especially with Jocky Scott and Ray Farningham, who I rated highly. And I finally had a chance of playing Premier League football. It was starting to feel like a dream that was really coming true!

The culmination of my lifelong ambition in football got increasingly closer when Jocky picked me in the squad for the opening day of the 1999/2000 Scottish Premier League season. And, in a lovely twist of fate, to further add to my already through-the-roof excitement at being involved, that first game happened to be a local derby against Dundee United. There is no way that I could have asked for any better start to my new career, as that particular fixture gave me a truly incredible experience that I could not have repeated at any other football club in the United Kingdom or even beyond.

Even though it was an away match, we actually held the team talk in the home dressing room at our own ground, Dens Park, still dressed in our club suits. Amazingly, we then walked to our opponents' ground at Tannadice Park to get changed! You see, Dundee and Dundee United are the two closest professional football clubs anywhere in the world, with

"BUZZING, BUSTLING, LITTLE, STRIKER SNAPPED UP FROM CLYDEBANK AND WHO CAN PRODUCE GOALS OUT OF NOTHING. HIS LAST-GASP, VOLLEYED WINNER AT NEIGHBOURS UNITED WAS ONE OF THE HIGHLIGHTS FOR DARK BLUES LAST SEASON."

10

| Date of Birth: | Place of Birth: | Height: 5ft 11ins |
|---|---|---|
| 7/11/79 | Dronskie | Weight: 11st 1lb | Position: Forward |

MICHAEL YATES

SQUAD NUMBER

STRIKER OR RIGHT-WINGER WHO PLAYED IN THE SAME LIVERPOOL YOUTH SIDE AS MICHAEL OWEN. MOVED INTO NON-LEAGUE FOOTBALL ON MERSEYSIDE BEFORE DUNDEE GAVE HIM A DEAL. THE GAMBLE LOOKS LIKE PAYING OFF.

25

*Nice barnet Yatesy!*

*My own Panini sticker*

Back Row: Frank Van Eijs, David McKay, Robert Raeside, Lee Mair, Steven Tweed, Robert Douglas, Derek Soutar, Jamie Langfield, Lee Wilkie, Jonathan Thompson, Gavin Rae, Kieran McGuinness, William Falconer
Third Row: Gavin Beith, Steven Watson, Shaun McSkimming, John Elliott, Lee Sharp, Steven Milne, Mark Slater, Finn Gilfillan, Michael Yates, Keith Gibson, Graham Bayne
Second Row: James Earlie, Roberto Matute, Jack Cashley (Masseur), Harry Hay (Sprint Coach), Kenny Cameron (Youth Development Co-ordinator), Jocky Scott (Manager), Jimmy Bone (Assistant Manager), Raymond Farningham (Youth Coach), John McCreadie (Physio), Billy Thomson (Goalkeeping Coach), Lee Maddison, Jonathan Kelly
Front Row: Paul Clark, Stephen Boyack, Colin Boylan, James Grady, Steven Robb, William Miller, Richard Montgomery,
Barry Smith (Captain), David Riley, Hugh Robertson, Graeme Thomson, Barry Forbes
Inset: Eddie Annand

their grounds being a mere hundred yards or so apart. The weather was really hot and sunny that day and the instant we finally stepped out into the street thousands of our waiting fans went absolutely ballistic. It was bedlam really and the police struggled to keep all of us players together in one group. Even though it seemed a bit like organised chaos, it was a happy kind of chaos and the vibe all around us was just fantastic. As we set off towards Tannadice, the whole scene must have looked like something straight out of the movies. Players and fans walking side by side, singing and chanting together, like an army marching to do battle with the enemy. It was like 'Braveheart Meets Premier League'! What an amazing, exciting, emotional experience that short but sensational stroll turned out to be.

I have to say that on this occasion Jimmy Bone did a great job of making myself and the other young lads on the bench feel comfortable. He encouraged us to go out and soak up the atmosphere during the warm-up. By the time we jogged out onto the pitch the cheering reached an ear-splitting crescendo and we could barely hear each other calling for the ball. At one point Jimmy made us all stop and gather around him: 'Listen to that noise, feel the excitement, take it all in. Look around you, this is where you want to be, this is what you are aiming for. Work hard and this is what you'll enjoy every week.'

Once the match kicked off, as much as I'd longed to get a start in that game, the fact that I was on the bench gave me a rare opportunity to experience the passion of the fans from very close quarters. The massive crowd was right behind me, no more than a couple of yards away. The crazy, fanatical supporters from both sides were totally psyched up for the big derby and roaring their heads off. The noise was deafening and the mood totally electrifying. I could literally feel the energy pulsating through my body.

'Wow!' I thought to myself, 'This is what it's all about, this is why I want to play at the top level.'

Around about the 70th minute, when we were 2 – 1 down, the manager told me to warm up and get ready to go on. There must have been a million things going through my mind while I was stretching and limbering up along the touchline but I could still hear the Dundee fans shouting encouragement at me. When I actually ran on to the field I was in a bit of a daze. Everything seemed to go silent and the players around me appeared to be moving in slow motion. That trance was soon exploded though when our keeper kicked the ball really high and I realized it was dropping right in my direction. Fortunately my football instincts kicked in immediately and, even though I knew there was a defender bearing down on me, I managed to keep my concentration and brought the ball down under complete control and turned away from him in the same movement. He brought me down from behind. As I picked myself up from the deck I thought, 'Phew, not a bad start!' Late on in the game I almost set up an equaliser when I drove the ball across the box into the path of Shaun McSkimming who could have knocked it in from six yards out, but their keeper got his finger tips to it and did enough to divert the ball away to safety. Overall, even though I was disappointed that we had lost, I was still reasonably happy with my own performance during that first short stint out on the pitch.

After all the euphoria of the Dundee United derby match, especially having done OK in my first game, even if it was only as a sub, I had extra motivation to push myself even harder in training. I was pumped up and looking forward to our next match, which was against Hibernian, especially as I had heard it was going to be covered on Sky TV. Now I know that might sound a bit shallow, but it's the truth. Wouldn't you like your family and friends to watch you playing football on television? During the build-up to the game I played well in all the practice sessions and I thought that there was a definite chance of me being in the starting eleven. Unfortunately Jocky Scott had other plans and he quickly burst my bubble by completely dropping me from the squad. I wasn't even on the bench. Bang! Back down to earth with a big bump. That was certainly one way to make me keep my feet on the ground.

One of the interesting aspects of Jocky's management style was that even though he had me regularly training with the first team, he still wanted me to use the youth team's dressing room. Looking back on that, from a coach's perspective, I now think that was a very good idea. He was helping me to stay focused on my job, while at the same time he was giving the other youth players a target for themselves to aim for. If you like, I was a sort of connection between the youth team and the first team squad. Plus, if I didn't get selected for the first team, I was still an everyday part of the youth squad and wouldn't feel out of place playing with them in the Scottish Under-21 League. It was a good system and it worked well for everybody.

Anyway, I'd been around the game long enough to know what kind of reaction the manager would be hoping to get from me after putting me firmly in my place; so I just kept quiet, got on with the job, worked even harder in training and kept on fighting to earn my start in the side.

# Jamie Redknapp
*Liverpool FC 1991 – 2001 and Former England International*

It can be difficult to accurately judge the future of many players at eighteen, simply because most lads don't really mature until twenty or later. Obviously the exceptionally talented players shine through very early, so it's no rocket science to pick them out. Anybody could see that Michael Owen was going to make the grade. Wayne Rooney was a boy in a man's body and always looked the part. Steven Gerrard was an interesting case because he lacked a bit physically and he didn't look like a natural athlete, but he could turn into Superman when he needed to. The first time I watched Stevie up-close was when Gerard Houllier sent him to train with the first team. Early on during the game I knocked a pass to him and waited for him to give it back, which is what most kids do when they first join in at that level. Not him! He just turned away and pinged a forty-yard pass right to somebody's feet. I said to him straight away, 'How good are you then!' It was easy to see that he was very special.

Clearly the majority of young players don't fall into the category of obvious future stars, and that is where the selection process becomes more challenging; but I have this strong belief that if you are good enough you will make it in the end. Even if a youngster has to drop down a division or two and then bounce back up again, if he has the right mentality and is hungry enough, then he will eventually reach the right grade. But if a player gets rejected at eighteen and just gives up, then he probably doesn't have what it takes to make it to the top anyway. Some deserving players occasionally slip the net, but not many.

To become a footballer you have to have a lot of dedication, you have to really want it. For a young man it's tough when all your friends are planning a night out for a few drinks and you have to say you're not going, because you have training the next day. And those decisions are even more difficult for local lads because they are surrounded by their old friends who still want them to behave like regular mates. They want you to still be one of them but the reality is you are not the same person any more. As a footballer you have to live a completely different life and keep yourself clean and in the best shape. All young footballers need to be patient and keep working hard, ready to grab any chance that comes their way.

It's not easy.

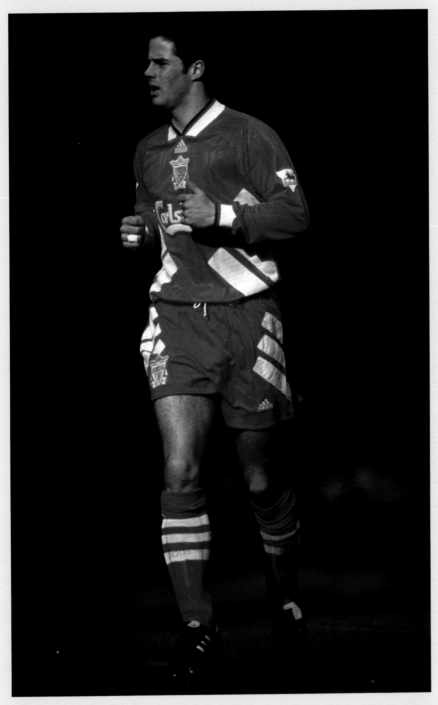

*Redders*

## Making My Scottish Premier League Debut

I soon reaped the rewards for my positive response to any earlier disappointments with the very next fixture against Aberdeen. As we finished training on the Thursday I bumped into Jocky Scott outside the first team dressing room and he asked me how I was feeling. I told him I felt really great. 'Fit and strong and enjoying my football.'

'That's good', he said, 'because you're starting on Saturday.'

Starting! Saturday!! Me!!! Even though that was exactly what I'd been praying for so long to hear, I was stunned when it actually happened. Before I could react properly and say thanks or anything he was gone; leaving me rooted to the spot, elated but speechless. This was it, my full debut for Dundee in the Scottish Premier League, away to Aberdeen at Pittodrie. It was a real struggle but somehow I managed to keep my head calm enough while I was still at the club not to embarrass myself in front of the other players or the staff, but the minute I got outside the gates I sprinted to a phone to call Mum and Dad to give them the big news. And loads of friends and other people after that as well! My brain was buzzing so much I was literally bouncing with excitement. Hopping like the Energizer Bunny, I couldn't sit still for hours.

We travelled to Aberdeen on the Friday and stayed overnight in a hotel. It took me ages to drop off to sleep but I still found myself wide awake an hour before dawn. My very first thought when I woke up was that I needed to play well so that I didn't let down my mum and dad who'd come up to watch the match. It was a very big thing for me to know that they would be there to be part of my first full game because I was always aware of the important role they'd played in me getting that far. The older I got the more I realized the kind of huge sacrifices they must have made for me over the years; and that still applies today. In fact, now that I am a parent myself, I am even more qualified to fully understand and appreciate the amazing efforts they made on my behalf.

The build-up to that full debut against Aberdeen seems to blur in my memory, but I do vividly recall that from the first moment the ref blew his whistle to get the match underway, play went zipping along at a really fast pace. Once again, like the previous occasion when I came on as sub, I was fortunate to be involved in a bit of positive action very early on; and that helped to settle my nerves. One of their players ran on to a good through ball and seemed to have lots of clear space between him and our goal; but I had already started tracking him back before the pass was made, so I was able to catch up with him and managed a solid tackle to halt the danger. It was a good first contribution and the Dundee fans got on their feet and made plenty of noise to show their appreciation for my efforts. Round One to Yatesy!

As the game went on I was seeing quite a bit of the ball and getting more settled all the time. At one point I put in a really good cross that rifled towards Willie Faulkner, but he was just beaten to the ball by a defender who headed it behind. The good news though was that we scored from the corner. When we celebrated that Dundee goal it was like I was living out another one of my dreams. As a schoolboy I had regularly fantasised about running towards my team mates and jumping up and down, fist pumping in the air and hearing thousands of fans cheering – and now it had actually happened. I loved it!

We won that match 2-0 and I put in a very sound performance but I had to come off after about 78 minutes, completely and utterly shattered. I was physically drained by the relentless speed and pace of the game and mentally washed out by the many emotional twists and turns that are part and parcel of a big debut match like that. Even if I never ever doubted it before, I now knew from painful personal experience just how super fit you must be to play at the top level of football. There is a massive difference between fit and match-fit for a Premier League game.

Despite feeling wrecked, I was still floating on a bit of a natural high. My full debut had been a fantastic experience and I was happy enough with the way I'd played. My confidence was given an extra boost when our press officer told me that the media had asked for me, as their choice of player to be interviewed, and they were all waiting for me in the lounge. Obviously I was flattered by this attention but, thankfully not for the first time, my education at Liverpool Football Club automatically kicked in and sent up a red warning flag in my head. All the values that the Liverpool Way had etched forever onto my brain suddenly started screaming at me to be careful. After all, I was just the new kid on the block and I'd only played one game; so who was I to be interviewed when our team was full of good senior players, including several seasoned internationals. With caution at the front of my mind, I stood up in the middle of the dressing room and, in front of all my teammates, I told the manager what was going on with the media and asked him what I should do. Jocky Scott looked at me a bit perplexed and said: 'Well son, don't be daft, if they've asked for

● Michael Yates (left) joins Willie Falconer in celebrating Dundee's opening goal ... drie. From facing the likes of Belper Town to lining up against Celtic. Yates ... n football has taken a dramatic change of direction (see story, left). Now turn to ... for full reports on how local teams Burscough and Skelmersdale fared in their ... on drives. Code NA

... WY ME? ... Dennis Wyness with Michael Yates

GOING NOWHERE FAST ... Kiriakov can't shake off his marker as yet another Dons attack fails

*My full debut in the Scottish Premier League. Great memories and a dream come true.*

■ FALCON SWOOPS — lanky hitman Willie Falconer is congratulated by team-mates after scoring in Dundee's 2-0 win over Aberdeen at Pittodrie yesterday

186

you then just go.' OK, fair enough. From my perspective it was no problem at all for me to have looked a bit stupid for asking the question; but it most certainly would have been a really big problem for me if I had not asked the question and ended up looking like a fat-headed 'Billy Big Boots' new boy!

Anyway, once I'd been given the go-ahead, I took a deep breath and walked into the press conference room. Nothing I had ever experienced in my life before had prepared me for what then faced me. It was like walking into a solid wall of noise and flashbulbs. The place was packed, the photographers were jostling for good positions, the reporters were all trying to get their question in first and I was literally stopped in my tracks – like a rabbit stunned in the headlights! It's worth bearing in mind that I'd never had any kind of lessons in how to deal with the media. It just wasn't done back then like it is at the Academy nowadays, so it was a case of sink or swim. I might have been a young lad doing my first interview but that didn't slow them down in any way at all. Even before I'd settled at the microphone, they started pinging questions at me from all angles, mainly asking my opinions about how the game had gone. Making a concerted effort to take things slowly, I gave answers that I thought were technically sound but in no way potentially controversial, generally talking about the pace of the game and my own contributions. Everything was going smoothly when one of the reporters popped up with a good one. He asked me how I was enjoying playing for Dundee and how had my life changed since I moved up to Scotland. Well that question was definitely a bit trickier than just talking about the game, so I gathered my thoughts carefully and hoped for some inspiration. And it came. I don't know where from, but it came. The words just flowed naturally: 'Well, let's put it this way. I am very happy and very excited to be here in Dundee. Two months ago I was preparing to play against Farsley Celtic in our local league and now here I am getting ready to play against Glasgow Celtic in the Scottish Premier League!' Of course the press boys absolutely loved that response and it was repeated in just about every paper or news story. In fact it was reproduced as the 'Quote of the Week' in many papers.

The upsurge in publicity resulted in more references to me as 'Michael Owen's former strike partner at Liverpool'. At first I enjoyed this label and I suppose it gave my confidence a boost, but after a while I felt embarrassed, simply because I was nowhere near as good as Michael and never would be. Unless of course I could have borrowed some of his lightning pace! To put that situation into its real perspective, by then Michael and I were both still eighteen but the difference was that he had already played for England in the World Cup in France and scored that wonder goal against Argentina. No further comment required! Later on I also got a bit fed up with the 'Owen strike partner' tag because I wanted people to recognise me for my own ability, not for the names of my former teammates – no matter who they were!

## An Encounter with the Mighty Celtic and a Liverpool Legend

After having successfully made my full debut against Aberdeen, I was even more pleased and reassured to be included in the team for the next match, just a few days later on the Tuesday. We were at home to Dumbarton in the Scottish League Cup and we won comfortably 4 – 0. Even though I didn't get on the score sheet, I knew I had played well and I felt as though I was starting to belong in the team. But the real significance of that recent run in the starting eleven was that the next league match was at home to Celtic – the big one!

During training that week Jocky Scott and Jimmy Bone spoke to me several times about man-to-man marking one of the Celtic players and I was also included as a key part of the set-piece practice routines. So, not surprisingly, I started to really believe that I was going to get a start against the Mighty Celtic. Sadly, when the big day arrived, I was only given a place on the bench. It was especially disappointing for me because John Barnes was the Celtic manager at that time and it would have been an honour to line up against a side put out by one of my former Liverpool heroes; a man who had provided me with plenty of inspiration and personal guidance as a young player.

Due to my former relationship at Liverpool with both John Barnes and Kenny Dalglish, who was then Celtic's Director of Football, the media asked me to do quite a few interviews and once again I ended up getting a lot of publicity.

Having to do those pre-match interviews, I arrived at the ground quite early. When I walked past the Celtic dressing room my eyes immediately latched onto their kit hanging on the pegs; those distinctive green and white hoop shirts, with the famous Celtic crest. It gave me a huge buzz to know I might get a chance to play against them that afternoon.

# BARNES STORMER

HE'S GOT A LOTTA BALLS: Michael Yates is desperate to kick-start his career at Dens

## Yates Den good

HOOPS head honchos John Barnes and Kenny Dalglish will have only themselves to blame if Michael Yates gives them another poke in the ribs on Tayside today.

For the 19-year-old, who made his Dundee debut in the

## INSIDE INFO COULD HELP

JOHN BARNES and Kenny Dalglish will have only themselves to blame if Michael Yates gives them another uncomfortable time on Tayside this afternoon.

For the 19-year-old, who made his first start for Dundee in the 2-0 win over Aberdeen last Saturday after being plucked from English

non-League football in the summer, admitted last night that he learned some of his trade from the two top men at Parkhead.

Barnes and Dalglish will be desperate to put their first set-back since their arrival – last Sunday's defeat by Dundee United down the road at Tannadice – behind them.

But Yates, who signed a three-year contract after impressing Dundee when he played with

"I have also watched videos of him in his playing days and the way he used to turn opponents and his one-touch passing were brilliant. You are going to

goals and a pair of clean sheets," he rapped.

"We didn't worry when we met Celtic last season and the situation is no different this time."

# Celts chiefs made Yates a success

By IAN STEWART

JOHN BARNES and Kenny Dalglish will have only themselves to blame if Michael Yates gives them another uncomfortable time on Tayside this afternoon.

SCOTT: Injuries have cleared up

been given. It is a huge step from playing against teams like Belper Town and Harrogate Town but I never gave up the hope of playing at a high level.

"The Premier League whether it is in Scotland or England is the dream."

Dundee boss Jocky Scott is hopeful he will have a full squad to pick from, with injury worries over Lee Maddison, Willie Miller and in-form ex-Celt Willie Falconer clearing up.

Striker James Grady, who missed the last two matches after a bout of flu, is fit enough to be included in the squad and Scott has also listed giant young central defender Lee Wilkie.

Scott was at Tannadice last Sunday and said: "They did very well and one of the keys to their successive was their discipline. As far as tactics are concerned, we may go the same route as United, but we also have alternatives.

BUT, whatever method we choose, the priority against Celtic is we have to be positive when we have the ball. We are going into the game with a fair bit of confidence after two wins which have produced six goals and two clean sheets.

"It is going to be a difficult game because we are meeting one of the two best teams in the country and I know they will be out to atone for the

## Yates hoping to come back to haunt Barnes

GEORGE GRANT reports

Young gun: Michael Yates

JOHN BARNES and Kenny Dalglish will have only themselves to blame if Michael Yates gives them another uncomfortable time on Tayside this afternoon.

For the 19-year-old, who made his Dundee debut in the 2-0 win last Saturday after being plucked from the obscurity of English non-league football in the summer, admitted last night that he learned some of his trade from the two top men at Parkhead.

Yates, who signed a three-year contract after impressing Dundee last season, is keen to continue his dream introduction to Scottish football.

The youngster seemed

destined for the top when he played in the same Liverpool youth side as Michael Owen and he recalled: "During my time on the YTS scheme at Anfield I remember playing in the same side as John Barnes on one occasion.

"It was a bounce match between the reserves and the youths which was arranged to help him get his fitness back after an injury. And I remember he helped me a lot during that match.

"I was playing up front while he was in midfield. He talked me through the 90 minutes and gave me a lot of good advice.

'He told me I was moving around too much and to stand still at times so that I could show myself and receive the ball from the midfield players.

"A lot of people might think it was a huge step for him to go straight from playing to such a big coaching job in the summer but it didn't surprise me because of the way I remember him from Anfield."

Dundee boss Jocky Scott is hopeful he will have a full squad to pick from, with injury worries over Lee Maddison, Willie Miller, James Grady and in-form Willie Falconer clearing up.

h the 90
e a lot of

s moving
h and to
so that I
self and
n the mid-

und the
t he was
er-figure

before he got the chance to cross Stanley Park and become a Reds schoolboy signing. He said: "My father and brother took me to Goodison from an early age and I remember how Kenny's team gave me heartache.

"I have also watched videos of him and I know he was magnificent. The way he used his body to turn opponents and his one-touch passing were brilliant. You are going to learn something from watching a player like him."

Yates wants to go on learning in his second chance at the highest level, after being spotted by

"During my time on the YTS scheme at Anfield I remember playing in the same side as John Barnes on one occasion.

"It was a bounce match between the reserves and the

mgu I umm r
was a huge step
for him to go
straight from
playing to such a
big coaching job in the summer, but it didn't surprise me.

6 I never gave
up hope of
playing at a
high level 9

189

The atmosphere during the warm-up was incredible, with a fantastic big-match vibe, just like the local derby against Dundee United. Later on, as both teams were leaving the dressing rooms to go out for the kick-off, I came through the door at the same time as John Barnes. He spotted me in the corridor straightaway, said hello and we started talking from there. By the time we were out on the pitch, and I was making my way with the other Dundee subs over to our dugout, Digger still had his arm around my shoulder. We walked together right along the touchline, chatting away all the time, with him asking how I was doing and making some joke about me not scoring that afternoon. It didn't even enter my mind that I was passing right in front of our home supporters and being pally with the opposition manager; it just felt great to enjoy a bit of banter with Digger again. When we reached the away team dugout he stopped, shook hands with me and wished me well, 'Hope you get on later Yatesy.'

And I did. After 72 minutes, when we were 0 - 1 down, I got the call from Jocky Scott to warm-up and get ready to go on. It was a massive occasion, so I suspect I must have been a bit nervous. Without doubt, I was definitely pumped up for it. Fortunately I got a few good early touches and, as usual, that helped me settle down quite quickly. Though I do also remember that there was a bit of a commotion and some pushing and shoving after I'd managed to get in a good, solid tackle on Bobby Petta. He was a Dutch international at the time so, even though it was a fair tackle, I suppose he didn't like being hit hard by a young lad. But it was just a quick bout of handbags, nothing more. The referee had a quiet word with both of us and that was that. Funnily enough I think it was Hugh Dallas, who went on to officiate in two World Cups and lots of big European games.

Shortly after that incident we got an equalizer through a lad called Lee Sharp and the Dundee crowd exploded into raptures. I can remember sprinting about 45-yards to join in with all the team to celebrate that goal. Then, as I was walking back to the halfway line, I looked up and saw John Barnes and Terry McDermott, another great former Liverpool player, locked in conversation, presumably talking tactics. There were only minutes left to play and Celtic started really piling on the pressure, so it was a case of backs-to-the-wall defending for our team. One specific moment in time that I do remember clearly was when I saw a ball coming in towards Mark Viduka and I decided that it was too risky to try to get in front and nick it from him, so instead I just went in hard against his back to get as tight as possible and stop him turning. Well I tell you what, it was like running straight into a brick wall!

Then, in the 89th minute, Celtic got a corner. Our whole team took up their defensive positions and the orders were buzzing around about keeping things tight and not giving anything away. There was all the usual jockeying for position, with lots of movement and blocking. Then the ball came sailing across to the back of the box, somebody headed it back into the danger zone and there was Henrik Larsson, ready to pounce and knock it into the net. Shit! My heart sank. To make my misery even worse, Larsson chose to perform his trademark tongue wagging goal celebration right in front of me. Great goal predator or not, I didn't enjoy that display one bit.

Before we had any time to regroup and respond, the ref blew his whistle to end the game and it was suddenly all over. We'd got really close to earning a battling draw with the Mighty Celtic but they had done their job very professionally, right to the very end, and got the late winner when they needed it.

There's no such thing as hard lines in football. You can only win, draw or lose – and we'd just lost. End of story!


## Scoring My First Goal in the Scottish Premier League

During the weeks following the Celtic match, Jocky Scott continued with his policy of starting me in some games but leaving me on the bench or dropping me from the squad for others. As well as being very frustrating for me, being in and out of the side definitely made it very difficult to maintain a good rate of progress. Nevertheless, as had become almost routine by then, I just kept working hard and waited for any opportunities to come my way.

Eventually, after two successive away matches on the bench, against Motherwell and Heart of Midlothian, the manager finally picked me to start the next home game against St. Johnstone.

And I scored!

On about the ten minutes mark, Steve Boyack picked up the ball and moved into space. As soon as I made a run, he knocked a pass out wide to me. One touch of the ball to bring it under control and I was moving at pace towards the box. Looking up to see what options were open, I

decided to drive it really hard into the danger area by the far post. After striking the ball, my momentum made me fall away to the right. As I was going down to ground I realized that the ball was flying towards the goal and bending into the far top corner. The keeper dived across to try to knock it away but he had no chance. One of those slow-motion camera moments clicked in as I watched the flight of the ball before it smacked into the back of the net.

The Dundee fans went wild. I can remember getting up off the floor and just standing there, my arms spread wide, looking at the crowd, hearing them cheering, and savouring that feeling of total exhilaration. Then all of a sudden I collapsed under an avalanche of bodies as my teammates jumped all over me in mad celebration. Brilliant! The only one who didn't rush over was Willie Miller, the wily senior pro, but he did walk up to meet me by the halfway line and congratulated me with a good old-fashioned slap on the back. Jocky Scott came out of his dugout to applaud me. Jimmy Bone, ever the professional, just shouted at me to keep concentrating and focus on my job again.

I stole a quick glance up into the stands to pick out my mum and dad, somehow managed to make eye contact, and gave them a quick wave of the hand. It was a very, very special moment knowing that they had seen me score that goal.

After the game I found out that my brother Geoff had been checking our match via Teletext back home in Burscough. And when it flashed up that I had scored, ever the madman, he ran out into the middle of the street to celebrate, shouting out, 'Our Mike has just scored for Dundee, Mike scored for Dundee.' I'm glad I wasn't there to witness that spectacle!

One thing I can remember really clearly about scoring that day is the incredible roar that went up from the Dundee supporters. It is impossible to describe just how thrilling it is to hear tens of thousands of people erupt into cheering because of something you've just done. And what really amazes me most about how I felt after scoring that first goal is when I think about what it must have been like for those players who've scored goals in big finals in the world's greatest stadiums. When I talk to Ian Rush about scoring winning goals in Cup Finals at Wembley, against Everton of all teams, in front of 90,000 screaming fans, I can't even begin to imagine how he must have felt. And what about Michael Owen knocking

*Opposite: GOAL - Yates in the 10th minute*

in the winner in the Cup Final against Arsenal at Cardiff? Or, better still, Steven Gerrard scoring that great header against AC Milan in the Champions League Final at the Ataturk in Istanbul? The immense buzz and adrenaline rush of scoring a goal under those circumstances must be impossible to measure. It takes a lot of experience to learn how to come back down to earth quickly and get on with the game. There again, those top players are able to take that massive emotional high and turn it into extra energy to push themselves even harder.

In my case, after all the goal celebrations had calmed down and the match was about to restart, it suddenly hit me that my legs had turned to jelly. I couldn't run properly, in fact I could hardly move at all. It took at least five minutes for me to regain my composure enough to start playing again. Even then, the rest of the game passed by in a bit of a haze, until Jocky took me off after about 75 minutes. Back in the dugout I started to think about the possible headlines in the next day's papers about me scoring the winner, maybe even with my photo on the back page. That kind of daydreaming is quite natural for a young player but the harsh reality is that football can quickly turn around and stamp on your dreams. St. Johnstone scored twice in the last 10 minutes and we lost 2-1. So no winning goal for me that day! I was devastated that we had been beaten. The press asked for me to do an interview again but this time I told Jocky that I was too disappointed to be able to cope with all the questions.

It was another harsh but valuable lesson in the 'ups and downs' of football success. And that's why most goal scorers will usually be quoted as saying: 'Well, yes, I was happy to get a goal today; but I'm much happier that the team won.'

## Haunted by an Old Ghost from the Past

Obviously grabbing that first goal in the Scottish Premier League really gave my confidence a boost and spurred me on to believe that I now had a genuine opportunity to nail down a regular starting place in the first team. My recent match performances had been very promising, training was going well, my mental attitude was right and I was growing in stature within the squad. I was a happy camper! By now I was on top of my game and bursting to play the following week's home fixture against Rangers; one of the matches of the season.

Life was treating me very kindly indeed until one morning during training I suddenly started to feel the recurring effects of an old back injury that I'd picked up during my schoolboy days at Liverpool. When I'd first noticed the back pain as a young teenager, I hadn't been able to pinpoint any particular incident or moment that had caused the injury. The same thing happened this time. There was no bad tackle, fall, slip, funny twist, pull or anything else that I was consciously aware of; the pain just seemed to appear from nowhere.

Desperate to play at the weekend, I convinced myself that I was OK and that I'd only strained my lower back by stepping up my work rate in anticipation of the big game against Rangers. The truth was the pain was agony every time I tried to sprint or turn quickly, but I tried to mask it as much as I could. In the end though, my conscience got the better of me and I told the trainer what had happened. The physio worked with me throughout the rest of that week and I responded well enough to the treatment to be included in the squad for the Rangers match. Unfortunately, or perhaps fortunately when I look back on it now, Jocky put me on the bench and I never got called on to play that day. So my big dream of playing against Rangers, the other giant of Scottish football, was relegated to a mere spectator's role from the dugout.

From that time onwards my first season with Dundee gradually declined into a living nightmare. My back problem persisted and, despite all the efforts of the medical staff, it gradually deteriorated. So while I found myself constantly struggling to attain full fitness, I was also forever fighting a losing battle for a place back in the first team. It was a very frustrating and demoralising situation. I made it onto the bench for a few more games and for a while there were some genuine hints of optimism. I even played a few more matches for the first team, including Motherwell away, but in the end my back got so bad that I couldn't even do any kind of proper exercise. Light running was just about OK, but as soon as I tried sprinting my back would just pack in and the pain would take over. Eventually, some time in December 1999, that miserable on/off period finally went from bad to worse when the injury forced me to stop playing altogether.

During my downtime, while only doing light training, I did my best to keep my spirits up and made a big effort to join in the banter and stay part of the dressing room. Just like I had done at Liverpool, I started doing my impressions to entertain the lads. On one occasion I even managed to

Photos courtesy of the Dundee Courier

get hold of Steve Boyack's mobile phone and, when he wasn't around, I changed his recorded voice message by doing my best version of David Beckham. After that, every time somebody called Steve and he wasn't there they got Becks on the line. Or so they thought!

What was really unusual about this particular joke was that it ended up being reported in the Scottish national press. The Mirror had an article about it saying how: 'Dundee star Steven Boyack last night revealed he has been receiving nuisance phone calls - from David Beckham! And thanks to Scouse team-mate Michael Yates he has not been able to get rid of the Manchester United star for the last month.'

Steve was then quoted as saying: 'Every time my phone's turned off and people try to get me they get this message. To be fair to Michael he is a good impressionist and has done it to a lot of the boys at the club. I think Eddie Annand has even had John Barnes on his messages, although I think most of it has been confined to the younger lads. I've no idea how to get it changed and I must admit I've taken pelters from some of my mates - but it's all in good fun, although sometimes you don't know what to expect.'

That short newspaper report gave us plenty to laugh about. We were all hoping that the reporter would contact me about the story so that I could answer the phone as Alan Hansen, telling the media to leave me alone!

Unfortunately there was nothing amusing about my back problem. The doctors in Dundee couldn't identify any specific cause of the acute pain; they just repeated my own amateur diagnosis that it seemed to be more of a flare-up of my old injury, possibly aggravated by general wear and tear. The damage had apparently been caused to my lower back and it had somehow affected my hips as well; but the fundamental problem was that every time I tried to sprint, my hamstrings would tighten and seize up. I couldn't even run fifteen yards without having to pull-up in pain. What made it all totally impossible to cope with was that the medical people couldn't prove what was in fact actually wrong. Which of course also meant that they didn't know how to treat it. So there I was, seemingly fit and strong but stuck with an injury that wouldn't go away and nobody could help me.

Once again in my short career, I was back asking that same horrendous, unanswerable question: 'Why has this happened to me now when everything was going so well?'

*Me celebrating with big Lee Wilkie, a great centre back who would win international honours for Scotland*

I was very, very down during that period. I couldn't play, I couldn't train, nobody could provide the right treatment, I was on my own away from home, I was depressed and my career was on hold. And all of that was compounded by the inescapable fact that prior to the injury, before the onset of all these new problems, I had been really flying. In fact I'd only just written a letter to my parents telling them how happy and excited I was; how I was really beginning to believe that this was it, this was going to be the real breakthrough for me in football. How cruel life can be!

After a couple of weeks of hopeless inactivity, I was at such an all-time low that my skin broke out in a weird rash; presumably all brought about by my stress and state of depression. And, ironically, the fact that my mum and dad were extremely worried about the whole situation didn't help; it actually made me feel even worse! Things eventually hit absolute rock bottom when I also went down with an unusually bad dose of flu. Even though some of the lads would occasionally pass round to my flat to check on me and try to cheer me up, I still felt completely isolated and unable to cope any more with the terrible circumstances that had been thrust upon me. In the end, Jocky Scott weighed up the whole situation and decided to send me home to recover. I was on the injured list for four months and missed the rest of the season.

In an effort to cheer myself up, I decided to go on a lad's trip that summer with my best mate Peter Norbury and a couple of other friends. We packed our bags and went off to Cyprus in search of sunshine and some fun. The resort we chose, Aiya Napa, was well-known as a party-capital and a popular favourite with the football crowd, so it was no surprise to find out that Rio Ferdinand and Ashley Cole were over there at the same time. Tony Warner, who I'd played with at Liverpool, was staying in the same hotel as us and he and I had some good chats about our time together at the club. One night at the hotel bar, Peter overheard a table full of girls seemingly talking about us. As soon as I turned around to have a gander, my eyes got no further than a gorgeous looking girl sat on a barstool. Not being a shy lad, but still feeling the old butterflies fluttering in my belly, I walked straight over, introduced myself and started chatting. Her name was Nikki and she turned out to be just as lovely as she looked, so I was absolutely made up when she later agreed to go out with me. Nikki and I enjoyed some good laughs and romantic moments whenever we spent time together. So, when the holiday sadly came to an to start my second season with Dundee, Nikki went home to Leeds, and we kept in touch for a while via text and the occasional phone call. But there then followed a long period when things went very quiet and our relationship, which had been inspired by a holiday-romance, just seemed to naturally fade away.

That was probably a good thing at the time because I had to focus on the job at hand.

I needed to win back my place in the Dundee first team!

## My Second Season at Dundee – Football Italian Style

At the end of the 1999/2000 season, despite the fact that Dundee had done well to finish in the top half of the Scottish Premier League, Jocky Scott was sacked as manager and replaced by an Italian, Ivano Bonetti. From a personal viewpoint, I was sorry to see Jocky go as he had given me my chance with Dundee and I had liked him as a man. But that is how the game operates. There is not a great deal of sentiment involved in the running of professional football clubs. The idea of a new manager taking over at Dundee gave me some room for concern but also excited me at the same time. My initial worry, like many players with the arrival of a new boss, was whether or not I would fit into his plans. On the flip side though, due to my interest in coaching, I was really looking forward to finding out what he would introduce to the club in terms of new training routines, style of play and match tactics. The idea of working with a European coach, especially an Italian, was something that I readily welcomed and I was looking forward to getting started.

Plus, of course, the appointment of a new manager also meant that I had a chance to make a fresh start after the misery of the last few months of the previous season.

As the start of the new season approached, because I had been sent home to deal with my back injury and recuperate from my depressed frame of mind, I was well rested, feeling fresh and raring to go again. While the other players had taken their annual holidays and enjoyed a well-earned break during the closed season, I had been doing lots of light exercise work and gradually rebuilding my fitness. Consequently, by the time the new manager arrived and we all reported back to Dens Park for pre-season training, I was already feeling as fit as a fiddle and ready for action!

When Ivano Bonetti and his coaching team, which included his brother Dario, took over at Dundee, it was like a breath of fresh air and I absolutely loved it. They introduced new playing systems, new coaching techniques and a whole new, much more dynamic approach to training. For me, with my coaching background, this was a very positive improvement. However, some of the more established, older pros were stuck in their ways and openly complained about the new regime. To his credit, the manager's response to their moaning was very simple: 'This is how you have to train from now on and if you don't like it you don't belong at this club.'

A perfect example of the Bonetti approach to training was when he arranged a week's stay for the first team squad at an upmarket health resort as part of our pre-season preparations. The new manager stunned a lot of the Scottish lads when he made that announcement, especially when he then told us in his lilting Italian accent that we were going to Borneo. Borneo? You mean like jungles and all that? Some of the lads must have had visions of themselves riding on elephants: at least until Ivano repeated himself, pronounced Bormio a lot more clearly and added that it was in Northern Italy, close to the Alps. Borneo or Bormio, I didn't really care which one, I just desperately wanted to go!

When the squad for the training trip was announced it included some new signings, like Marco de Marchi, Georgi Nemsadze and Chris Coyne. Happily, my name was on the list too. When our plane took off for Italy on a Friday afternoon in early July 2000, I was flying in more ways than one. Everything I'd witnessed so far had convinced me I was going to enjoy the new Italian style Dundee FC.

My career was getting nicely back on track.

Bormio was a spa town high up in the mountains of Italy and we checked into a specialist health resort that was accustomed to hosting professional sports teams. Even though there was strict control of what we ate and drank, we still had some fun enjoying different forms of exercise, like going on bike rides, in addition to our regular football training. After the first couple of days of the camp, the manager started to talk to me quite a lot, congratulating me on my progress and encouraging me to keep going. He kept mentioning my role in the pre-season games that we were scheduled to play, so I was growing increasingly confident about my position in the team for the upcoming season. Thriving under this new management regime, I was enjoying every minute of every session. There was one particular drill, when we were working on different methods of crossing the ball from wide positions, and I was totally on fire. Time after time, I kept pinging the ball in with pinpoint accuracy. Dario Bonetti, the assistant manager, was delighted with me and told me so several times.

At the end of that session we had a practice match and my good form carried over into that game. At one point I picked up the ball and drilled a long, diagonal pass to the opposite wing. Disaster! Something in my lower spine popped. It felt like a knife going into my back. Instantly dejected, I knew straight away what had happened. Oh shit, here we go again!

The biggest difference between this breakdown and the other previous occasions was that the manager himself took complete control of the situation. He told me there and then that we needed to find out once and for all what was the fundamental cause of my back problems. So, while we were in Italy, instead of me playing in any of the pre-season friendly games, Ivano arranged a car and driver and sent me to Bologna F.C.'s first team facility to visit an orthopaedic back specialist who he had worked with before. Eventually, after they had carried out numerous tests, they came to the conclusion that the root of all my back problems was a damaged sacroiliac joint. The doctor then prescribed a series of exercises to increase my lower back strength and improve my flexibility, plus he recommended a course of treatments at an osteopath to ensure that I was aligned properly. Clearly I was thrilled that at long last a solution might be in sight but, at the same time, I couldn't help thinking, 'well if they can do all this now why wasn't it ever done before'? I suppose the answer to that is because Ivano Bonetti was the first person involved who had his wealth of knowledge and experience in this kind of injury.

Mum and Dad still have a newspaper article in which Ivano gave me a bit of a glowing report, saying how he had been impressed by me both as a player and as a man; and how he respected me for my attitude to work and my approach to dealing with all the people around me. Clearly, especially at that difficult time, this made me feel good about myself and it helped me a lot. The respect was mutual and he grew even more in my esteem by being willing to give me whatever time I needed to recover from my back injury and get fit again. I can remember the first game of that new season was against Hearts and the manager called me in for a meeting. He told me that I had done well during my recovery period but, no matter what I thought, his opinion was that I wasn't fit enough yet to play in the

# Yates injury casts shadow on first win of Bonetti era

By Dan Stewart in Borno

THE NEWS that Michael Yates had suffered a potentially serious back injury cast a shadow over a 5-0 victory for Dundee against Polisportina San Giuseppe at the picturesque Borno Stadium last night.

Yates, who missed the final 2½ months of last season with injury problems, has been told to rest for the remainder of the Dark Blues' pre-season training camp and is to be sent to a specialist on his return to Scotland after reporting a recurrence to medical staff.

The fact he had been one of the most impressive players on the trip before his setback did little to cheer him as he watched his teammates canter to a win against opposition from the Italian fifth division.

"It is just so frustrating for me," said Yates as he gazed out over the snow-capped Italian Alps. "The arrival of the new coaching staff wiped the slate clean for all of us here and I had been really pleased with the way things were going.

"I don't think it is exactly the same problem as I had last year as the pain is nearer the centre of my back this time where before it was more off to one side.

"That said, it is close enough to be worrying. I get pain every time my feet hit the ground and I am told that could mean a problem with one of the discs in my spine.

**Michael Yates.**

"Apparently I am to see a specialist as soon as I get back but at the moment there is nothing to do but wait and keep my fingers crossed that it is nothing too bad."

New Dark Blues boss Ivano Bonetti was quick to give his player a vote of support, expressing his sympathy for Yates but also satisfaction at his side's success in their first outing under his charge.

"We do not know yet how serious Michael's problems are but I feel confident that he will be OK even if he has to sit it out for a while," he said.

"At 20 years old he is a young boy with a long future in the game in front of him.

"He has impressed me very much in this training camp, not just as a footballer but as a

man. He has the right attitude—the hunger to do well—which I always look for in my players."

Bonetti got his new side off to the perfect start in last night's match, winning the sixth minute penalty for handball which allowed Willie Falconer to open the scoring.

Steven Milne on 19 minutes, Marco de Marchi (24), Georgi Nemsadze (25) and Hugh Robertson (65) also grabbed the chance to get themselves on the scoresheet but with the semi-professional Italians tiring badly later on it should have been much more.

"This was really a training exercise for us but as such it went well," said Bonetti, who substituted his entire starting 11 at half-time to give himself a chance to see as many players in action as possible.

"The movement, the passing everything we have been working on was there, which pleased me.

"It is not exactly as we would like it yet but then you would not expect it to be.

"You have to be ready for the start of the season proper, not the pre-season, and I have every confidence that we will be."

Dundee have arranged a game against a regional select for next Saturday, again to be played at the Borno Stadium, and may also try to fit in another match in midweek.

game. He reassured me that he was happy with my performances so far and was prepared to wait for the right time for me to make my comeback. Ivano told me I should go back home for the weekend and enjoy a break. So I did.

After returning to Dundee, I trained properly for the remainder of that week, happily with no sign of any lingering issues or niggles. True to his word, Ivano then told me I would be on the bench for the next game against Dunfermline. I don't think I'd ever been so happy about just getting a place on the bench! As I continued to prove my increasing fitness in training, he gave me another two games as sub, against Hibernian and St. Mirren, but on both of those occasions I was given a run out for the last twenty minutes or so. A few weeks into the season, despite my lengthy absence due to injury, not to mention the influx of new talent, once I was fully fit, I did get picked for the first team again. My first game in that 2000/2001 season was against Montrose at home in the Scottish Cup. We won 3 – 0 and I played well.

After that decent performance I came off the bench to play a part in the next five consecutive league games, including a good 3 -0 home win over arch local rivals Dundee United. But the most outstanding game I remember from that spell was my first match against Rangers, on 9th September 2000. We earned a hard fought 1 – 1 draw, which was actually a very creditable result as the previous season Rangers had done the double, winning both the Scottish Cup and the Scottish Premier League by a ridiculously wide margin of points! To give a clear idea of the quality of that Rangers team, their bench that day included Claudio Reyna, Peter Lovenkrands, Tugay and Ronald de Boer. Half way through the second half, the Rangers' manager Dick Advocaat, sent on de Boer to try and drive them on for a winning goal. That resulted in our manager, Ivano Bonetti, then instructing me to go on and shadow him. That turned out to be quite a challenge. What a player Ronald de Boer was! Other than that first time I ever played against Steven Gerrard as a boy, no other player made as big an initial impact on me as de Boer did that day. He'd start off on a run and I would literally be wondering where he was going. His positional play was outstanding and he had fantastic vision. Definitely one of the very top players I ever faced in a match.

# Jamie Carragher
*Liverpool FC*

When I was a kid I sort of just knew that I was one of the better players in my age group, especially when I made in into Lilleshall, and I always believed I could make the grade. So, when Liverpool gave me a professional contract at sixteen, I didn't really see that as any great accomplishment. It was just the next step that I needed to take before I could play for Liverpool's first team. I don't want that to sound big-headed in any way, it's just that I was confident that I could challenge for a place straight away. I didn't just want to be a professional; my real target was to play for Liverpool.

My own son, James, is part of the Liverpool Academy set-up and he goes there three nights a week and Saturday morning for coaching and plays a game on Sunday, which adds up to about eight hours of coaching and playing per week. In my day, at his same age, we got one hour in a gym! So the kids today definitely get more exposure to good coaching, and the modern facilities are incredible, but I actually think it's more difficult for a local lad to make it in the game today. When I was working my way up through the ranks we had some good foreign players in Liverpool's first team but none at the youth levels. Nowadays the Academy brings in some of the top young prospects from all around the world, so clearly that must reduce the opportunities for locals to break through. It has to be the right approach for a big club like Liverpool, who need to attract the game's best players, but it does mean that a local lad will have to be a really exceptional player to force his way into the first team. Even then, no matter how good the Academy might be, any club still needs a manager who is willing to give the youngsters a chance.

At the same time, I also think it can be very difficult for the young foreign players as well. They have to leave behind their own family and come to our country to learn a new language, get used to a new way of doing things and deal with lots of big changes. It was hard enough for me just to move to Lilleshall, so it must be really tough for these young foreign lads to swap countries at age sixteen. Maybe one solution that would help the local lads as well as the players from overseas would be to have a minimum-age rule, stating that foreign players could only be signed after the age of eighteen.

Photo courtesy of Liverpool FC via Getty Images

*Jamie Carragher*

People like to make out that foreign players are given better treatment and more chances than local players because the club has spent lots of money on them and wants to get value for their money; as well as to prove that it was a good decision and not bad judgement. That might well be the case but I'd also like to point out that it's no different when clubs buy British players. The same situation exists because the club still needs to show that they didn't waste their money. If two players are fighting for the same position and performing to a similar level, then some managers will find themselves under pressure to choose the one who cost a fortune rather than the local lad who basically cost nothing. Unfortunately it's the way of the world for local players.

## Squeezed Out by the Foreign Invasion

After the Rangers game I played against the likes of St. Johnstone, Motherwell and Dunfermline; but, as the season went on, the club started to bring in a lot of new foreign players and the fight for places got even more intense than usual. Soon it became quite apparent that Ivano Bonetti was intent on building a team based around his foreign contingent.

One of those incoming foreign players was none other than Claudio Caniggia. I suddenly found myself playing upfront alongside one of the world's top players, a man who had starred in two World Cups for Argentina. Quite a pedigree! Claudio didn't speak much English back in those days and, as he was generally a quiet person, he tended to keep himself to himself. So it was a bit out of character when he burst out laughing and got all excited after answering his mobile on the team bus going to play a game at Hearts. I'd never heard him talk that loud or that long, so I asked him if the call had been from a close member of his family or a good friend. 'Yes', he confirmed, 'my best friend, Diego Maradona.' OK then!

In a match against St. Johnstone, I was brought off the bench to replace him. It's funny what you remember from your past, but I can still clearly visualize him running towards me and taking off his famous headband. Then, as he reached me, he stopped and purposefully took off his gloves before shaking my hand and wishing me well. That simple gesture of courtesy has always stuck in my mind because it so clearly demonstrated the kind of person he was. He was a good man; I liked him a lot.

While I still thought I was performing well and seemingly getting good reports from the coaching staff, there was no regular place for me in the starting eleven and I was forever in and out of the side or left on the bench. The same thing happened to a lot of the Scottish lads, who suddenly found themselves being squeezed out of the team. Even Lee Wilkie, who was a Scotland international at the time, ended up struggling to get a place. Being left out of the team was clearly bad for my development as a player and my game naturally began to suffer. The final straw was when the club then signed another batch of young players, all Italian like the manager, and I was left even further out in the cold. In my estimation, those young Italians were not better players than myself or the Scottish players, but they definitely got more favourable and preferential treatment than we did. It left a very bitter taste in our mouths.

Ultimately, towards the end of my second season, I got a call from the club secretary telling me not to report to training with the first team but to go with the under-21s instead. It was bad enough to get that kind of shattering news from anybody but it felt even worse coming from the secretary and not the manager, or at the very least one of his coaches. When I asked why I was being left out, the secretary merely said that Mr. Bonetti had filled his squad and there was no room for me and four of the other lads. That hurt a lot, especially because I knew deep down inside that there were some foreign players still in that squad who did not deserve to be there instead of me. It was very frustrating and really tough to take. But that is football, that is what happens and you just have to cope with the crap that is thrown at you. If the manager had already made his decision then there was nothing I could do to change his mind. In many ways it was actually a lot worse for some of the Scottish lads who were retained in the first team squad. In Scotland back then there was a rule that each team had to at least have a minimum number of local players on the bench; so the manager would randomly pick a few as subs and they'd end up just sitting there, knowing they had no chance of actually getting on the pitch. They were just there to satisfy the rules and regulations, not to play. Now that would have really driven me insane.

To add to my frustration and make me even angrier, I had just got my fitness back, I was almost twenty-one and I was playing some of the best football of my career. It didn't make sense. Even the reserve team coaches, Ray Farningham and Steve Campbell, told me openly that they couldn't understand at all why I wasn't in the first team. When I dropped down to the reserves, playing alongside the likes of Kenny Miller, I was running games. I was performing really well and impressing the team managers, off the field as well as on it. I know for a fact that they admired my attitude in the face of adversity and really appreciated the way I made a point of working with the young players around me, trying my best to help them along the way as well as myself. I was truly behaving like the model professional as well as playing well on the pitch.

But it was all to no avail – there was just no way back into the first team squad.

The door had been slammed in my face. It was a closed shop.

# Jason McAteer

*Liverpool FC 1995-99; Republic of Ireland International*

Photo courtesy of Liverpool FC via Getty Images

My route into professional football was definitely unusual for this day and age. I was never taken on by any academy and it wasn't until I was twenty that Bolton Wanderers eventually picked me up when I was playing for Marine Reserves in the Lancashire League. Three seasons later I was playing for Ireland against Italy in the World Cup Finals in America and the following year I joined Liverpool. Quite a journey!

So, even though I had some contact with YTS trainees at all the clubs where I played, I didn't get to truly understand the difficulties faced by released players until I was made Reserve Team Coach at Tranmere Rovers. Working with those two-year scholarship lads turned out to be one of the most enjoyable experiences of my career. By the end of the second year, I had to identify who I thought should be kept on and who should be released. I recommended that we retained about six of them.

The day of their meetings I went along to offer a bit of support to those who needed it. But I couldn't believe my eyes when they all started to come out one by one, white faced, in shock, devastated by the news of their rejection, eventually collapsing in floods of tears. I was able to cope with the first few lads and tried to console them, but even I ended up in tears when the rest of them continued to file out in that same sad state.

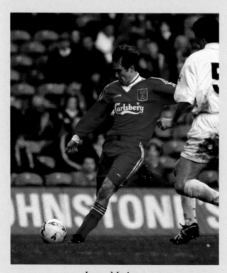

*Jason McAteer*

It was one of the saddest days I've ever known in football and that memory will always stick in my throat. We tried to find other clubs for them but soon discovered the obvious fact that it wasn't just Tranmere that had released players, every club throughout all the leagues had done the same! So there were literally a thousand kids all looking for a new league team to play for; and all those teams had just released players themselves so they were in no rush to sign on new ones. Clearly it was a system that couldn't work.

To some extent I can personally relate to the huge problems that released players have to deal with, because even seasoned professionals face similar challenges when they have to stop playing. When my last contract finished it was like somebody flipped a switch. One day I was a professional footballer, enjoying the rush of playing in front of 45,000 fans, and the next day it was all taken away from me. The amazing life that I'd enjoyed for the last fifteen years was suddenly gone. All the banter and daily routines that I'd thrived on for so long just disappeared. I ended up in a state of depression for over a year and had to undergo professional counselling. Luckily my mum was from a counselling background so she was able to spot all the signs and point me in the right direction. I am not ashamed to say that at my lowest point I was so desperate that I considered ending it all. Had it not been for my son, and me wanting to take proper care of him, I might not be around today.

In simple terms, because of my acute depression, I couldn't find any answers to life's everyday problems; and it's much the same for these kids. One day they are the elite and 24-hours later they are rejects. How do they handle that? It was very difficult for me as an adult, even with all of my experience of life. And at least I had enjoyed a good career and made myself financially secure. But what about these kids at eighteen who are only just starting out? Very few of them have the mental strength to pick themselves off the floor and keep moving forward.

I know that the clubs, the FA and the PFA are all trying to help these kids; and I know that ultimately it's down to each individual to pick up the pieces and find a new road to go down; but I still think the game in general needs to do more to support these released players. There is no shortage of money in football, so we just need to find the right answers. At the very least, the young players need to be made more aware of the difficult challenges ahead of them and given more protection after they leave the club. They are at a very vulnerable age, at a time when it's tough for anybody to find a new job, even people leaving university with a degree. So what chance do these kids have? Maybe there could be some kind of 2-year grace period after being released, when they are given enough money to live off, as well as some opportunities to rebuild their life: maybe a job at the club, trials at other clubs, further education or training and an introduction to other careers. Clearly after a certain time period, if they don't reach the required criteria, then they'd have to be left to their own devices.

But we must find some way to give them more support and more time to sort themselves out.

*Versus Dumbarton in the Scottish Cup*

Back Row: (From left to right) Juan Sara, Chris Coyne, Steven Tweed, Jamie Langfield, Robert Douglas, Derek Soutar, Craig Ireland, Lee Wilkie, Willie Falconer.
Middle Row: Jack Cashley (Masseur), Dario Magri (Club Co-ordinator), Enzo Romano (Fitness Coach), Marco De Marchi, Mark Slater, Graham Bayne, Michael Yates, Hugh Robertson, Gavin Rae, Harry Hay (Sprint Coach),
Billy Thompson (Goalkeeping Coach), Dario Bonetti (Asst. Manager)
Front Row: Walter Del Rio, Steven Milne, Patrizio Billio, Fabian Caballero, Barry Smith, Ivano Bonetti (Manager), Marcello Marrocco, Alessandro Romano, Giorgi Nemsadze, Javier Artero, Shaun McSkimming.
Inset: Claudio Caniggia, Luis Alberto Carranza

*The Dundee first team that included Claudio Caniggia*

## My Parting Shot from Dundee

At one point Ivano Bonetti did inadvertently give me a chance to vent some of my pent up frustration and make a bit of a personal statement. I don't know why he did it but he arranged a full-scale match, on the actual Dens Park pitch, between the reserves and the first team, complete with all the foreign players. For me this was a golden opportunity to show the manager that he'd been wrong to cut me from the first team squad and I was really psyched up for the occasion. As we lined up to start the game, I noticed that their keeper was standing slightly off his line. So, probably because I felt I didn't have anything to lose and could afford to be a bit cheeky, I decided to pull out my old party trick from my schoolboy days. The ball was tapped straight to me from our kick off and I absolutely smashed it from the halfway line at the first team's goal. With months of festering anger behind my shot, the ball flew like a rocket, straight as an arrow, over the keeper's head and right into the top corner of the net. Nobody moved. There was a stunned silence while they all tried to take in what they had just seen. Even the great Claudio Caniggia, the man who'd seen it all, was staggered. He just looked at me with this incredulous expression on his face, as if to say, 'Did you really just do that?' Of course I lapped up every second of the moment. It felt so good to be able to stand there and eyeball the lot of them, silently letting them all know, 'Yep, that was me, Mike Yates. Cop for that Bonetti!'

What I had just pulled off certainly must have rattled the manager because he instantly started shouting and gesticulating in that crazy Italian way, then promptly disallowed the goal. Can you imagine it: a manager disallowing a goal from the sidelines, not because there was anything wrong with it from the perspective of the rules but simply because he didn't like it. He didn't like the fact that this young reserve had comprehensively beaten his first team keeper all the way from the halfway line! Bonetti said the goal couldn't be counted and made us start all over again. It was actually quite bizarre, watching as all the players had to line up and kick off for a second time, but I was absolutely thrilled because that was exactly the kind of impact I'd hoped to make.

Anyway we played out the first half, things went well for me during the game, and I was still feeling cocky when we changed ends after half-time. If the manager thought he'd had the last laugh by disallowing my goal in the opening seconds of the game, then he was soon in for a big shock. When the first team kicked off the second half, we somehow got possession of the ball very quickly and it ended up at my feet. So I glanced up and, sure enough, just like before, the keeper was off his line. So I did it again! Bang! Just like that, straight into the net! The first team players were all blown away for a second time but for this one, rather than a stunned silence, most of them cheered me or in some cases just burst out laughing. Perhaps he was too embarrassed to disallow the second goal, or maybe he even felt obliged to respect what I'd done, but Ivano let that one stand. I'd successfully made my point. Two goals from the halfway line, at the start of each half, wasn't a bad effort from a young first team reject!

However, it wasn't just the spectacular long-range shots that pleased me about that match, because I had also played well throughout the whole game. When we finished, Ray Farningham, who had played himself for Dundee and was a well-liked and highly respected coach, once again expressed his amazement that I wasn't in the first team squad and suggested that I was being wasted in the reserves at Dundee. A week or two later he approached me about the possibility of me moving to Montrose, where he knew the manager. Ray's opinion was that even though playing in Division 2 might be considered a step down, it would still be better for me to be playing regular first team football; especially when compared to training all week merely to then have a weekend at home, since the under-21's only played on Monday nights. He told me that I could still train at Dundee and then just travel to Montrose to play the actual matches. Ray thought that if I did well I might at least be spotted by another club and be given a chance to move on.

And moving on sounded like a really good alternative!

Since it seemed as if nothing could be any worse than my situation at Dundee, I agreed with Ray's assessment and decided to give it a go at Montrose. Unfortunately, while the theory was good, the reality proved to be horrendous. No disrespect intended to Montrose but at that time their club set-up was like a non-league team in England. To make matters worse it's situated right on the coast and when I went there it was absolutely freezing, one of the coldest places I'd ever been to. I was travelling for hours between Dundee and Montrose, all for nothing really. The pitch was constantly frozen rock hard but we still trained on it simply because there was no choice, no other alternative. It was like training on a car park and probably did the players more damage than good. Again I don't want to sound like a football snob, but after the high standards that

I'd been brought up with at Liverpool, Montrose seemed like a disaster zone. The amateurish approach to the poor conditions even made me lose respect for the manager because I couldn't understand why he made us suffer through it all.

Anyway, after a week or so, I played in my first game for Montrose and put in a decent performance. It was a tough fixture and we did well to salvage a 1 -1 draw after going down to ten men after 25 minutes. A week later we played away at Peterhead and drew 1 – 1 again, with me playing well for the second time. After that, for whatever reason, I was dropped to the bench. Well that was the end of Montrose for me. The whole situation was taking too heavy a toll on my mental state and I couldn't take any more, so I packed it in.

By now I was at a very low ebb and feeling very sorry for myself, so I did what most young people do under those circumstances - I went back to the sanctuary of my parents' home. Mum and Dad were their usual supportive selves and gave me the good, sound advice to return to Dundee and ask them to release me from my contract so that I could look for another opportunity at a new club. At the same time, George Norrie, the scout who had sent me to Dundee in the first place, recommended me for a trial at Stockport County, who were playing in the old English second division at the time.

As expected, Dundee willingly agreed to let me go for the trial at Stockport, so I packed up all my belongings from the flat, gave my month's notice and got ready to return to England.

Despite the disappointing end to my two seasons at Dundee, I'd enjoyed some wonderful experiences at the club and I knew I'd matured a lot as a person. While things hadn't worked out as well as I'd hoped as a player, I had successfully achieved a number of my personal ambitions.

It was the right time to bid farewell to Scotland.

# Clarke Carlisle
*Former Professional Footballer 1997 - 2013; England Under-21 International;*
*Former Chairman Professional Footballer's Association*

Since I presented the BBC documentary, Football's Suicide Secret, I have had hundreds of phone calls from players who can personally relate to that programme. It is an extremely serious issue that football has never given any credence. So, now that the real dangers of mental breakdown and suicide have been exposed, it is vital that we address this problem.

Pressures within the game have increased dramatically since the inception of the Premier League. The massive income the league generates has resulted in players being paid huge salaries. However, while their wages have shot up, so too have the levels of intense scrutiny they are subjected to. Footballers are studied 24/7 by an often unforgiving public and a press culture that is desperate for sensational headlines. It has become impossible for footballers to enjoy a personal life outside their own home. To compound matters, footballers have been designated as role models. This is a ludicrous burden of over-expectation to heap on any player, especially youngsters. That level of expectation is way out of proportion for the demographic of our profession. What other industry would expect workers between the ages of 16 to 30 to act as role models for society? Furthermore, because players earn so much money and are constantly under the microscope, they are judged with different moral standards. That is unfair and piles enormous pressure on them.

Stardom has forced footballers away from the man in the street. Yet, ironically and alarmingly, complete strangers can use Twitter to invade a player's private space and dispense all kinds of vitriolic insults without any fear of recourse. Faceless hatemongers can post horrendous comments that are seen by millions of people or send disgusting text messages. Imagine being verbally abused in your own home by hundreds of people every day!

The intrusion into a footballer's life is endless and it is very difficult for players to truly get away from the game because they are not allowed to develop their own identity. From an early age players are told how to do everything: when to get up, what to eat, what to wear, how to train, when to rest, what kind of smoothie to have, when to go to bed .... everything! So later, when you take away a player's football identity, you are left with a confused and empty vessel. Football dominates 95% of a player's life and then it ends and he suddenly has nothing.

*Clarke Carlisle challenging Wayne Rooney*

Footballers are treated more like assets than human beings. Clearly, while we obviously still need to focus on creating good players, we must also do a lot more to develop conscientious young men who can make well-informed, well-balanced decisions about their own life. And we can only achieve that goal by firstly making them aware of the fickle and finite nature of our profession. Football has become an industry of sycophants and bull-shitters. Too many coaches are telling kids that they are part of an elite group and that they will make it to the top. And the longer they remain in the system the more they believe it. Then along comes an agent who'll promise them a top deal with a fantastic salary and a life of luxury. More often than not they are filling the kids' heads with complete rubbish and there isn't a hint of reality about it.

The biggest change I would make in football is that it should become mandatory for any player, throughout his career from the age of 16, to undertake some form of education or training for a job outside of football. It should be easy enough to introduce this kind of system. Let's say we choose an allotted time on a Thursday afternoon and every professional player at every club up and down the country has got to spend an hour doing some form of training that could at least provide the basis of a new employment option if ever required. No single club would be disadvantaged because everybody would be doing the same thing at the same time. And, collectively, our industry would be making a huge contribution to the wellbeing of each individual in the game.

Football needs to fuel aspirations but it also needs to administer a healthy dose of realism. We must get the balance right.

## Discovering the Reality of Life in the Lower Divisions

George Norrie's recommendation turned out to be a good move because I really liked Stockport: the facilities, the manager, the players, everything about the place. I enjoyed training with the first team, which included some good seasoned pros like former Manchester City keeper Andy Dibble. The football was good and I hit some top form in the trial matches, scoring in a couple of reserve games and generally fitting in well. Then I played in a first team game at Stockport when the coaching staff experimented with a new formation, playing three up front. Well I'd already learned from the Italians at Dundee how to play in that set-up, so I slotted in easily and put in a strong performance. After the match the manager, Alan Kernighan, told me he wanted to sign me and I replied that I would be delighted to do so. That very same day I was in the car, just about to leave Stockport's ground, when I heard that the manager had been sacked and was being replaced by Carlton Palmer. And that was the end of my contract before I'd even signed it! So, once again, through no fault of my own, another chance had gone.

After that disappointment I went to Hartlepool for their pre-season training. Early on I played an away match against Blythe Spartans and did really well. Even though I didn't manage to score I did make a big impression, including hitting the woodwork three times. My dad watched that game and when I came off he made the comment that I'd have no problem getting signed – and from him that was a bold statement because he never gave away compliments easily and was rarely so definite about anything to do with football. Deep inside myself I knew I'd put on a good show in that game and so, all in all, I was very confident that they'd want to sign me. All the more reason that it was a huge shock to me when I got a phone call telling me that the manager didn't think I was good enough for them, that I was not what he was looking for. I was really pissed off by that. I couldn't stop myself from blurting out: 'Well what the hell is he really looking for then?'

I was fit, I'd worked my nuts off and done well in pre-season training, I'd played a really good game for them, I fitted in happily with all the other players and I knew that I was good enough to do a job for them. Once again, it just didn't make any sense to me.

That was when I started to get disheartened with the game and decided that I couldn't carry on travelling from club to club, trying to get signed. Especially when it seemed that no matter how well I performed there was just no way I was going to be taken on. I consider myself to be a modest person, and I've never been one to think too highly of myself, but I knew that I was good enough for them. It was just that my face didn't fit, for whatever reason. It was at this point in time that I became convinced that some managers in the lower leagues preferred to keep their mates happy rather than sign players based solely on their talent. It all left me completely disillusioned with the game. That feeling of despair, thinking that no matter how well I performed these teams would just not sign me, eventually became too much for me to handle.

Out of frustration I turned once again to George Norrie, ready to tell him that I felt like packing it all in. He calmed me down and then wisely suggested that the best step for me was to go back to my roots, where it had all started. George suggested that I went to Lancaster City, located closer to home, who played in the Unibond Premier League, a league above Burscough. He encouraged me by saying that they had a good manager and even though they were only semi-pro they did have enough money behind them to pay me a decent wage. But then he also put me off a bit by commenting that I might have to find some other job to do on the side, to top up my wages. That made it a really big and difficult decision for me. Essentially I would be stepping down from full-time professional footballer to become a part-timer. Realistically that meant if no bigger club came in for me then I would eventually have to find a full-time job to support myself. And that was a really weird thing to have to think about! In the end, what made that decision easier for me to make was that I was technically still employed by Dundee and they agreed to terminate my contract and pay me off. That lump sum of money bought me extra time in the sense that I could start playing for Lancaster in the hope of being picked up by somebody, secure in the knowledge that I had enough cash to live off for a while if things backfired. So I signed for Lancaster.

I scored two goals in the very first match; one from the penalty spot and the second a spectacular overhead bicycle kick. Tongues started wagging straight away about this lad who'd come to Lancaster from Dundee and had once been at Liverpool as Michael Owen's strike partner. I scored more goals in the following games, success started flowing again, and I had the football bug back!

It was around that same time, with the gods once again looking down upon me favourably, that I unexpectedly heard from Nikki, the girl I had

met in Cyprus. Completely out of the blue, she sent me a text saying that she was on another holiday and had just seen something that reminded her of me. That random text was enough of a spark to reignite the old flame and, after just a few more messages, I soon found myself on my way to Leeds! Not long after that first trip to Nikki's home, we started seeing each other regularly and gradually settled into a steady relationship. The timing was a lot better than when we'd first met, when I'd still been a player at Dundee, simply because I now had greater freedom to enjoy our life together. Having said that, my weekends eventually took upon epic proportions and, with me travelling all the time between Ormskirk, Leeds and Lancaster, I started to clock up more miles than a long distance lorry driver! Reality soon checked in when I became more and more aware that all the driving was costing me a fortune in petrol money; a fortune that I really couldn't afford. That problem was soon solved though, in a really very special way, when Nikki and I got married on the 15th of May 2004.

Just a few months later, I got a strange phone call from the new Mrs. Yates. I had just walked off the pitch after training when my mobile rang:

'Hiya Dad.'

'No Nikki, this is Mike.'

'Yeah, I know. Hiya Dad!'

'Dad?'

Stunned silence.

'What? Do you mean? OMG! Yeeesssssssssss! Me? A dad!'

Nikki could not have given me any better news that day because I was so unbelievably happy and proud to find out that I was going to be a father. I suppose the fact that I had always been part of a good, solid family, meant it was almost a natural progression for me to want to have a child of my own. One thing was for sure, even at that very early stage, I instinctively knew that I'd do my absolute very best to be a good parent.

Being blessed with the new responsibility of raising a child made me consider my current situation and my future more carefully. It was quite obvious to me that while playing part-time for Lancaster was hugely enjoyable, it was not financially rewarding. It was just not good enough at that stage of my life! My Dundee money was rapidly running out and I still didn't have any other job.

All of this was weighing heavily on my mind when we went to play an away game at Droylsden. It was then that fate unexpectedly stepped in when I literally bumped into Iain Brunskill who, unknown to me, was their assistant manager. I'd known Iain from my days at Liverpool where he was a coach, but I had no idea that he'd started working with Droylsden as well. Anyway, after the game was over, he offered me a lift home. Needless to say, we had a good laugh talking in the car about the old times at Liverpool and so on. But he was really shocked to find out that I didn't have any job to support my modest income from part-time football; and equally surprised to hear that I wasn't working as a coach anywhere, especially as he rated my ability.

Two days after that chance meeting, Iain telephoned and told me to meet him at the Liverpool FC Academy. When I got there Steve Heighway was already expecting me and immediately offered me a job. He made it clear that it wasn't the same position that I had held before; but as the Academy had grown they did need an additional part-timer, especially for community soccer schools and overseas jobs. So we shook hands on it and, for the second time in my life, I accepted his offer to work as a coach instead of playing football.

This was destiny playing a massive role in my life once more.

I was going back to Liverpool Football Club.

**Geoff Yates:** 'Mike was always the first lad into the dressing room and always the last one out, so I often found myself standing outside, just killing time, waiting for him so we could go home. I remember once getting a bit impatient and as young Steven Gerrard came out I asked him if Mike was still in there. He must have picked up that I was bit flustered and, with a cheeky grin on his face, he came back with: 'Don't worry, he'll be out soon. He's just putting his lipstick on!'

**Cheryl Yates:** 'Mike once had a big game coming up for Burscough and he'd been talking all week about how important it was for him to do well. On the morning of the match, while it was weighing heavily on my mind, it suddenly dawned on me that it was Tuesday, the traditional day for praying to St. Martha to ask for a favour to be granted. So I decided to pray for a blessing on Mike that night. It wasn't something that I did a lot but I put my heart and soul into that particular prayer. I just asked that he played well enough to get a bit more publicity, in the hope that a big club might come along and sign him. He scored three goals that night and was featured in the newspapers for the next ten weeks straight!'

## Nicola Yates

When Mike and I started going out together he was playing for Lancaster. I like football, so it was easy to go and watch him play. It was a bit frustrating though, because even I could see he was reading the game better than other players, he was anticipating things quicker, expecting the movement of the ball that he would have been used to as a pro. If I had taken all those knocks I'm not sure I would have maintained the same passion and enthusiasm for the game that Mike still has, he has never let it get in the way of his life and I admire him for that.

Mike really 'Knows' Liverpool Football Club, what it stands for and what it means to the fans and indeed the city, he is very, very proud of the club. There is no doubt that Mike is a fantastic coach, he is great with people which is an asset in today's world. Ever since Mike joined the commercial side of the club, representing the club globally, he has had some fantastic ideas, all for the good of LFC ... he does a great job in his current role but I know he misses the pitch!

Both Devon and I are extremely proud of everything Mike has achieved in football but more importantly, Mike is a brilliant dad who is always very generous with his time.

*Me & Nicola*

# Part Four
# The Prodigal Son Returns

## Learning to Coach the Liverpool Way

Even though the coaching job at Liverpool was supposed to be part-time, I actually ended up working every day from Monday to Friday and attending pre-Academy matches on Sundays as well. So they really kept me busy. Fortunately I was still able to carry on playing for Lancaster. We had training after work on Tuesdays and Thursdays, with matches on Saturdays, so it all suited me down to the ground really.

The big thing here of course is that it was just a fluke meeting with Iain Brunskill that resulted in me going back to Liverpool and I have been with the club ever since. I definitely think it was fate, something that was meant to happen.

Even though I had to start all over, back where I was when I first began coaching as an eighteen year-old, working with the schools and the pre-Academy kids, it was fantastic just to be part of the Liverpool set-up again. It's such an amazing club that it is hard to imagine working anywhere else. And that was one of the biggest challenges I faced when trying to establish myself as a player at all the other clubs; none of them were anything like Liverpool.

Starting to work with successful, well-established coaches like Steve Heighway, Hughie McAuley, Dave Shannon, John Owens, Paul Lever, Steve Hanlan and Robbie Johnson, all coaches who'd been in the game for a long time, I quickly learned that the most important aspect of the job was how to get the right messages across to the kids. It wasn't just about teaching them the right football skills, it was also critical to teach them good life skills that would help them in their development both as a footballer and a person. In simple terms, we had to teach the young lads the Liverpool Way from a very early age. Luckily for me, because I had been so involved at the club for most of my life, nobody needed to teach me what that actually meant because I already knew it like the back of my hand. In fact my whole life has been based on the Liverpool Way.

The Liverpool Way can mean different things to different people from different parts of the club. For example, you could mention the Liverpool Way to Ian Rush and his first reaction might be to say that it means a winning attitude on the pitch, where the players work together with a never-say-die spirit and a burning desire to win. On the other hand I might

*Opposite: Ian Rush*

Photo courtesy of Liverpool FC via Getty Images

say that the first thought that springs into my mind is the way that Liverpool players behave off the pitch as well as on it, because that is just as important to us as coaches when we are delivering messages to the youngsters. It could even be as simple as politely holding a door open for somebody. From a player's perspective, it is the value of hard work and togetherness, the capacity to overcome difficulties and, above all, the principles of fair play and dignified behaviour both on and off the field. Essentially, it is just the right way of doing things. So, although different people might offer a variety of interpretations, ultimately it is all of these factors that come together to represent the Liverpool Way. And once you are a player, a coach, an employee or even a supporter of Liverpool Football Club, then you are automatically an ambassador of the Liverpool Way.

One of the most important lessons I had learned when I first made the transition from player to coach, back when I was released, was that whereas players just turn up for training, coaches have to be there well in advance. They need to have all their preparation in place and be ready to deliver the session. I can remember that when I started coaching I didn't really understand that big difference and so I often found myself running late. The senior coaches let me make my mistakes for a while, which is a great way to learn, and then eventually pointed out what I was doing wrong. It was actually Frank McParland who pulled me aside one day in the Portakabin at Melwood to explain what I should be doing. It was an excellent lesson about responsibility: a lesson that I learned very quickly and have never forgotten. One of the messages involved here is that a coach should always be there to welcome the kids. It is a crime for a coach to arrive late and find the players waiting.

Now that I was back for my second stint as a coach, I was once again struck by the incredible attention to detail that went into the sessions, as well as the simple but effective techniques that the coaches used to get their messages across.

Dave Shannon was always telling players to ping in their passes, so to help them remember he wore a Ping cap! On one occasion I was assisting him in a session when he was coaching how to deliver a disguised reverse pass and I'll never forget what he said to get the message across. In fact I still use it to this day! He turned to the players and said: 'Imagine you are playing at Anfield and attacking the Kop end. Your chest should be facing the Main Stand, because everybody thinks you're going to play a ball out to the right wing. But when you actually play the pass, you reverse it straight to the striker's feet in the middle. That means when you finish the pass your chest should end up facing the Kop.' So Dave's painting a picture of playing at Anfield that the young players can visualize easily and that helps them to understand. I have always remembered that lesson.

All of the coaches had similar techniques and it was a pleasure to learn from them.

In terms of how we actually coached the kids at that time, we certainly had a fixed structure and we had to cover all the basic areas of the game like passing, running, dribbling, shooting and defending; but we also benefitted from a freedom to work within that system to best meet the needs of the players. Back then we had a printed manual that laid out the required criteria of any coaching course; but fast-forward to today and there is no comparison to the depth of detail and amazing resources that coaches can now call upon. Thanks to advancements with computers, we have easy access to all the components of the five basic coaching session elements of Warm-up, Technical, Technical Progression, Game Related and a Game. Plus everything we do nowadays is recorded and stored on the computer so that we can refer back to what we have done already as we move further into the programme. This level of organization also means that we can monitor each player's progress over the years from pre-Academy all the way to under-18s. Each age group does essentially the same coaching courses but obviously at a more advanced level each year. And while the physical and technical requirements increase and the coaching gets more demanding, it's still the same key messages that are being driven home year after year.

When a new coaching programme was introduced at the Academy I can remember Kenny Dalglish reminding us that no matter how much the game may have progressed over the years, you still have to get the ball from A to B and players have to make an angle to receive the ball. He was emphasising that it is still a relatively simple game. All that really changes over the years is how are you going to use fresh ideas to get that same message across to young players and teach them how to do it effectively. A big challenge for coaches today is how to deliver the constant repetition of the right messages without it becoming monotonous.

A good way to achieve this target is to help the young players to fully appreciate that they are not the only ones doing these repeated drills. It can be a real eye-opener for a young boy to do his own session in the morning and then watch the senior players being coached in the afternoon and see that they are being drilled with the same messages. That is a very practical and easy to understand way for them to appreciate why they need to constantly practice the basic skills of the game. It is that repetition of the right messages, clearly with increasing progress over the years, which will ultimately deliver a top footballer. Instead of under-11 players being left to wonder why they keep on having to repeat the same drills, when they'd really prefer to be playing a game, it is of huge value to actually show them that they are no different to the more accomplished players. It helps to establish the right kind of discipline and focus. And that's another example of the Liverpool Way.

I first started working with the pre-Academy kids alongside Karl Robinson, who is the current Manager of MK Dons, and Gareth Evans, who nowadays is based in the USA as an Academy Technical Director. Both Karl and Gareth played for the club. In fact Gareth came through the system in the same team as Steven Gerrard, Michael Owen and myself. Anyway, in my early days we all worked together with the pre-Academy group who are actually under-8s. The really significant thing about this age group is that the boys have free licence to play for any club at any time. So they could literally train with Liverpool on Monday, Everton on Tuesday and Manchester United on Wednesday. Obviously a lot of them do go down that road so that they can try out each of the clubs.

From day one in my coaching career, because of that unusual situation, this always made me think that this is actually one of the most important age groups, one where we definitely need to do our best job. Clearly the club wants to attract the very best young players to the Academy and then we want to keep them, not lose them to our rivals. Happily, thanks to the whole Liverpool Way package, which caters not only to the kids but also their parents, we tend to retain the vast majority of our brightest prospects. And that is absolutely vital at the end of the pre-Academy under-8 year, since that is the first time that the boys can actually be formally signed on to the club.

It is worth mentioning at this stage that the spreading of the Liverpool Way doctrine was not only limited to young players, as we also started to host commercial events for adults. Some time around 2004, the club launched the 'Anfield Experience', which was really more about having a bit of fun than any kind of serious coaching. It was open to Liverpool fans from all around the world, who would pay a fee to participate in a day of

LFC activities. A typical programme would start with breakfast at the hotel in the company of a couple of Liverpool Legends, followed by a ride out to the Academy on the actual Liverpool first team bus, with the former players telling a few stories along the way. The likes of Steve Hollis, Karl Robinson, Gaz Evans and myself would welcome the group when the bus arrived and then show them around the facility before going into the indoor arena. The Legends, usually Phil Neal and Ronnie Whelan, but also others like Jan Molby, Alan Kennedy and Dave Johnson, would describe the training sessions back in their day. They would then set the group off jogging around the perimeter and do some basic stretches and a few traditional warm up exercises. At that point, one of us younger coaches would interrupt the session with something like: 'Hang on a minute! When was the last time anybody won a match without a ball at their feet?' Then it was our turn to explain the more modern approach to coaching, emphasising how much more ball work we do. Then we'd do some actual ball drills with the group to demonstrate how we warm up the kids nowadays. Inevitably somebody like Phil Neal or Alan Kennedy would always have a smart reply, such as, 'But we used to enjoy jogging around the pitch to warm up, it was like a social occasion with really good banter. And it didn't do us any harm. Look at all those trophies we won.' And on and on would go the comparisons, with plenty of jokes and old tales pitched in too!

The two elements that were most common to both generations of coaches were #1 the correct way to pass the ball and #2 the consistency of the messages sent out. Some things never change! After the coaching demonstrations the group would be split into two teams – usually England v Rest of the World – to play a game. Finally, to end the day, the Legends would tell entertaining stories and answer questions about some of the famous matches they'd played in for Liverpool. It was a relatively simple format but it was a winning formula – the fans always loved those Anfield Experiences.

While there is no doubt that I thoroughly enjoyed life at the Academy in those days, the one thing I did miss was interacting with the first team players on a regular basis. Having literally grown up at Melwood, where the young players were in constant contact with the first team squad, it felt strange to now be almost entirely separated from them. In fact we rarely saw any senior players at the Academy, unless it was for some pre-arranged visit or the season-opening Press Day: a one-off training event that was specially arranged to allow the media an opportunity to get some photographs of the squad, particularly any new players.

It was after one of those pre-season sessions, in August 2004, that Michael Owen saw me in the office as he was leaving and as usual popped in to say hello. After exchanging the regular 'how are you doing?' and a bit of basic news, Michael really shocked me by telling me that he thought it was a good time for him to change clubs. Even though I'd heard a whisper that there was a chance he might be moving on, the thought of him actually leaving Liverpool Football Club after all those years still seemed somehow not quite right. I didn't repeat what he'd told me to anybody else, just kept it to myself, but within a few weeks Michael was on his way to Real Madrid. He was such a phenomenal player that I was very sorry to see him leave. But there again, each player has his own personal motivations and I am sure that Michael had very good football reasons to make his decision; no doubt including wanting to test himself against the very best players in the Spanish League. And I certainly believe that he did successfully prove himself during his time playing for Real Madrid.

Some players feel compelled to try playing at a top club in a foreign league, with Ian Rush being a good example when he went to play in Italy for Juventus. Others are more inclined to stay on home territory. In this day and age, there are very few professionals who complete their career as a one-club man; so Liverpool is extremely blessed to have two players of the superb quality of Steven Gerrard and Jamie Carragher who have remained 100% loyal to this club.

Towards the end of my first year back at Liverpool, my own playing career took a major turn when I left Lancaster. I had gradually found myself growing more and more unhappy with the team's coaching and tactics. Then, when I started to openly voice my concerns and opinions in the dressing room, the manager obviously took exception to my criticism and his way of dealing with it was to start leaving me out of the side. It wasn't the first time that I had upset a manager like that but I can honestly say that I was never insolent with any of them. I just gave my views as a qualified coach who also had plenty of experience as a player.

Things eventually came to a head when Lancaster's chairman started to talk to me about becoming his new manager or first team coach and, inevitably, the old Chinese whispers started around the club. The existing manager heard the rumours and exploded. Needless to say he never picked me again for the team! He was soon sacked but the chairman also resigned and the club found itself in a bit of turmoil. Around that same time, John Davidson, who I'd known at Burscough, was signed on as manager at Witton Albion and he invited me to join him. So I decided to give that a go.

But, no matter how much I was still enjoying playing the game and welcomed the extra money, I was acutely aware that I needed to focus on becoming a better coach.

That was now the key to my future in football.

## Expanding My Knowledge

In 2005, after serving my time with the pre-Academy, I was promoted to work with the under-9s, to replace Dave McDonough as assistant to Steve Hollis. Interestingly, Dave went on to become First Team and Opposition Analyst at Liverpool under Rafa Benitez.

The great thing about this new position was that I had the opportunity to plan and deliver my own sessions and, very significantly, I was now actually working alongside Steve Heighway, Hughie McAuley and Dave Shannon: the same top men who had coached me between the ages of eight to eighteen. Even though they were still mentoring me, it really felt as if I'd now completed the full circle and crossed the line to become one of them.

That year turned out to be a good period in my life because I really enjoyed coaching that age group, plus of course we all had the added bonus of that absolutely unforgettable Liverpool comeback victory against AC Milan in the Champions League Final in Istanbul. I feel truly blessed that I was actually there in the Ataturk Stadium that night to personally witness one of the greatest moments in the entire history of Liverpool Football Club. I still get goose bumps just thinking about it now!

However, the ultimate icing on the cake was when our daughter was born on June 29th 2005. Watching Nikki give birth to our child was absolutely amazing and awe-inspiring. It made everything else that had happened to me before seem quite insignificant. Devon's arrival into the world instantly gave my life an entirely new focus. It was no longer about me; it was now all about her.

Recently, while stuck in traffic taking her to school one morning, I

*Devon*

told Devon, now aged eight, my story of that wonderful final in Istanbul. She listened intently to every word I said, no doubt surprised by the passion in my voice and captivated by the drama of it all. When I finished, she asked me if that had been the best day in my life. So I answered her truthfully: 'Well, it was definitely one of the best days of my life up until then. But it didn't last long, because just a few weeks after that night in Istanbul you were born. And that became the best day of my life forever!'

The way her shy little smile lit up her face was just brilliant: a magical moment for any dad.

While on the subject of memorable cup final wins for Liverpool, I have got to also make mention here of that other incredible come-from-behind victory, the 2006 FA Cup Final against West Ham - The Gerrard Final! The club took some staff members to that final and I travelled on the train from Lime Street to Cardiff with the usual suspects: Iain Brunskill, Steve Hollis, Gareth Evans and Karl Robinson. We had a laugh on the train and then savoured every minute of what proved to be a truly pulsating final. The Reds went 0 – 2 down, battled back to all-square, (Cisse and Gerrard), only to give away a third goal. We were losing 2 – 3 with a minute to go. Up steps Captain Fantastic himself and fires in a last ditch equaliser from 30-yards! We eventually went on to win 3 – 1 on penalties. Stevie G was brilliant that day, presenting a master-class in how a captain should lead from the front.

The train was rocking on the way back to Liverpool and we were in full flight, belting out all the victory songs, when Gaz Evans' mobile suddenly rang. It was James Parry, to tell us that his dad Rick, the club's Chief Executive, wanted to know if the lads would like to go to the players party at Alma de Cuba! Well, errrr, let me think about that one!!! So, as soon as we got back to Lime Street, we made our way straight to the nightclub. When we arrived, Rick met us with James and took us upstairs to the VIP lounge. The players were all sat around with their wives, fully enjoying their celebrations. James then asked what we would like off the menu. So we tucked into a three-course meal, with drinks flowing and the FA Cup on show. All great stuff!

We made a point of not bothering any of the players, thinking it would be best to just leave them in peace to enjoy their night on the town! But I do remember having a chat with the Club Chairman, Mr. David Moores, about the game. And Peter Crouch, who is a really great guy, asked Karl and I how things were going, probably because we had helped him with a training session for Blue Peter about four months earlier! In fact that day at the Academy was a shining example of Crouchy's class act as a person. The TV session finished about 2:00 pm and Iain Brunskill asked him if he could possibly hang around to meet the pre-Academy kids when they came in later for their training. The only problem was they weren't due until 4:30 pm! 'No worries', says the big man, 'I'll go and have a cup of tea while I'm waiting.' He sat patiently in the canteen for over two hours. Then, at 4:30pm, when all the young players were gathered in the dressing room, in walks Peter Crouch. All 6' 8" of him, towering over all these little eight year-old boys! The kids were totally blown away.

Anyway, back to the FA Cup victory party. Later in the night the players went downstairs to show off the cup to the fans who were enjoying their own celebrations in the bar below. The lads all gathered around Stevie G as he hoisted that lovely shiny cup in the air and a massive shower of ticker tape came pouring down on everybody. It was epic!

The only liberty I took that night was to ask Steven to join us for a photo of him with the cup …. one to keep forever!

'No problem Yatesy. How are yer?' enquired SG.

'Fine, thanks mate. And you?'

What a stupid question to ask the guy who had just won the FA Cup and played an absolute blinder. How do you think he's feeling you nugget.

But what a day and what a night!

Around that time I was still playing for Witton Albion. I had enjoyed my two seasons there because we had a good team and I was playing well. Sadly, and surprisingly, that all came to a sudden halt when John Davidson got the sack, despite the fact that we'd finished sixth in the league. I would have stayed at Witton but the new manager was another one of those who moved in with his own group of players and started picking his mates and mates of mates and so on. It was the same old sad story that I'd come across at a few other non-league clubs and by that time I didn't have the patience to try to fight it any more. Even though I was well aware that this kind of negative experience is just a part of football, indeed life in general, it was still far too unfair for me to force myself to cope with it at that stage of my career.

In the end I decided to stop playing altogether, so that I could concentrate on my coaching. That turned out to be a very good decision

*Another memorable day and night in LFC history! Bottom left to right: James Parry, Gareth Evans, Me, Iain Brunskill, Steven Gerrard and Karl Robinson*

*Magnus Alford and I with the LFC under-13's before a game at the Academy versus Man City.*

because it also allowed me to spend more time with Nikki and Devon and enjoy the pleasures of family life.

My next step up the ladder at the Academy came in 2007 when I was appointed as Assistant Coach to Magnus Alford with the under-13s. This was another good move for me because it involved older players and therefore required a different level of coaching and the need for me to find new ways to get the right messages across and provide the best forms of motivation. Fortunately, because I'd been through the system myself, I knew just how critically important that under-13 year can be for those young players. I could look back on my own experience and remember what it felt like to know that you were just one season away from signing schoolboy forms for Liverpool Football Club – or not being signed! It's always a massive age-group year. So it was easy for me to relate to those lads and fully understand what was going on in their heads; and that definitely helped me appreciate the job I had to do on their behalf. I instinctively knew how critical it was to keep them fully focused and on the right track. Just as importantly, I was also highly aware of the kind of mental turmoil that a lot of their parents would be going through. My mum and dad have spoken to me a lot about what it was like for them when I was at that stage of my football development, so I was well equipped with a good insight into the kind of concerns that can crop up in a parent's mind.

Another huge advantage of having gone through the system myself was that I could also draw on my own experiences to help boost a young player's confidence whenever required. A simple but effective example of that method would be making a quiet comment to a player out on the pitch that might be something along the lines of: 'Well done son. I can remember Steven Gerrard passing the ball like that when he was your age.' Just a straightforward comment, no great effort required, two seconds work – but worth a million pounds to the kid's confidence. Plus, of course, statements like that play an important role in reminding the young players of the rich heritage that they are privileged to be part of, and hopefully inspiring them to emulate the success of the senior players.

Those positive messages are vital, especially at Liverpool. It's like saying to a youngster: 'Steven Gerrard was in your situation twenty years ago. Do you want to be in his situation twenty years from now?'

Speaking of inspiration, there were of course many times when the shoe was on the other foot and it was the kids who actually inspired me.

That particular crop of under-13s was an especially strong group and they were truly a pleasure to work with. We played matches every Sunday and even went on a number of tours. It was incredibly rewarding to be able to watch and witness them develop as footballers and young men.

One of my all-time favourite, everlasting memories is an away game we played at Manchester United with that under-13 team in 2008. Any match between Liverpool and United is a big match, no matter what age group, and the pre-game atmosphere is never less than electric. It would be very easy for any player at any level to feel apprehensive about an away match against United but that particular day it was obvious that the Liverpool lads were well up for the occasion. Far from being intimidated, they were chomping at the bit to get the match underway. It was a brilliant day for football, with a bit of rain leaving the pitch in perfect condition. Both clubs were desperate to win and, typical of this fixture, the rivalry was intense: all the more so because the sidelines were packed with staff, players and parents from both teams. We had all the right ingredients for a classic encounter. Once the game got underway though, it soon became clear that the Liverpool team was simply unstoppable that day. It was one of the best performances I have ever seen in my whole career from any under-13 team, truly exceptional quality. Once the goals started to fly in and the shouting and cheering grew louder and louder, more and more of the United staff started to come out to the pitch to see what all the commotion was about, including Brian McClair, the former United and Scotland player who was their academy director. Even if he found it hard to swallow the result, I am sure that he must have been highly impressed by the Liverpool performance as he watched our lads eventually romp to an 11-1 victory. As coaches at this age level, we are always aware that the result is less important than the overall development of the players but I still maintain that a huge victory like that in such an important fixture can only be beneficial for a young boy's confidence and future progress. Psychologically it was such a massive benchmark moment for them. So, even though we did our best to keep their feet on the ground and not allow them to get too carried away with themselves, I can assure you that when those kids turned up for their next training session they were absolutely buzzing. It boosted them to a new level at a critical time in their development.

There is no doubt that the many positives those players gained from that match have remained with them to this day. In fact, when I recently visited the Academy one of the lads from that team who is still around today brought up the subject of that amazing match as soon as he saw me. 'Heh Yates, remember that time we stuffed United 11 – 1?'

An unexpected turn of events in 2009 encouraged me to take my own boots out of mothballs and make a comeback as a player in non-league football. Nikki was unfortunately made redundant and I decided that I needed to make a bit more extra money with my feet while I still had the ability and fitness. That was when the wheel went full circle and I signed on once more for Burscough, where the whole adventure had started in the first place. Andy Much, the former Wolves player, was the manager and he was happy to welcome me back to the club, especially as they hadn't won a single home game for the season.

The first match I played was away to Blythe Spartans and good fortune was on my side. With my very first touch of the ball, I put in a cross for the opening goal and then I later laid on the second as well and we won 2 – 0. It was a great result for Burscough and a very encouraging start for me personally. The positives continued in the next game, a mid-week away fixture at Gainsborough Trinity, where I set up two more goals and grabbed one for myself in a 4 – 1 win. Next up was Stafford Rangers at home at Victoria Park, where the Burscough fans hadn't seen their team win for a long time. Once again I had a good game and managed to set up another two goals in a 3 – 0 victory. The crowd loved it all and the local press went to town the next day – full of headlines about Mike Yates, the former Liverpool player, the local hero, who was back home again after ten years away and helping Burscough return to winning ways.

Of course I thought the good publicity was brilliant and it definitely helped re-ignite the fire of enthusiasm inside my belly. All of a sudden life was great again: off the pitch with my wife and daughter and on the pitch with Liverpool and Burscough. I was enjoying my coaching and I was thrilled to actually be back playing. It made me realize how much I'd really missed the passion and competitiveness of the game. There is no question that it was all good fun at that non-league level, but equally there is no doubt that it still had a good edge to it. By the time 3 o'clock came around on match days and I had my boots on ready to go, I was well up for it and looking for a good battle. I suppose I felt a bit blessed to be getting another chance like that and I savoured every moment of every match. Once you've got a good taste for the game you miss it whenever you're not playing. I still miss it now!

Life at Burscough was going very smoothly when, once again, my story took an unexpected twist. Nikki was away from home one day when we had a training session and I couldn't find anybody to babysit Devon. So I called Andy Much to tell him sorry, that I couldn't turn up that night. He said no problem because that had been the agreement when I signed on, but could I please come to the ground for twenty minutes anyway as he wanted to talk to me about something important. He sounded a bit cautious and I found myself thinking 'oh no, not again'. Anyway, I loaded Devon into the car and drove to Victoria Park.

As soon as I sat down in Andy's office, with the baby on my knee, he shocked me by offering me the job as his assistant manager. Andy explained that he had been monitoring my progress carefully, that he knew I had a good football background, he admired the way I handled myself around the club, respected my ability as a player and coach, and liked me as a person. He told me that he thought we could work well together and his plan was for me to start as assistant manager the following season. The idea of helping to manage Burscough really appealed to me a lot and I was delighted to accept his offer right there and then.

As I drove away from the ground I was happily thinking that this was just about perfect – coaching at Liverpool, the club of my dreams, and playing and managing at Burscough, the club of my youth.

My excitement didn't last long though. Just two weeks later we were relegated after losing the last game of the 2008/9 season. Andy Much got the sack and his departure saw my Burscough management opportunity instantly turn to dust.

I scored in that last match but, sadly, it ended up being my last kick in competitive football.

The following year, just before the start of the 2009/10 season, Rafa Benitez, the Liverpool manager at the time, made it a priority to try to improve the tangible results of the Academy, which hadn't provided the first team with a key player since Steven Gerrard. One of his first big steps was to appoint fellow Spaniards Pep Segura and Rodolfo Borrel to replace the Dutchman Piet Hamberg as Technical Director at the Academy. As with any other shift in a management regime, this revised structure resulted in a change of the coaching philosophy. With Hamberg's Dutch influenced approach it was all about individual skills and protecting the ball, essentially the Coever Coaching system. Whereas, with the arrival of the two Spaniards, we reverted to the kind of passing game that has always been the hallmark of the great Liverpool sides. So then the coaching became more about passing, movement off the ball, making angles to receive a pass and so on.

And I have to say that, from my perspective anyway, this was a very good development at the club. Nowadays, when you watch the youngsters training, you can really see the positive results being achieved. Apart from physically being able to perform the practice drills to a highly accomplished degree, the kids today are also taught to understand the When?, Where?, Why? and How? to do things out on the pitch. All of those important messages are constantly being reinforced, even from as early as age 5 – 6, and you can clearly see the outstanding progress that is being made. It's all very exciting and fascinating at the same time. Everything is going in the right direction. Frank McParland, my first boss in the Community Section, is now the Academy Director, overseeing the whole programme. The system is working really well and it is benefitting the coaches as well as the players, with more youngsters like Raheem Sterling, Martin Kelly, Jon Flanagan, Andre Wisdom, Jack Robinson, Jordan Ibe and Conor Coady now breaking into the First Team.

I think it was Rafa Benitez, when he arrived as manager, who brought with him the concept that any successful academy must have a clear line of work and a single person responsible for technical supervision. With that in mind, he appointed Pep Segura to co-ordinate a plan to ensure that all the coaches at Liverpool followed the same line of progression.

While I strongly believe that all the coaches at the club should be working together towards the same single, well-aligned mission, I don't think that just because there is a change of management at the Academy that I should just forget any ideas that I've learned from previous head coaches. On the contrary, I actually think it is a strength to build up as broad a knowledge base as possible, to be better equipped to reach the final goal of transforming young boys with potential into top class footballers. Consider the simple example of baking a cake. Five people could use the exact same recipe and ingredients to bake five cakes - but you will almost certainly end up with five cakes that all taste and appear a bit different to each other. It's the same with coaching young footballers. We all must use the same recipe and have a distinct goal but, provided you stick to the common line and don't wobble off course, then how you achieve that target depends on your own personal input and individual style.

I think I am very fortunate to have been a coach at Liverpool during this particular era because I have been exposed to a wide variety of international coaching techniques and given the opportunity to work alongside some of the world's top youth coaches in what was relatively speaking a very short space of time. From Steve Heighway and all my other British colleagues at Liverpool, to Piet Hamberg and then Pep Segura and Rodolfo Borrel, I have been constantly surrounded by the best in the business. Any time I go back to the Academy, Rodolfo, who is now the Technical Director, is always willing have a chat with me and keep me up to speed with all the latest developments and programmes.

Working alongside such a variety of top coaches has allowed me the privilege of learning from each of them as I've gone along and to pick out the most outstanding aspects of their individual styles and add them to my own personal coaching repertoire.

### Enjoying My Life as a Coach

It was at the same time as the arrival of Pep Segura at the Academy that I was rewarded with my first opportunity to work as a head coach. Ever since I'd returned to Liverpool, my day job had always been community oriented. We'd run tournaments at the Academy, put on coaching clinics at schools and generally do whatever PR we could for the club; but at the same time we'd be looking out for any good prospects, who we'd then recommend to the scouting department. Then, when our daytime commitments were completed, we'd have to go back to work with the Academy players of an evening. This meant that our working days were very long, usually twelve hours from 8:00 am to 8:00 pm. On top of that we had our own group's Academy fixtures every Sunday and occasionally we would also have to go to watch another age group or a youth cup match during the week. It really was a demanding job – but I loved it!

So, even though I was already finding it a big challenge to juggle my time and manage all of my responsibilities, especially with regards to my family, I was absolutely thrilled when the club invited me to take charge of the under-10s for the 2009/10 season. I worked with Darren Hughes as my assistant and I enjoyed every minute of my coaching duties. It really felt special to lead a group like that. When I look back on it now, I realize that I actually felt honoured to have the opportunity of working with a group of boys who represented the best of the best footballers in their age group in and around Liverpool. There is something incredibly rewarding and enjoyable about being able to pass on football knowledge and advice to young boys and see it being applied by them almost immediately because they just 'get it' straight away. And, having quickly picked up whatever we were coaching, they could then remember it at the next session. That is a privileged position for any coach in any sport anywhere in the world. Those kids thought they were lucky to be at Liverpool, but meanwhile I thought I was lucky to have them there with me. It was a win-win situation all around.

I used to love Friday afternoons when you'd see the ground staff mowing and preparing the under-10s pitch for the upcoming match and the playing surface would look as good as Anfield. That always gave me a big buzz, especially when we were due to play Everton or United. It was a fantastic experience for me to watch the squad making gradual progress over the course of a whole season; never more so than during the Sunday matches when our kids would pit their skills against the best players from the whole North West of England. Very often those occasions would be given an extra, special dimension by having Kenny Dalglish watch the match alongside me in the dugout. Kenny genuinely enjoyed watching the youngsters play and if anybody ever caught his eye he'd ask me his name and store it away for future reference. It used to amaze me how many names he could remember, even after only watching the kids a handful of times. He'd often come into my office on the Monday morning to chat about our game and individual players. Then, the following week, he'd be back out there looking to see if those same players stood out again. I have to say, it gave me a boost to have a man of Kenny Dalglish's calibre taking such a keen interest in the work we were doing.

As I have said before, whoever Liverpool play against it is always like a cup final for the other team. Everybody wants to beat Liverpool. So, just before every game, I would always tell the lads on our team to look at the badge on their shirt and remember who and what they were representing. I'd point out the amazing facilities they were using, the fantastic quality kit and boots they were wearing, and generally talk about how lucky they were to be playing for Liverpool Football Club. I'd let them know that every player on the opposing team would love to take their place. Then I'd remind them that no matter who we were up against, because of all of those reasons, our team would face a very tough and challenging opening

10 to 15 minutes play in every single match. So the only way to meet that kind of challenge was to match them for commitment and work rate, then gradually raise our own game and outplay them. All the same messages that I'd been given as a kid! But the very last thing I used to tell them was to think about everything they'd learned in training, relax and go out and enjoy playing their football.

Back in my day as a young player we'd generally only play against other teams from the North West, so the likes of Bolton, Crewe, Everton and the two Manchester clubs. But today the lads will also go off during school holidays to play in mini-tournaments, often in London against the likes of Chelsea, Arsenal and Spurs, but occasionally overseas in Europe. This is fantastic exposure for young players and something that really helps to accelerate their development. I can remember in 2008, when I was coaching with the under-15s group that included good young players like Connor Coady, John Flanagan, Jack Robinson and Thomas Ince, we went across to play in a tournament in Italy. Apart from the obvious challenge of having to play top Italian sides in their own backyard, our lads were at a big disadvantage because of the different age group structures of the two systems. Whereas we use August to August as our cut-off dates, the Italians and most of the Europeans use January to January. This means that our boys were usually almost a year younger than the Italians they were playing against and, at that age, this also translates to a big difference in physical size and strength. But, despite being generally younger and smaller, our lads were always able to hold their own out on the pitch. I have to say that one thing you could always be sure of with our Liverpool teams was that the players had plenty of heart and were never intimidated by the opposition. We always played a good level of quality football and gave every team a good run for their money. So, even if we were not quite equipped to actually go on and win the tournament, it was still a very positive experience for those kids – both as developing footballers and as more worldly young men.

The following year, 2009, we went back to Italy to play in another mini-tournament and my lasting personal memory of that tour will always be looking proudly at our Liverpool boys standing in the tunnel ready to go out and play the quarter-final against AC Milan. The two teams were lined up next to each other, us in our classic red strip and them in white.

*Opposite: Me in Italy with Conor Coady & Tom Ince. Photo by Robbie Johnson*

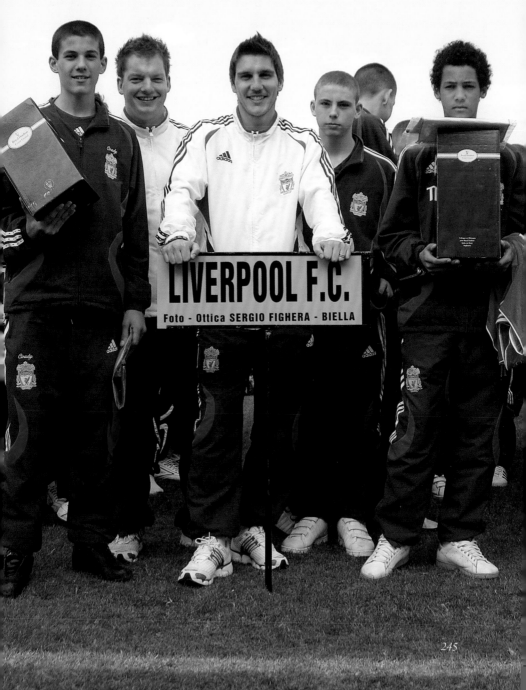

Photo courtesy of LFC and Nick Taylor.

It was Istanbul all over again! What an experience for all of those youngsters, on both teams. I couldn't help looking at them all and wondering how many of them might be doing that in the real thing in a few years time. We lost the game but we certainly played well enough to win the respect of everybody who watched our performance. And, regardless of the result, it was a huge step forward on the players' path towards their goal of becoming professional footballers.

All of the recent developments within the structure of the overall coaching and development programme can only be good for the lads today. While the system in place during my time as a young player going through the Centre of Excellence was clearly right for the time, and did successfully produce some top class players, there is no doubt whatsoever that the kids today benefit from superior facilities and equipment and are offered many more opportunities. They literally want for nothing. Everything is there for them, on and off the pitch. All of their needs are taken care of by a cadre of highly qualified professionals: not just top football coaches but also medical staff and personal development officers. They even have their own kit man at the Academy who looks after that side of things for them. At the start of the season each player is given a kit bag full of boots, shorts, shirts and so on. And if anything needs replacing they just have to ask. Need a new pair of boots? No problem, here you go son. Clearly this is a far cry from my day. In those days, and it is really not that long ago, if our boots split we were expected to take them to somebody like Sammy Lee, who would either just tape them up himself or send them to the cobbler to be repaired. That definitely doesn't happen in these days where sponsorship is such an integral part of the game and even young kids have boot deals.

While there can be no doubt that having a steady supply of top quality equipment can only be good for the boys, and although it might be easy to accept that young players today are not expected to do menial tasks around the academy, I can still look back on my own similar experiences with nothing but affection and appreciation. Not only were we taught how to respect and look after our own kit, at the same time, we were also taught the value of respect by being required to look after the kit of the senior players and staff. It certainly worked for me. In fact I don't know anybody from that generation of footballers who doesn't think it was a

*Opposite above: Coaching the LFC under-10's ... I loved coaching this group!* • *Opposite below: 'Flanno', Jon Flanagan, popped back into the academy to meet the kids on our programmes.*

good part of their development. I truly enjoyed taking good care of my own boots and I felt hugely privileged to be given the chance to also look after the boots of a top pro like Jamie Redknapp. It was an extremely positive way of connecting young developing players with established first team players. By putting us into everyday contact with the seniors, it made it an easy, almost natural progression for our heroes to also become our role models. And I firmly believe that all boys benefit greatly from the presence in their lives of a strong male role model who can set a good example for them to follow and emulate: not just in terms of football but also life in general.

Perhaps the biggest difference today is the massive amount of public exposure that the young Academy players are given. When we were doing our YTS years there was virtually no media coverage whatsoever of the players, so even a rising star like Steven Gerrard could slip under the radar and make his debut as a virtual unknown to most people. Today, no doubt due to the extensive reach of the Internet and social media such as Facebook, Twitter and so on, the young players are already minor celebrities. Even their matches are covered live on Liverpool FC TV; so the fans might have watched them play many times before they even penetrate the First Team squad. Stevie G has actually said in an interview that he thinks that this aspect of the modern game puts much more mental pressure on today's Academy lads than he ever experienced. To counteract these trends, the Academy now formally coaches the youngsters on how to handle the media and helps them to gradually become aware of how to manage the publicity.

As a recent case in point, in December 2012, the Liverpool under-19s travelled as far away as Singapore to play in the NextGen Series and when the squad arrived they were met by thousands upon thousands of local Liverpool supporters at the airport, with some even carrying banners bearing Adam Morgan's name. Liverpool academy chief Frank McParland was quoted in the Daily Mail as saying: 'We played in a tournament and it was beamed on TV to 50 countries. You could see it was difficult for some of the lads to comprehend but it's all part of the education. Welcome to being a player at Liverpool Football Club.' Frank later also told me that during that tour the coaches had actively encouraged the players to sign autographs, pose for photographs and interact with the fans, as a practical way to help them learn how to deal with the challenges of living constantly in the public eye. Clearly that situation is a million miles away from what

I experienced. But, as always, it is another example of Liverpool trying to equip the young players with the right skills that they will need in the future, not just to survive but also to thrive.

Even the traditional Liverpool Way has been obliged to adapt to suit the new demands of the modern game!

### Back to Community Coaching and Lessons From Soweto

In 2010 there was another major adjustment to the structure of the coaching staff at the Academy that resulted in Steve Hollis and I being transferred back into the Community Coaching Department. Some people might have considered that sort of sideways move to be a disappointing development at that stage of my career, but I certainly did not. As far as I am concerned, that department represents a very important aspect of life at Liverpool Football Club. Knowing how essential the fan base is to Liverpool and its future, I am fully aware that it is imperative for the club to be seen to be doing good work amongst the local community. So, even though I might have enjoyed carrying on coaching at the Academy, I had no problem making this switch and I still got stuck into my work full of enthusiasm every day. I think Steve had the same attitude and we both went out into the community to do our very best for the club. A large proportion of our job involved going into the schools throughout the term and running coaching clinics and competitions during the holidays. I have to be honest and say that this was not as exciting as working with the elite players at the Academy but it was still very rewarding to see the response we would get from the kids, and even their parents, just because they were working with Liverpool FC. It was a very humbling way to be reminded just how important this club is to the people of the city of Liverpool.

Not long after we'd got started, in a very interesting turn of events, Steve Hollis and I were invited by the club and Oxfam to go to South Africa to do some community coaching in Johannesburg and the townships of Soweto. It was just prior to the 2010 World Cup and the idea was that we would work alongside the Oxfam staff as a way to raise awareness of the work they were doing in Africa. Amongst other projects, we assisted Oxfam with their Anti-Xenophobia Campaign by working with groups that were trying to promote greater participation of young women in football. I don't have any statistics to quote, but suffice it to say that at the time there were an horrendous number of young girls being regularly raped and beaten in parts of the townships. The simple idea was that by getting them involved in organised football, apart from giving them a healthier lifestyle and something positive to focus on, it also literally took them off the streets and thereby reduced their vulnerability. In essence, it meant that the girls were now part of a team set-up and responsible people were actually looking out for them, so they were no longer isolated and easy prey. It was shocking to hear about what was happening to those poor young women but that made it all the more rewarding to be able to work with them and make our own small contribution towards giving them a better chance in life. It felt really good to know that we were making a tangible difference.

When the club had asked me to move back into working within the community, I had never resisted that decision or questioned the relevance of the role I was given. Nevertheless, working in the townships of Soweto still provided me with a tremendous degree of vindication and an unshakeable sense that I really was 'doing the right thing'. When you arrive in Soweto you cannot escape the poverty; it totally engulfs you. Poverty is a way of life in Soweto and people adjust their values accordingly. So, when a boy literally owns only the shirt on his back, even though that shirt is a 12-year old hand-me-down, you know that he values it just as much as if it was the latest Nike straight out of its wrapping. Now, against that background, try to imagine my contrasting emotions when I saw a boy like that come running towards me, pulling at the front of his shirt, trying to shout something to me and laughing his head off all at the same time. I couldn't understand a word he was saying and I had no idea what he was so excited about. It wasn't until he was literally pushing his shirt into my face that I could finally recognise the shape of the Liver bird on the long-faded crest on his now washed out, almost pink shirt. A Liverpool shirt in Soweto! I didn't know whether to laugh or cry. The boy was so excited and proud that he had a Liverpool shirt and he just wanted to share that bond with us, the club's representatives, all wearing our own Liverpool shirts, right there in his home village. I was just as excited and proud as him but felt terribly guilty at the same time. It was a gut-wrenching flashback to my earlier life-changing experiences of all the hardships in Armenia! How is it possible for some people to have so much while others have so little? I was desperate to give him a new shirt and anything else I had with me. Sadly, since I was advised that doing that could have ended up being a problem for him, I could not. The rules of life can be very complex in the townships of Soweto.

Later that evening, back at our hotel and once again surrounded by the luxurious trappings of a wealthy society, I couldn't stop thinking about how Liverpool Football Club must maintain contact with all of our supporters, even at the most humble of levels; not just in the UK but all around the world. I know from personal experience that many people are intimidated when they walk into the club's corporate headquarters on Chapel Street in Liverpool city centre, literally just around the corner from the famous Liver Buildings, with the even more famous Liver Birds perched high on the roof. Even accomplished people can sometimes feel a bit nervous when they walk into the heart of Liverpool FC and are surrounded by legendary memorabilia and super-sized photos of the club's greatest players and managers, complete with long lists of the many trophies and honours won during a truly illustrious history. Liverpool FC is not just a football club: it is a living dynasty; it is a huge element within British heritage; and it is a spiritual life raft that keeps many people afloat when they might otherwise sink. And that is precisely why LFC constantly strives to engage with people and communities at the grassroots level. That is what makes our club so great. It's all about the people. I see this first hand on a regular basis but never has the importance of that philosophy been made clearer to me than during my time in Soweto. My personal opinion is that those of us who are fortunate enough to be employed at Liverpool, in whatever capacity, have a moral responsibility to do whatever we can to deliver the club and its values into the lives of our supporters.

As part of that same trip we were also given a special guided tour around the brand new Royal Bafokeng Sports Complex close to Rustenburg, which was due to serve as the England team's headquarters for the 2010 World Cup. We visited the Royal Bafokeng Stadium where England would soon play their opening game, as well as all of the training pitches. It was an incredible experience for us to get a private, insider's preview of such an amazing football facility. To cap it all off, we actually stayed at the Royal Bafokeng Hotel, the England team hotel, before they did. In fact our stay there was a bit of a trial run for the hotel because it was so new it had literally just been opened. We even used some of their conference facilities to run a couple of Coach Education Courses for coaches from around Rustenburg. Just before we checked out at the end of our stay, Steve Hollis and I wrote good luck messages for Steven Gerrard, Jamie Carragher and Glen Johnson and left them at reception, so they would get them when they arrived.

The South Africans were generous hosts and they did all they possibly could to make us feel welcome. Sadly though, despite all the very special treatment and wonderful hospitality we benefited from, it was still impossible to escape the harsh facts of the real everyday situation. Just a few hundred yards away from that magnificent stadium and the superb hotel, both spanking new and both lavishly appointed at a combined cost of many millions of South African Rand, we saw some of the worst squalor I could ever have imagined. The brutal contrast between the vast wealth epitomised by the stadium and the abject poverty of the neighbouring townships was simply staggering. No matter how I tried, I couldn't shake off the belief that it was just plain wrong. And the more we saw the more I felt that way. We visited the home of one of the young coaches and she was living in a single room with about another seven members of her family; and not just brothers and sisters, uncles and aunts as well. To make matters worse there was no running water. And the main money earner in the house was making a living by selling peanuts at the side of the road, ironically opposite the entrance to the stadium.

Even though I already knew full well that these things happen all around the world, that personal real life experience in South Africa really made a big and lasting impact on me. Now, thanks to football, I can totally understand why Oxfam works so tirelessly to raise global awareness about these devastating social inequalities that still exist in some countries.

My Soweto lessons reconfirmed my belief that we should use the power of the Liverpool FC badge to do good whenever and wherever we can. Liverpool Football Club represents such a massive brand that, whatever we do, it will always have a major influence on people, literally millions of people around the world. So, as a club, we must always be careful to ensure that whatever we do is deemed to be positive. While successful modern football clubs are by necessity multi-million pound business empires, there is still no escaping the fact that ultimately it is still all about people: people working at the club, people in Liverpool and people all over the planet. We need to address the needs of all of those people.

*Opposite above: Steve Hollis and Me at Royal Bafokeng*
*Oppposite below: Members of the Orange Farm community and founder of Let Us Grow Mama Rose Thamae. Me holding little Tupraya (To pray). Photograph: Neo Ntsoma/Oxfam GB*

# Clive Cook
*Education and Welfare Officer, Liverpool Football Club*

We know that as well as developing professional footballers, we also have a responsibility to produce decent human beings.

So, off the field, we put a big emphasis on offering our lads a true perspective of the realities of life - and we do this through life-skills classes and the actual experience of doing community work.

Our lads go to Alder Hey Children's Hospital each month, to local homeless shelters and to other projects around the city. They see for themselves that there is real suffering out there. When our players go to a local homeless hospice to help other volunteers serve food and drink they go in covertly, without club tracksuits on. The reason why there is never any reference to Liverpool Football Club during these visits is because it's not a PR exercise, it's just the right thing to do - to help others. Some people are born into poverty, they don't get what so many people take for granted like warmth, shelter, love and care. They don't choose this life.

So we feel that it is vital to let our youngsters personally experience these negative situations, otherwise we may give them a false sense of perspective, both about football and real life.

That way, during times when they are feeling down because of injuries, loss of form, or de-selection, all of which can affect confidence, they can better appreciate that what they may perceive to be big issues aren't actually as bad as some of the wider issues of life.

And the lads who do this community service appreciate its importance. They've all commented on how it's such a great thing to do and how rewarded they feel afterwards. They also learn that it's a privilege to represent Liverpool Football Club; and that privilege comes with responsibilities both on and off the pitch.

# Nick Levett
*The Football Association's National Development Manager (Youth and Mini-Soccer)*

In my personal opinion, the aim of developing a top quality young man as well as a top footballer should be high on the list of every Academy, Centre of Excellence or grassroots club. We know from evidence that less than 1% of the children who play football in England are going to go on to become a professional footballer, but 100% of them are going to be citizens of this country. We have a responsibility to develop well-rounded, young people and football can be an excellent vehicle to do this. Over the last few years the FA has developed coaching courses that have fundamentally changed how we coach children; focusing on putting the learner at the heart of the process. This is vital. We are about developing children holistically, in all areas of their life, not just their football experience.

In this regard, some adults might need to redefine or broaden their expectation of 'winning'. It is simply more than three points and goal difference. Winning might be those kids that get to football early, have packed their own bag, cleaned their own boots and generally taken more responsibility for themselves. It might be the children that have increased their self-esteem and confidence levels, or got faster and quicker through physical activity. This is humanistic coaching and something I firmly believe we all have a role to play in, whether at a professional club or grassroots club.

Sometimes we lose sight of the fact that each individual is a child first and an athlete second. We need to be more patient and recognize that the desire for short-term success is not part of developing players. It's like being a gardener. You can't just magically create flowers. They need to be watered and nurtured gradually. Young players are the same; they need to be cared for along the entire length of their journey.

I think we are moving in the right direction with the Elite Player Performance Plan. But this is a long-term system, so we must not dismiss the plan after a couple of years if it hasn't yet produced a World Cup winning team. We must have a long-term vision, one that is also fully aligned with developing the best workforce to support young people. And this might require a focus on learning rather than football, because if we support young players to be better learners then they will become better players anyway.

## Promoted to the LFC International Football Academy

The South Africa trip definitely triggered a lot of new thoughts in my head, which in turn inspired a lot of ambitious ideas. As soon as I got back home to Liverpool, I started thinking about different ways how the club could use its massive influence to make some positive contributions within the global community, while generating some income at the same time. Steve Hollis and I both had some interesting ideas about how we could move the club forward in terms of the football programmes we were running. We soon found ourselves bouncing fresh concepts between each other whenever we were together, gradually turning our daydreams into feasible plans. The only problem was that most of our schemes wouldn't work in the Community Coaching Department; so there was no real fit between our job and our ideas. To try to solve our predicament, we decided to share our thoughts with members of the Liverpool Football Club Commercial Team.

Most of our suggestions were based upon the sort of programmes that we were already involved with, such as coach education and soccer schools, but we also raised the subject of an enhanced, online coaching session-planner that we had been working on for quite a while. Anyway, the Commercial Team was sufficiently impressed with our proposals that in March 2011 Steve Hollis and I were invited to undertake a three-month secondment to that department, to allow us the time and resources to do more research into our potential projects and then deliver actual detailed plans. Steve and I really enjoyed that three-month spell and I'd like to think that we did a good job of preparing and delivering a number of financially viable schemes that could also meet the community spirit and PR requirements of the club. Somebody must have been impressed because within a relatively short period of time I was offered a new and exciting position within the newly formed LFC International Football Academy department.

Wow!

As soon as my appointment had been fully confirmed, it really struck me that I was once again setting out on yet another exciting adventure in my already richly varied and eventful career at Liverpool Football Club. This was clearly not just another sideways movement; this one was definitely a very significant step up the ladder. The big question this time though was not only where would this new road lead me to, but also just how far could it take me? Or, indeed, how far could I take it?

The original Liverpool FC Soccer Schools were essentially an offshoot of the Academy itself. There was such a high demand for places at the Academy that we could never possibly have accommodated all of the boys who wanted to participate. Even the parents of lads who were already part of the Academy would often ask if there was any way we could do anything for their other sons. What became obvious was that Liverpool had spent millions on building this magnificent facility but it wasn't being used all the time and, meanwhile, there were droves of lads longing to get in.

The coaches started to talk about this more and more, especially people like Stewart Gelling, Iain Brunskill, Gareth Evans, Steve Hollis and myself, and then one day Steve Heighway walked into the office just when we were all in full flow on the subject. So, there and then, we suggested to him that an obvious solution to the two-pronged problem was to run LFC Soccer Schools during the school holidays that could cater primarily to young players who hadn't been able to make it into the Academy's elite programme but would still love to get a taste of the action. In basic terms, let the kids pay to play.

Steve agreed and invited us to write some coaching sessions that would fit the bill. The only thing he told us was that he didn't want any fancy frills involved, just good solid football coaching. So, in the end, we created three-day programmes that had the same basic content and sessions that we used with the elite players. The only major difference was that we reduced the required performance levels to better suit the lesser ability of these kids.

As anticipated, those Soccer Schools proved to be extremely popular and, as usual, we had more applications than places. After that level of success locally, it was something of a natural progression to then launch LFC Soccer Schools overseas, especially in locations where we already had a strong Liverpool connection and a well-established fan base. It was for that reason that Dublin was chosen as the location for one of the very first overseas LFC Soccer Schools. We used our scouts in Dublin to find the best venue for us and to recruit the right kind of kids for the training camp. Such was Liverpool's popularity that, yet again, it was easy to attract a full complement of participants and it proved to be a huge success all around. From the club's perspective it was not just about making money, it was really all about offering a service to our supporters overseas and establishing a new kind of PR activity. After that initial success, our overseas Soccer Schools became so popular that the growing demand started to put a strain on our regular coaching staff and resources. We couldn't do our own jobs and manage these extra camps at the same time. It became increasingly clear that we would have to use outside coaches to run the camps or find some alternative way of operating them. And that is precisely why the club decided to establish the Liverpool FC International Football Academy.

In simple terms, what we then launched is a partnership system whereby a client pays a licence fee to Liverpool, which gives them the right to host their own series of Soccer Schools under the LFC brand over a period of twelve months. As part of the deal we send over our coaches to teach their own local coaches how to best manage the schools, what to incorporate in the coaching sessions and how to get across the right kind of messages and values. In effect, we are exporting the Liverpool Way.

When I first came on board at the International Academy my role was to rewrite and improve the existing content, as well as to create new content for the coaching programmes. Since then I have also written an International Academy Manual, which is essentially an A to Z of how to set up a football academy.

Today, one of my major roles is educating our own coaches on how to effectively deliver the Liverpool Way to an international market. The rapid development of the Internet has certainly made my job easier when trying to work with coaches who are based overseas. Thanks to an online session planner that we brought into the club, I can now sit at my desk in Liverpool and update a coaching manual for somebody thousands of miles away, anywhere in the world.

Gone are the days of a hard cover manual that we'd have to keep re-printing and shipping. Nowadays any overseas coach can e-mail me in the morning with a request for some kind of special session, say a shooting drill for a group of advanced under-16s. I can go online to review what they have done already, then custom design a detailed session for them. Once finished, I simply post it online and all the coach has to do is download it, ready to use that same afternoon. It's quite incredible really, particularly because this allows us to retain a kind of hands-on level of input even though we might be working with somebody on the other side of the globe.

Our Liverpool FC International Soccer School partners have enjoyed such great success over the years that some clients have now become a bit more ambitious. A recent trend has seen several Soccer Schools asking to be allowed to expand into an actual Academy. This of course represents a whole new ball game, with significantly more work and responsibility involved; and, by extension, a lot more money is required to cover costs! For any partner to be able to acquire a licence to facilitate the transition from Soccer School to Academy, the client would first of all have to substantiate their financial capacity and also prove that they can provide all the appropriate, high quality facilities that the agreement demands as a standard requirement. Once the physical set-up is fully operational, we would then send a coach from Liverpool FC to work on the ground with the local coaches, to ensure full adherence to all of the club's exacting standards.

In August 2011, I had the great pleasure of travelling to China with Ian Rush. While the main purpose behind the visit was really to promote the concept of the soccer schools, with Ian serving in his capacity as an official Ambassador for Liverpool Football Club, we also used it as a good opportunity for me to work with their coaches and give them a first-hand demonstration of the Liverpool Way. Rather than simply explaining what we expected from them, we decided to actually show them by running a number of practical sessions. Based on the original programme, I had been allocated three days to work with twenty Chinese coaches. However, as soon as we arrived in China, I quickly realized that this was nowhere near enough time. So, in a last minute effort to make it more effective, I asked the local organisers to draft in fifteen young players on the last day so that we could stage some real coaching sessions. I literally sat all the coaches down in a row alongside the playing area and then I went about my work with the kids, just as if it was a regular session. The coaches got a lot out of the demonstration, the kids enjoyed it immensely and I found it all really rewarding.

That group of Chinese kids were not the greatest natural talents I've ever worked with but they were certainly very enthusiastic, well disciplined and hugely respectful. It was a genuine pleasure to work with them and very encouraging to see just how much they valued and appreciated what I was trying to teach them. All in all it was a great experience for me and I couldn't help thinking that with their very positive attitude towards learning, once they have the right coaching programmes in place, it won't be long before we are seeing some top players coming out of China. In fact the whole approach towards football in China is geared towards producing world-class players.

When I was a young boy growing up the Liverpool Way at the Centre of Excellence and Melwood, I could never have imagined, not even in my wildest dreams, that one day I would be exporting those same LFC traditions and values to all kinds of exotic locations around the world.

The circles of life really do revolve in mysterious ways!

## My Role at the Club Today

One of my colleagues in the department, Adam Flynn, is the International Academy Head Coach and he focuses on organising and looking after all the international coaches for the overseas programmes. It is good having Adam around as we know each other well from the past and we have always been happy to work together. In fact I had actually coached Adam during my first spell at the Academy, when he was in the under-14s. Almost bizarrely, I was only eighteen myself at the time. Later, when I came back to Liverpool after my spell at Dundee, my return to the Academy coincided with Adam switching from player to a coach in the community department and I was the one who mentored him in his early days. So our paths have crossed several times during our careers.

One of our main areas of collaboration in the International Department has been to create the Coach Education programmes.

Occasionally we get the welcome opportunity to host some of the international coaches from overseas right here in Liverpool. The obvious very big advantage of that situation is that we can actually take them to the Academy and Melwood and let them see for themselves how our coaching system operates. That first hand experience is immensely valuable as a teaching tool. We also show them around Anfield and immerse them in the Liverpool Way culture, including watching a game if there is one scheduled at the time.

In February 2013, Adam and I both thoroughly enjoyed hosting a group of coaches from our LFC International Football Academy partners from North Texas. They were all good people and very keen to learn more about coaching, so the sessions had plenty of energy about them. What made it extra special for us was that their Technical Director is Jimmy

*Opposite above: Not as flexible as I used to be!*
*Opposite below: High fives with the local kids in China ... great kids!*

Photo courtesy of Robbie Johnson

Melia, a Liverpool Legend from the early 1960s. Jimmy is a likeable person and it was fascinating to listen to him talking about the start of the Bill Shankly era and his personal experiences with the great man himself. When Jimmy shared his memories of how the club functioned back then, one thing that really stood out was that although the overall structure has altered considerably, the essential values have not. Even the coaching messages were incredibly similar.

We took the Americans to watch Liverpool play Zenit St. Petersburg in the Europa Cup and it turned out to be one of those extra-special European nights at Anfield. Fighting to overturn a 0 – 2 deficit from the first leg, the Reds tragically gave away an early goal and at 0 – 3 all seemed doomed. But, lifted by the crowd, the lads raised their game and banged in three goals to win 3 – 1 on the night and level the aggregate score 3 – 3. Sadly we went out on the away goals rule but it had still been a great match to watch and a truly fantastic experience for the overseas coaches.

Just after the game finished my mobile rang. It was Ian Rush asking me to bring Jimmy Melia to the Carlsberg Lounge because there was somebody who wanted to meet him. When we got there it turned out to be none other than Ian St. John, Ron Yeats and Ian Callaghan – three Liverpool greats who had all played alongside Jimmy. He was absolutely thrilled! As a bonus, he also got to meet Luis Suarez who came in to collect his Man of the Match Award.

The following day we were back at Melwood and, even though there was no full first team training that day, a few of the players had come in for various reasons. The American coaches were blown away when Steven Gerrard stopped to say hello to me and then agreed to have his photo taken with the group. I think that was the highlight of their trip!

Perhaps the most significant aspect of our department's role is that we actually generate income for the club; but it is equally important to me that we also have a major responsibility to take the club to the people. In fact, apart from the first team and the Academy, we are the only department that directly reaches out to people and gives them an opportunity to get actively involved with the club; to actually experience the Liverpool Way. And that is extremely important to me.

In terms of promoting the club, even though I am technically the LFC International Academy Programme Manager, I do still get the opportunity

*Opposite: King Ping ... You can't beat striking a football!*

to contribute to our domestic development programmes as well. One of my absolute favourite innovations was when we developed the idea of hosting a Liverpool FC Soccer School on the actual pitch at Anfield. It had never been done before, possibly because in days gone by the pitch was sacrosanct and never to be trodden on by mere mortals. So, even though this was a novel, benchmark event for the club, we just instinctively knew that it was destined to be a massive success. And it was!

While this new event was clearly a profitable income generator for Liverpool, the greatest benefit for the club was definitely the satisfaction of creating such an amazing experience for all those young people. For me it's all about providing opportunities for as many local kids as possible, giving them a better chance in life. And that is the same philosophy that Jamie Carragher is applying to his '23 Foundation' and Steven with his 'Steven Gerrard Foundation'.

Adam Flynn and I had loads of fun coming up with extra ways to make it an unforgettable, lifetime memory experience for anybody who participated. First of all we decided to involve the parents by inviting them to sit in the paddock to watch the sessions taking place on the pitch, including a penalty shoot-out in front of the Kop.

To create an even more realistic match day atmosphere, we also arranged for George Sephton, the legendary 'Voice of Anfield', to MC the night, welcome people, commentate on what was going on and, of course, play some music.

But the real icing on the cake for the kids was that we got them to line up in the players' tunnel, complete with the famous 'This is Anfield' sign. To top it all off, we played the iconic Liverpool anthem 'You'll Never Walk Alone' as they walked out on to the pitch. The first time we did that routine it was an unbelievably magical moment. In fact I couldn't really tell you exactly how impressed the kids were because I was absolutely mesmerized myself!

We made a little piece of Liverpool FC history on that first night and I am very proud to have been involved.

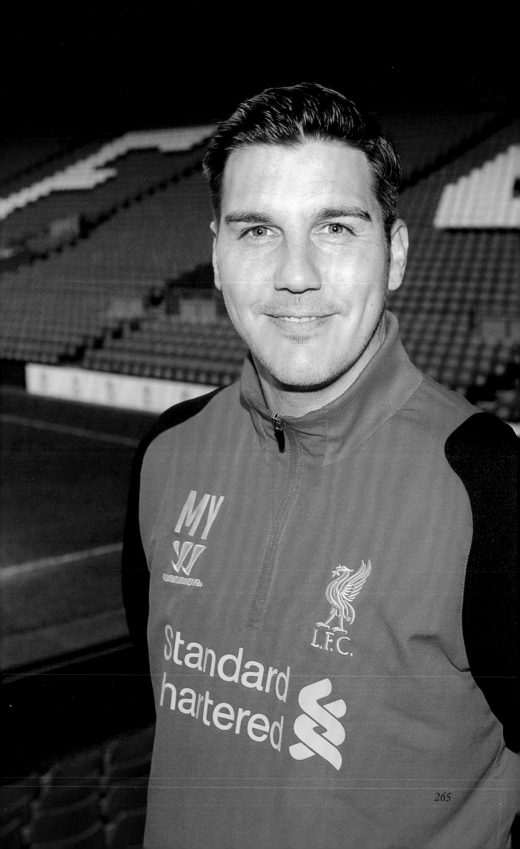

# Jimmy Melia

*Director of Football, Liverpool FC America; LFC Legend 1954-1964*

I grew up in the famous Scotty Road area of Liverpool and played football at every opportunity I could find. By the time I was fourteen I'd been playing regularly for England Schoolboys so, when I was ready to leave school, I took the advice of one of my teachers and joined Liverpool Football Club as a member of the ground staff.

In those days the apprentices were just as much labourers as we were players. It was part of our regular routine to do odd jobs around the ground, such as painting the stands and doing maintenance work wherever required. During my first year we even dug all the trenches to build the foundations for the first ever set of floodlights at Melwood.

Bob Paisley used to be in charge of our work group. He'd only just stopped playing and his main job was first team trainer, but he still got involved with all the jobs himself. We used to have to clean the players' boots and wash their socks, by hand. And Bob would be there, sleeves rolled up, working alongside us. After training and matches we'd have to prepare the bath for the first teamers, get their clean, dry towels ready, and even dry them down when they got out. Imagine asking a kid to do that today!

Compared to today's standards it was a bit like hard labour, but we just took it all in our stride because it was expected of us. It certainly stopped anybody becoming a big-head.

I signed professional forms on my 17th birthday, for the standard wage of £3 a week. Back then the team was picked by the Board of Directors, not the manager. The only way I discovered that I'd been selected to make my first team debut was when I read about it in the Liverpool Echo. But what an occasion that turned out to be. We beat Nottingham Forest 5 – 2 at Anfield. Billy Liddell, who was a cult hero, scored a hat-trick and I managed to bang one in at the Kop end from one of his crosses. What an amazing feeling that was for an eighteen year-old!

To really put things in perspective when comparing the game now and then, when I first started playing nobody at the club owned a car. From the players to the manager, we all walked to the ground or came on the bus. I can remember one occasion when we spotted a car in the car park and Bob Paisley asked who it belonged to. When he found out that it had been parked there by a new player, who was only eighteen, he went totally berserk. It turned

*Jimmy Melia*

out to be Johnny Morrissey, who had been given a car for his birthday by his dad, who was a 'well-off' docker. Bob gave the shocked young lad a total dressing down and ordered him to move the car immediately and never bring it back!

By the time Bill Shankly came to Liverpool in 1959, we'd established a reputation as a decent Division 2 side of 'also-rans'. We could always get close to promotion, but never clinch it. Shanks soon changed that. We had always been a fit and strong team, thanks to our excellent trainer Reuben Bennett, but when Shankly arrived he was like a breath of fresh air, delivering a whole new way of thinking to the club. The very first time I met him was when he walked into Melwood, already kitted out for training, with a bag of balls slung over his shoulder. My eyes lit up when I saw that because I was a ball player. You could tell straight away that things were going to change.

Bill Shankly launched the Liverpool passing game. He taught us to always keep the ball moving, play short passes, find the nearest man as quickly as possible, maintain possession, never give the ball away. He was incredibly passionate about football and had a brilliant knowledge of the game. His infectious enthusiasm and confidence rubbed off on all the players and Liverpool walked the Second Division in 1962. Then, helped by a couple of key signings, we won the First Division title just two years later in 1964. And everybody knows how immensely the club has grown since then.

Bill Shankly was a visionary and I learned a huge amount about the game from him and his coaching staff. When I left the club after ten years, I took the Liverpool Way with me and applied it to my life wherever else I went in the world as a player or a manager. I am still using it today in my current role as Technical Director at Liverpool FC America in Texas

The operation is two-fold. Firstly, we want to produce players that are good enough to represent Liverpool at some level. But, at the same time, we also want to enhance Liverpool's popularity and get young fans buying into the club's philosophy.

It's very exciting for me at this advanced stage of my career. In many ways, I've come full circle.

## The Story Behind 'You'll Never Walk Alone'

Most people today know that 'You'll Never Walk Alone' is the Liverpool anthem but few know the history behind it, which means that they cannot fully appreciate its deep significance. YNWA is not just a song; it's a culture. It is so symbolic of the Liverpool Way that I think it is essential to educate our young players about its relevance. This is especially important for our current generation who have not seen Liverpool win a Premier League title. We need to let them know just how great this club really is and help them appreciate the rich heritage that they have been fortunate enough to inherit. So, at events such as the Anfield Soccer School, or any other time I get the opportunity, I always make a point of talking at length about 'You'll Never Walk Alone'. Few football clubs, if any, anywhere in the world and at any time in history, are so readily identifiable by their fans' adopted song as Liverpool and YNWA. With the inimitable Kop leading the singing, this globally famous football anthem is performed with emotional reverence and heartfelt passion as a sacred ritual at the beginning and end of every match, as well as in response to any highs or even lows during the course of play.

It might be hard for young people today to fathom this, but the love story between Liverpool FC and 'You'll Never Walk Alone' began way back in 1963, over fifty years ago. That was the year that the club installed the first tannoy system in the ground and started to play music before kick-off. The DJ back then used to play the Top 10 from the charts, in reverse order, with the number one hit being played last, just as the players were getting ready to kick off. As fate would have it, the number one song at the time was 'You'll Never Walk Alone', performed by a band from Liverpool called Gerry and the Pacemakers. The song stayed on top of the charts for four consecutive weeks and quickly became a firm favourite with the Kop: partly because it was a great song to sing along to and partly because the lyrics were perfect for motivating the team. By the time the DJ stopped playing the song because it had dropped in the charts, the fans had already adopted it as their permanent anthem. The story then goes that Gerry Marsden gave a copy of the song to the legendary Liverpool manager Bill Shankly, who immediately fell in love with it too. A short while later, when 'Shanks' was the featured guest on the celebrity radio

*Opposite: Bill Shankly, hand on heart, leads the team out at Wembley*

show Desert Island Discs, he picked 'You'll Never Walk Alone' as one of his all-time favourite songs. That seal of approval from the boss was the absolute clincher for the already converted Anfield faithful and YWNA has been the official club anthem ever since.

Unusually for a football team's song, the use of 'You'll Never Walk Alone' has travelled far and wide around the world as the anthem of choice for numerous other sports teams. In addition, because of the powerful emotional support offered by this truly inspirational song, which has today become synonymous with Liverpool Football Club, it is also frequently used at peace rallies and memorial services. I'd like to think that this is another good example of the Liverpool Way quietly spreading a positive influence beyond the world of football.

Given the song's theme about overcoming adversity, coupled with the deeply engrained never-say-die attitude of Liverpool Football Club, it is no surprise that some of the greatest renditions of 'You'll Never Walk Alone' have been performed during matches when things were going very badly out on the pitch.

In May 2005 I was blessed to have been present in the Ataturk Stadium in Istanbul on that immortal Champions League Final night. When the half-time whistle blew, the entire Liverpool contingent was in a serious state of deep shock. How could we be losing 0 – 3? That wasn't written in the script, we were supposed to be destined to win! I felt more confused than deflated. What was going on? Then, out of all the miserable silence, a single voice started to sing the first words of 'You'll Never Walk Alone'. Everybody in that area joined in. The singing spread like wildfire. Within seconds it seemed like three quarters of the people packed into the stadium were holding up red scarves and singing like they'd never sang before. It was raw emotion. At first the voices sounded like they were offering up some kind of funeral chant but that gradually strengthened into something more like a statement of intent, a reassurance that the fans would stick by the team no matter what. Incredibly, this passionate rendition of YNWA just kept going and going, possibly the longest version ever; and the longer it lasted the more it became a powerful message of defiance. Ultimately the anthem became a challenge: a challenge to AC Milan, a challenge to our own players and a challenge to destiny. How dare you think that we're beaten already!

A song cannot win a football match. But that night, beyond any shadow of doubt, that truly extraordinary performance of 'You'll Never

Walk Alone' did reverse the mood inside the stadium. It was an awesome display of collective positive thinking resulting in positive change. Gone was the inevitable expectation of an AC Milan victory; back came a glimmer of hope. Come on Liverpool!

Whether or not Steven Gerrard actually heard the fans' incredible singing at half-time or sensed the shift in the mood, when he came out for the second half he certainly embodied the fighting spirit that YNWA represented that glorious night. Eight minutes later Stevie G scored his fantastic header and the rest, as they say, is history.

You'll Never Walk Alone.

**Geoff Yates:** 'As a father it is very hard to see your son being knocked back and badly disappointed. Apart from being left on the bench to make room for some trialist or other on a number of occasions, I can especially remember Mike being totally deflated when he was left at home at the last minute when the team went off to play a tournament in Paris. He was young for the group but we were made to believe he was going. That would have been a big opportunity for his development, so it was a huge disappointment for him. It's a tough system and I don't know how he survived it all sometimes. Even now I am very proud that he just took those setbacks in his stride, kept his head down and kept going.'

**Cheryl Yates:** 'We were devastated for Mike when he broke his wrist. Talk about terrible luck and terrible timing! The posters had been up all around our town for weeks advertising the big Burscough v Liverpool match. The build-up in our area was amazing. Just about everybody knew that Mike was probably going to play, so wherever I went that's all people spoke about. They were all so proud of how well he'd done at Liverpool. By then we really felt as though he had a real chance to make it and that match could have been his big moment. It was very hard to swallow when the accident happened. As a parent, you feel the disappointment so much for your son that it breaks your heart. I still ask myself what if? But everything happens for a reason in life.'

# Ian Rush
*Liverpool legend 1980-87/1988-96; Official LFC Ambassador*

When Liverpool first tried to sign me as a teenager I turned them down, simply because I didn't think I was good enough. I am the second youngest in a family of ten kids and our dad brought us up to respect other people and never get too big for our boots; so I suppose I was naturally modest. Plus I didn't know enough about the game to appreciate my own ability.

Dad worked at Shotton steel works for his whole life and three of my brothers joined him. I probably would have ended up working there too but football gave me a chance to have a different kind of future. Having said that, while I was playing for Chester City as a teenager I thought that when I eventually packed it all in I'd still end up going to the steel works.

When Liverpool came back for me when I turned eighteen, the salary they offered me made me think that I should give it a try, because if it didn't work out I'd still get a few bob and could always get a job at the steel works. The decision was finally clinched when Chester's manager told me to have a go because they'd take me back if I wasn't happy.

When I made my debut for Liverpool I had no clue I was even playing. I was in the dressing room before the game with the rest of the squad, which was the normal routine, but not really paying attention to Bob Paisley when he read out the team sheet. It was only when I realized that he hadn't called out Kenny Dalglish at number seven that it struck me that I might actually have heard my own name. But I didn't really know, so I turned to Terry McDermott next to me and asked him if the boss had called out my name. He just said 'yeah' and carried on getting changed, as if nothing had happened. No fuss, no big scene.

I was going out to play for Liverpool, wearing the famous #7 because Kenny was injured, so they kept it all very low key and didn't give me any time to get nervous. They made sure I didn't get too excited with myself. That was just the Liverpool Way of doing things.

Nowadays I enjoy travelling around the world and visiting new countries in my role as a club ambassador. Liverpool Football Club is a global brand and we are known as a family club, so when we interact with all of those international soccer schools and their young players we need to make the right impression and leave behind happy people and a worthwhile legacy. To achieve that successful level of PR we obviously need to take the right kind of Liverpool coaches with us. They have to be good coaches who are also good people and, above all, they must have a genuine passion for the club.

Mike Yates is a prime example of the kind of person we need doing this job. He is a good coach, with all the right people skills, and he truly understands the game. He has been involved at Liverpool since he was a lad and has personally experienced many of football's ups and downs. He grew up playing alongside the likes of Steven Gerrard and Michael Owen, so he knows what it feels like to play at that level. And even though he might not have been as good as them as a player, Mike has gone on to build a new career for himself and shown that he is

*Ian Rush*

very good at what he does. He is not a failed player; he is a successful coach for Liverpool Football Club.

Mike Yates still feels just as proud when he pulls on that red shirt and goes to work.

# Part Five
# My Personal Views

## Developing Young Players in the Modern Era

The recurring question of how can we best develop young footballers in our country is one of the most debated and potentially controversial subjects under scrutiny in the game today. And instinct suggests to me that it will continue to be so for quite a few more years to come.

In an era when technology is developing at an incredible pace but traditional values are on the decline, and where long-term investment in human development is sometimes sacrificed in favour of short-term profit, our young players need more care and guidance than ever before.

Not so much as footballers, more so as people.

As I have already said in earlier parts of this book, thanks to the enormous amount of money that is now an integral part of the modern game, including the ready availability of sponsorship deals, any player who earns a place at a football academy will lack for nothing. From a steady stream of top quality kit to training at a superbly appointed facility, the young players of today can enjoy arguably the best coaching environment that has ever existed in the history of the game in the United Kingdom.

The use of the latest science and technology has rapidly become a huge part of football and this has added considerable scope to the way coaches plan, deliver and keep a record of their sessions. Everything is recorded on video, both training and games, and then archived for analysis and use in future coaching. This visual record allows a coach to show young players action shots of themselves, so that they can see what they are doing well or needs to be improved. And to reinforce any messages being delivered, the players are given a DVD or a memory stick to take home and watch. To further consolidate the lesson, the clip might include some 'best practice' examples. For instance the footage might show Lionel Messi driving into the box, beating three defenders, but still having the vision and intelligence to lay the ball off to a teammate for a simple tap-in and a guaranteed goal. Watching real examples on a video is a very effective way for kids to learn – and a very efficient tool for the coaches to use.

Computer technology has made it possible for coaches to keep an accurate log of all the games and training that any player has been involved in during the season. Known as a Player Performance Clock, this programme assists the coach in planning future sessions and provides reliable reference material to monitor the player's progress. The system can actually collate all the individual's weekly ratings and produce a performance graph, which is automatically shown alongside the average trend for that age group, to provide a means of comparison and an easy point of reference. This clock is continuously updated and follows a player throughout the entire time at the Academy, thus ensuring a complete set of records and valuable statistical information.

Given the exceptionally high standards of the training facilities at today's top clubs and the new efficiencies created by modern technology, combined with the fact that there are more qualified coaches in the game than ever before, it seems to me that the actual football coaching of young players is making steady progress.

My personal view is that the football academy production line is working fine: but we still need better ways to deal with the finished products at every level.

Nowadays we all have regular access to a steady stream of football-related articles that can provide a potent mix of 'the good, the bad and the ugly', especially via the ever-present electronic media. British football is currently under the microscope to an unprecedented degree and it is undeniably apparent that the game still needs to take more measures to promote the good, improve the bad and clean up the ugly.

At the national level, one of the main areas of concern is the lack of English players graduating from academies to play in the Premier League and, by extension, the perceived resultant weakness of the England team. General consensus tends to lay the blame for this problem squarely at the feet of those clubs that prefer to buy the best young players from around the world, rather than invest more in the longer-term development of local academy players.

The obvious point here is that we have to give more consideration to our own young footballers and create ways to allow them greater opportunity to test and prove themselves at the highest level. In that regard, I agree with what Gary Neville recently had to say on the matter in an article for The Mail Online:

*"The best clubs always have a core of players at the club that set the tone for the dressing room and establish standards for the long term. Usually they are home grown or at least from the same country as the club they play for. At Chelsea, they haven't brought through their youngsters but John Terry, Frank Lampard and Ashley Cole have been vital to their stability.*

*Think of AC Milan in the Nineties. They had superstar Dutch imports in Frank Rijkaard, Ruud Gullit and Marco van Basten; but the heart of the club was Paolo Maldini, Alessandro Costacurta, Franco Baresi and Demetrio Albertini. There are exceptions, such as the Arsenal Invincibles of 2003-04, but I would argue that is not the rule.*

*Look at the leaders in the major leagues around Europe: Barcelona have used 22 players and 15, or 68 per cent, are Spanish; Juventus have used 27 players and 63 per cent are Italian; United have used 25 players and 52 per cent are British; while Bayern Munich have used 25 players and 45.4 per cent are German.*

*Surely the penny must be dropping that the path to long-term success requires a core of players developed within the club that provides stability? Maybe the introduction of UEFA and the Premier League's Financial Fair Play rules will demonstrate to clubs that you cannot always be spending £35million on a player to fill a gap.*

*The Premier League's insistence on leaving eight slots free in 25-man squads for home grown players is a step in the right direction because British football needs to do all it can with the law to encourage its own. And maybe clubs will recognise that building a British core to their team is in their interest because they will see how fragile a club it can be with players who don't have long-term ties. Maybe we are witnessing a return to clubs based on more organic values.*

*Otherwise we risk seeing an ever-decreasing number of British players as clubs opt for what seems like a cheaper and quicker fix."*

(Mail Online, Saturday, Apr 13, 2013)

In direct response to this kind of serious situation, many individual clubs, the Premier League, the Football Association, the Professional Footballers Association and a host of other stakeholder organisations have already taken a number of positive steps to establish improved systems that are more supportive of the long-term development of young players. One of the most ambitious and far reaching programmes to be introduced recently is the Elite Player Performance Plan (EPPP), a youth development scheme initiated by the Premier League. With the overarching aim of boosting the potential for more home grown players to break into first team football, the main focus of the EPPP is to give clubs greater access to players so that they can have more time to coach and prepare them effectively for a career in the Premier League. Importantly, this also includes the introduction of more robust educational and career support programmes, to offer a more holistic approach to player development.

The EPPP is a welcome initiative and I definitely support its long-term goals. In fact, in my opinion, Liverpool FC was already implementing most of these new initiatives before it was introduced, so the club has generally been somewhat ahead of the game. The main areas of change I see are the day release programmes, whereby all players are given the opportunity to come in for extra work in the afternoons. These are technically based sessions, so they all add up on the Player Performance Clock and are documented in their hours of practice.

Another positive advancement has been the introduction of the Barclays Under-21 Premier League, an innovation that had been previously recommended for several years by many leading names in the game. The fixtures are scheduled to not clash with first team matches. This means that any young players who are already in the senior squad but do not get selected to play, can still get a competitive game with the Under-21s. Amongst other benefits, this new competition gives the trainees more breathing space after the age of eighteen and provides a better environment to help them with their transition from the Academy to the Premier League.

The Football Association's long awaited opening of St. Georges Park, as a purpose-designed, headquarters for the England squad and a central facility for national coaching and player development, is a sound concept; and in time it might well prove to be a success.

However, my own view is that as well as paying attention to the top tier, we also need to do a lot more right down at the basic, grassroots community level.

Footballers from my generation and earlier all have happy memories of groups of kids going to the park, or anywhere else with a bit of space, putting down coats as goal posts and playing matches that sometimes went on until way after dark. There were no coaches, no adults, no referee, no formal organisation and no strict rules: just a bunch of kids having fun. By the very nature of their spontaneity, those impromptu matches encouraged players to use their imagination and be creative. Nobody would be telling us how to play; we just played! We copied fancy moves that we'd seen our heroes do on TV. Or we invented new tricks and tried different ways to dribble past an opponent. In essence, we learned how to play the game by enjoying ourselves.

Sadly, those carefree days of epic matches in the park have long gone. In modern society, most parents are not comfortable with letting their children stay out alone for any length of time because of the fear of security risks, regardless of where they live. Perhaps the football authorities, along with property developers and local councils, should consider takings steps to address that unfortunate situation. How about opening 'Safe Soccer' community centres around the country, where parents could drop off their kids for a few hours and collect them later? These locations would not offer any formal coaching or controlled games, just pitches for the kids to play on. But they would employ suitably qualified personnel to ensure the safe and secure environment that parents quite rightly demand. It happens already with swimming pools, where kids can just go along and have fun in the water while lifeguards keep an eye on them. So, why not similar centres for football?

Although it somehow tends to slip under the public radar more than most of the other challenges the game faces today, I personally believe that the most pressing issue for football to deal with right now is how we can improve the way Premier League clubs prepare young players for the inevitable reality that the vast majority of them will be released by the age of eighteen.

Since academies are attempting to produce players who are capable of eventually graduating into the first team, they are obviously obliged to encourage self-confidence and instil self-belief into their charges. Young footballers must believe 100% that they can make it to the top, if they are to stand any chance at all of doing so. That being the case, it is inevitable that any young players who rise successfully up through the ranks of the academy system will automatically aspire to sign a professional contract and play first team football. As part of a natural process, they start to believe that their football dream is going to come true.

And yet statistics show quite clearly that only an extremely small minority of those trainees will ever enjoy the ecstasy of achieving their goal.

The rest will be released and forced to endure the heartbreaking repercussions of shattered dreams.

A few resilient youngsters can take being released in their stride, find a new avenue to go down and continue happily on their journey.

*Opposite: Robbie Fowler giving 100% effort*

The majority of released players find it to be a difficult and stressful situation, but they manage to bounce back and build a new life.

However, the remaining unfortunate souls find the sense of rejection to be far too traumatic and suffer a variety of negative after-effects ranging from low self-esteem to dropping completely out of the game, to alcohol or drug dependency problems. Very sadly, in the extreme worst-case scenario, an alarming number of young, former footballers find themselves on the wrong side of the law and in jail.

So the unenviable catch-22 situation that football finds itself in today is, how do you prepare young people for success as first team players but, at the same time, also prepare them for the 'failure' of being released?

For us at Liverpool Football Club that process starts at the very beginning, as soon as the kids join the Academy. Mindful of the fact that less than 1% of the children that play football in England are going to go on to become a professional footballer but 100% of them will have a role to fulfil in society, we focus on developing well-rounded individuals. To accommodate that philosophy, the fundamental culture of our coaching is to teach, train and win, in that order.

When working with the younger children our priority is to provide them with a platform to show off their potential and learn new skills and techniques in a fun, inclusive and safe environment. It is very important that while the kids are learning the game and keeping fit and healthy, they are also enjoying themselves. We know that if we see plenty of smiling faces, then we are doing a good job.

The long-term aim of our coaches is to not only develop the players' abilities on the pitch but also to inspire them off the pitch, by introducing them to a positive experience that will help shape their development into young adults. We want to give them personal skills that they can use for the rest of their lives, either in or out of the game.

In essence, the development of footballers is important but the development of people is paramount.

To ensure delivery of this more holistic approach, Liverpool Football Club has established a dedicated Education and Welfare Programme, which monitors the welfare and academic progression of the players from the Elite Development Squad, the under-18s and the under-9 to under-16 schoolboys.

The current head of the programme and Academy Manager is Phil Roscoe, a man with valuable experience related to this field. Prior to his appointment, Phil had spent six years as a lecturer in sport development and fitness at a further education college in Merseyside, plus he has also been coaching within academy youth football for over fourteen years, spending the last seven at the LFC Academy developing various age groups. Phil describes the role and aims of the programme as follows:

*"Within the Academy we provide a very structured and focused programme which not only gives players the best chance possible to progress within the football industry but also educationally as individuals. This is achieved on a post-16 level by providing the players with an opportunity to develop academically and vocationally, by undertaking educational programmes such as A-level, BTEC, NVQ and key skills. The players will also take part in external qualifications, which will provide a mechanism for them to improve their individual skills such as communication, organisation and leadership. Within the U9-U16 age group programme I monitor the welfare and educational progression of each boy through regular correspondence with their schools, parents and age-group coaches. This excellent and continually developing relationship allows each registered player at our Academy the best chance to progress as a player and improve within their schooling. This also allows the players from a very early age to identify the expected educational and behavioural traits needed to develop as a Liverpool player and achieve their maximum potential within their school environment."*

Something that I have learned from chatting with Clive Cook, who is the Education and Welfare Officer, is that no matter how much work and preparation goes into preparing players for the prospect of being released, how well they handle the situation will ultimately depend primarily on their own mental strength.

There have been cases where released players have declined to accept offers of trials at other clubs, not because they didn't want to play anywhere else, but rather because they were just in too much of a state of depressed shock to think clearly. Under those circumstances Clive can allow the individual as much time as is available to think about it, but will then at some point need to adopt a more blunt approach and remind the player that the clock is running down on his options. If you miss this second chance then there might not be any more coming along!

The longer a released player takes to decide what to do next, the more difficult it becomes to move forward again. Liverpool Footbal Club makes a point of keeping in touch with all its released players and continue to offer support to those who need assistance. But, as Clive has pointed out to me, the club can only do so much; after that it is up to each person to take charge. Unfortunately, quite a few of them break contact and just try to disappear; perhaps due to their dejected state of mind, resentment, frustration and even embarrassment.

At the end of the day, it is all down to the mentality of the individual.

This is something I can directly relate to, because Steve Heighway gave me an opportunity, a second chance if you like. He let me go as a player but then offered me a role as a coach. Once he'd taken that step, there was nothing else he could do. From that point on, it was entirely down to me to take it or to leave it. Fortunately, even though at the time it was not really what I wanted, I did accept that second chance. And I did give it my best shot!

As well as working hard to quickly learn how to do a good job in my new coaching position, I also made a pact with myself to carry on playing with the same determination and enthusiasm that I had always shown at Liverpool. So, when I went to play non-league football at Burscough, I applied myself 100% to performing at the highest possible level I could reach in that environment.

Victoria Park might have been a million miles away from Anfield in terms of prestige and glamour, but because I continued to push myself and maintained all the same high standards I had been taught at Liverpool, my quality shone through and I was eventually rewarded with trials at Dundee in the Scottish Premier League.

It seems to me that not all released players understand that football trials are called trials for a very good reason – players are examined and scrutinised by a jury of experts who will eventually give a verdict that will officially seal their fate. They will either be found guilty of lacking ability and commitment or they will be given their freedom to start a career at a new club.

Unfortunately, I have come across certain young players who didn't understand that basic fact. They thought that being invited to trials by what they perceived to be a lower echelon club meant it was almost a formality that they would be signed. That is a huge error! It doesn't matter where you are going, you will still be inspected in minute detail and compared to the best players already in that team. So there is no room whatsoever for complacency, particularly regarding effort and attitude.

And that same philosophy still applies if you do succeed and get signed on. In fact more so! When Dundee offered me a professional contract I was absolutely thrilled, but I didn't let myself get too carried away by the excitement. Getting into a squad is a lot easier than getting a starting place on the first team. Once again, I have noticed that some academy players who have been released and then picked up by other clubs often underestimate the challenge that still awaits them. Even though you might have been a solid player at a Premier League academy and are now moving to a Championship side, there is no guarantee at all that life is going to be any easier for you. On the contrary, it will definitely get a lot tougher. You will now have to battle with two or three other players, probably all a lot more established than you, for that one position. And their livelihood absolutely depends on it, so they are not going to just step out of the way for you. You must fight hard to win a place in the team and you have to work even harder to earn the right to keep it.

That crucial message was driven home forcefully to me time and time again when I started training with the Dundee first team squad. I was a new boy amongst a band of seasoned professional men and I had to battle for every single scrap of a chance.

There are of course some great examples of players who have dropped down from Premier League academies and then gone on to have happy careers in the lower leagues, with some even climbing back up into the top flight. So any released player who wants to keep playing football should feel encouraged about the opportunities and possibilities that exist. Just never lose sight of what you have to do to get there – and to stay there!

Coaching has provided me with a great career and a very enjoyable life, so I can highly recommend it to anybody. In fact I would advise all footballers, including the ones who make it to the top, to acquire as many coaching qualifications as they can. All players need to prepare themselves for 'life after playing' – which one day will arrive just as surely as night follows day, whether it be by choice through retirement or by necessity through injury or ill-health.

The Professional Footballers Association has a special Coaching Department whose primary role is to prepare PFA members for a secondary career within the professional game, often in coaching but also management. With statistics showing that over 70% of the members express a desire to stay in football when their playing days are over, it is no surprise that the

PFA advises players 'to search out these qualifications while you are still playing, not when your career is over or coming to an end'.

To make it easier for players, both young and not so young, to plan ahead, I'd like to see the introduction of more careers guidance into football. There is even scope for the production of some form of careers manual, to allow easy reference to the kind of jobs that are available in the game. Beyond being a player or a coach, there seems to be a huge amount of other career avenues open to anybody who has a passion for football. Straight off the top of my head I can think of physiotherapy, fitness training, sports science, journalism, TV and other media, PR, marketing, IT, hospitality, turf management and on and on. The full list of potential careers must be immense.

The essential point for injured or released players is that it is possible to stay in the game, follow your passion and still enjoy a very rewarding career in football. There are lots of niche opportunities out there, you just need to get out and find the right one for you.

**Geoff & Cheryl Yates:** 'Parents of Academy players need to be as dedicated as their sons. Our social life became Mike's life; our free time became Mike's time. You have to be prepared to sacrifice as much as the kids. You have to live with all their disappointments as well. It's a hard road for everybody. Mike's football journey started at the age of seven; and between those early days and his YTS years there were an awful lot of ups and downs. Liverpool is a fantastic club and it was all an amazing experience for him. By a twist of fate, he found himself in an age group that contained an incredible amount of talent. It was a truly exceptional team and they played superb football. There can be few generations that will ever have two players like Steven Gerrard and Michael Owen developing at the same time. It was a thrill for Mike to be an important part of that outstanding period.

If a parent was to ask us today for advice about what club a seven year-old should sign for, we would highly recommend Liverpool without hesitation. However, we would suggest they also consider going to a lesser club, where a boy might have a better chance to shine.'

# Michael Kinsella
*Founder of OnSide*

Football needs to clean up its act by doing more to look after the thousands of young players who get released by clubs each year.

I know what I'm talking about. I've lived the life of the young football apprentice and suffered the consequences of being released. I've been involved in crime and paid the penalty with jail sentences in Spain, Holland and England. I've witnessed my own brother almost slide down the cracks after being released by Everton and then forced out of the game by injury. While I was in jail, I finally got the proper education I'd never been given before; and I devoted myself to unearthing the facts about what really happens to rejected footballers like my brother. Since being released, I have personally met hundreds of former players who desperately need help.

XPro, a charity representing ex-professional footballers, estimates that only 4% of players who sign on as Scholars at age sixteen are still playing with professional clubs at eighteen. Perhaps even more alarmingly, only 2% of those who sign professional contracts are still in the game at twenty-one. A 98% dropout rate! What can they do instead of playing football? Where do they go? What happens to them?

Right now there are 147 ex-professional players in prison; and all but four of them are in for selling drugs. Plus there are another 189 in the young offenders system. That has to be way too many!

Starting OnSide was my way to try to help these kids have a better chance at making a new life for themselves; by giving them some kind of an education, teaching them a trade or somehow keeping them in the game.

As a country we need to be much more aware of what is going on. And we need to do something about it. I love football but it's got a massive problem concerning released players; and it has a massive responsibility to take care better care of these kids. I'll never leave this issue alone. I'll keep knocking on all the doors until the right messages reach the right people. And I'll keep going until they do something worthwhile and introduce a support system that really works.

The game has got to stand up and be counted.

**3/Sport/Football**

THE INDEPENDENT
MONDAY 11 FEBRUARY 2013

# SAFETY NET FOR GAME'S LOST SOULS

Michael Kinsella (right) and brother Gerard in Liverpool
MIKE POLOWAY/UNP

## Ex-con Michael Kinsella, once a Liverpool hopeful, has launched a scheme to keep former players from drug crime, writes **Simon Hart**

Michael Kinsella took a stroll down Memory Lane last month when he stepped inside Anfield for the first time since his days as a promising young goalkeeper with Liverpool Schoolboys in the early Nineties. The 35-year-old also visited Melwood, Liverpool's training ground, where he met Jamie Carragher (right), an acquaintance since they turned out for the same Sunday league team in their early teens. They were together not to discuss old times, though, but because of Carragher's support for a project Kinsella is putting in place to provide a safety net for some of the lost souls discarded by football's dream factory.

With the backing of the former players' charity XPro, Kinsella has established Onside (On Sport Intervention Development and Education), a scheme to combine educational courses with football training for those who fall out of the game. "It is just about mentoring them and having something there for them for when they drop out," explains Kinsella, who knows only too well the pitfalls that can await a young man cast through football's exit door.

Kinsella trained with Liverpool and had spells with Bury and Tranmere Rovers but got no closer to the big time than a pre-season outing with the Birkenhead club before, with his hopes "fizzled", he became a drug dealer. "I got disheartened, had a few little chances again where I got offered contracts but my head was gone," he remembers.

Kinsella saw the inside of jail cells in Spain and the Netherlands, and in 2007 earned a 10-year sentence for his involvement with a Merseyside drugs ring. "I've lived the two lives and you live the same life: you go and have everything you want. That is why it is so easy to fall into. The only thing is the bizzies [police] are only going to come for you for one of the things."

According to Kinsella, there are 129 ex-players currently in prison, all but four serving time for drugs offences – including Michael Branch, the former Everton and Wolves forward jailed for seven years in November. It is a depressingly well-trodden path – with Branch the highest-profile victim since Mark Ward, another former Everton player – and no surprise at all to Kinsella.

"Another one has just been arrested who played with Jamie Carragher and

Michael Owen when they won the FA Youth Cup. I am trying to help lads now who have played international football, who are selling drugs. They haven't got a club. I can't name them but I am trying to help them.

"Young lads sign a decent two-year contract on one or two grand a week [but then] come out of football, get an injury and think, 'That's the life I wanted, I want a car', and there's only one other way they know how to do it."

Kinsella's goal is to help to provide an alternative. "My gran and granddad died while I was in prison. It changes your mindset and that's what I want to show to people – you don't have to do [crime] to have a life."

He was let out of prison each day for six months before his release late last year to work on the Onside project and has wasted no time, setting up an office at Liverpool Hope University and attracting interest from prospective partners, including Virtual Learning UK, with whom he also wants to provide online courses for prisoners. There are plans too for a football-based pilot course for the unemployed with Liverpool City Council.

Kinsella's determination to make a difference has been cemented by his success in helping his younger brother, Gerard, to rebuild his career. After rejection at 19 by Everton, the club

who nurtured his talent from the age of seven, Gerard went to Plymouth with hopes of earning a contract but suffered a cartilage injury and ended up with nothing. "It kills you. It happened so quickly," the 21-year-old, now at Fleetwood Town, says of rejection and the loss of the focus that football had provided.

Gerard concedes that he came "very close" to stepping into a world of crime, but for his brother's intervention. "I heard he was in and out of cars with some of the lads in our area, the local drug dealers. I found out about it, made a few phone calls and told them to stay away," explains Michael, who, though in prison at the time, arranged for an old friend to help his younger brother. "He put Gerard on a bricklaying course. After that he did a personal trainer diploma. Then he started training again and went on a trial for Fleetwood and signed a two-year deal."

The elder Kinsella's conviction – shared with XPro's founder Geoff Scott, a former Stoke City and England Under-21 defender – is that football clubs are failing to prepare their youngsters for a life outside the sport. He did 17 different courses in prison and speaks about education with all the zeal of a convert. "If you sign a scholarship at a football club you've

## Jamie Carragher, an old Sunday league team acquaintance, supports the project

missed vital years of getting an apprenticeship – be it as a joiner, in construction, plumbing, whatever it is."

Onside's planned first intake of 25 will train and play friendly matches, with the aim of finding students a route back into the game – but, crucially, they will earn the qualifications they did not gain as teenagers. Gerard Kinsella, recalling his Everton experience, explains: "One day a week we went to a college and did a Sport BTEC but nobody was interested. We were still in that bubble thinking we were going to be footballers."

The cold statistics tell otherwise. XPro estimates that only 4 per cent of players who sign on as scholars at 16 are still playing with professional clubs at 18; moreover, only 2 per cent who sign professional contracts are still in the game aged 21. Closer to home, Kinsella recalls how 13 members of his Liverpool Schoolboys squad joined clubs but only two had prolonged careers in the game, while six went to prison. Hence the interest from his old pal Carragher, who was interviewed by the BBC about Onside last week. "He's supportive because he knows it should be there," Kinsella adds. "It wouldn't get to the point where so many people were interested if it were not needed."

# Top Ten Tips for Young Players

### 1. Enjoy your football

Play as often as you can, practice as much as you can and always try to have fun. You don't know it yet but you are creating memories that will stay with you for the rest of your life. So try to enjoy yourself at all times.

### 2. Listen to your coaches

They hold the keys to your overall development, so always pay careful attention to what they tell you. Your coaches know a lot about football, so learn from them. Don't be afraid to ask questions .... I know you want to!

### 3. Take criticism the right way

The person criticising you is doing it because they see potential in you and want you to be the best you can be, not because they don't like you. Criticism can be constructive, so accept it whether you like it or not!

### 4. Always give 100% effort

Don't commit the crime of one day having to say 'if only I had tried harder'. You will gain great respect by working hard. And later in life, whatever the outcome, at least you will know that you gave it everything.

### 5. Stay positive and mentally strong

Some day you will question yourself and your ability, it's part of the ups and downs of football. The people who succeed are the ones who can handle both the good and bad. Keep moving forward at all times.

### 6. Keep the 3Ds: Discipline, Dedication, Desire

You can have all the talent in the world but without these qualities you are going to fall short in anything you do. But with the 3Ds you can overcome all your challenges and stay on the right path.

### 7. Make the most of every opportunity

No matter what level you play at, you won't be able to play forever. So always grasp your chances with both hands and give it your best shot at all times. One day you will realise just how lucky you are!

Photo courtesy of Robbie Johnson

## 8. Remember who you are, what you are and who you represent

Keep your feet on the ground, stay true to yourself, don't get carried away with things people might say to you. Always be loyal to your family, your friends and your club.

## 9. Educate yourself

You can't play football forever and you must also prepare for the possibility of being released or getting injured. It is essential to have a back-up plan. Work hard in school, learn a trade and get some coaching qualifications.

## 10. Be prepared

Football is a wonderful rollercoaster ride of highs and lows. Be prepared to make it to the top and have to deal with the pressures of being a player. But also be fully prepared for the reality of not making it or something going wrong.

# Richie Partridge

*Physiotherapist at LFC Academy and a Former LFC Trainee and Professional Player*

I don't think I was ever inspired by anyone or anything to become a professional footballer. All my friends and me ever did when we were growing up was to play footy in the park or on the street as much as we could. When I got slightly older it became apparent that I was half decent at playing. And then, when invitations started to come in for trials with top clubs, I started to think how good it would be to play football for a living!! Needless to say, I was absolutely thrilled to be signed on by Liverpool.

I think that in this day and age, with all the glaring publicity involved in the modern game, it is far too easy to forget that superstars like Michael Owen and Steven Gerard, deep down, are just normal lads who enjoy normal things and want their lives to be as normal as possible.

They are extremely fortunate that they have done what every boy dreams of, but it's not luck or talent or ability that has been the key to their success. It is the combination of hard work, dedication, professionalism, commitment and sacrifice that separates the 'very good players' from the 'elite'.

*Opposite: Back row left to right: Steve McManaman, Jamie Carragher, Dominic Matteo, Steven Gerrard; Front row left to right: Michael Owen, David Thompson, Robbie Fowler*

# Jamie Redknapp

*Liverpool FC 1991 – 2001 and Former England International*

It's very scary that many parents today seem to think that being signed on as an apprentice at a football club is not only a guarantee of a good future life for their son, but also for them. Too many mums and dads just see it as a quick ticket to a fancy car, big new house, holidays overseas and a life of luxury. And of course that is the last thing any young player needs. The support of a well-grounded family is essential for any youngster to successfully work his way through the challenges of the system. All lads need good, open, honest advice to help them stay on track; and footballers more than most because of the glamour of the game.

I was lucky in that regard because I had a dad who'd played professionally and was a manager, so he knew exactly how to handle me. When I was about eighteen, my family all went to Spain on holiday together in the summer. By then I'd played for Liverpool Reserves and had been knocking on the door of the first team; so I naturally felt good about myself and the way my career was going. I wasn't a flash kid and I don't think I actually said or did anything that was particularly out of order, but my dad saw something developing in me that he didn't like. So, out of the blue, he asked me who did I think I was and reminded me that I hadn't done anything yet other than play for the reserves. Then he finished off with, 'When I look at you it makes me think you've still got a long way to go, so you'd better get your head down and keep working hard'. I didn't say a word back to him, but the next day I got up early and went for a run. And I repeated that every day for the rest of the holiday. After starting the new season with a more focused sense of purpose I soon earned myself a regular place in the first team.

We all need somebody to keep us in check and provide the right kind of motivation, whatever we do in life.

# Top Ten Tips for Parents of Young Players

## 1. Support
Parental support is an essential component of any young player's development. They need your backing and guidance through both the good times and the bad. Be there for them, talk to them and, most of all, listen to them!

## 2. Encourage
The more encouragement young players get the better. But try not to overstep the mark and start pushing them into doing things. Encourage them to practice more but don't force them – they have to want it for themselves.

## 3. Observe
It is vital that all parents keep a careful watch on their children under any circumstances, but it is especially true for young footballers. Be sure to monitor their eating and sleeping habits and look out for any health issues.

## 4. Be honest
It is good to praise them whenever possible for their effort and improvement, both on and off the pitch, but do not fall into the trap of telling them they have performed well when they have not. They need to know where they stand.

## 5. Promote enjoyment
Keep a regular check on whether they are enjoying their football and if they aren't, ask them why. Remind them that they should be enjoying themselves. It's good for them to relax and play with a smile on their faces.

## 6. Leave the coaching to the coaches
One coaching session per day is enough, so they don't need another one in the car on the way home. Enjoy chatting with them about what took place during the session but try to avoid giving opinions.

## 7. Give them responsibility
At the end of the day, all young players need to be able to take care of

themselves. So encourage them from an early age to look after their own kit, clean their own boots, pack their own bag and be ready on time.

## 8. Teach them to ask questions
Coaching sessions are full of valuable information and if players are unsure about anything they should ask. The ability to ask questions is a strength, not a weakness. Tell them to ask how they can improve.

## 9. Develop independence
Encourage them to be themselves at all times. Help them to understand the value of being your own person, capable of making your own decisions based on your own values. Tell them to 'Dare to be different!'

## 10. Be prepared
You will have to make many sacrifices during their journey and you will share all their ups and downs. Be prepared for when they make it; but also be prepared for when they don't. They'll need your support whatever happens!

# Philly Carragher
Jamie Carragher's Dad

Dads of academy players should be really careful what they say to their sons and about their sons. Over the years I've seen too many examples where the dad has gone round telling everybody that his kid is going to make it and play for Liverpool; and then of course the exact opposite happens and the poor lad is released early. There is enough pressure on the players already without parents piling any more on them like that. It's not right. It's a long journey and the closer the player gets to the top then the tougher it becomes. If you build a lad's hopes up too much and he gets let go, it can be totally soul destroying. Just let the kid enjoy himself and if he's got what it takes he will make it in the end.

Having said that, I always felt that our James had a good chance to break through, to some level anyway. He stood out head and shoulders above other lads. I had good enough knowledge to be confident that he was going to be alright. I didn't know whether it'd be at Liverpool or not, but I knew he was going to play at a decent standard. But I always kept that opinion to myself, I didn't go around talking about it or telling him what I thought.

You can identify the exceptional players from the age of ten. It's easy to recognize that the Gerrards, Rooneys and Bales are going to make it. You can see that from an early age, provided of course they stay on the right track.

You don't need scouts to spot the best young players in the country; they are already on the radar. It's the regular lads, the ones who will eventually develop into the average Premier League, or lower league, players, who need the most support.

And today especially, you have to be a really top class player to break into the first team at a club like Liverpool. If you just look back to the locally born strikers who've made it in the modern game – Rush, Fowler, Owen – they were truly exceptional talents. It's very hard for today's local players to even get close to that standard. James knew what he wanted and he had the drive to push himself hard enough to achieve it. Any player needs that extra bit of 'bottle' to succeed and stay at the top. And that can't be coached! Fortunately my lad has plenty of it and that is the main reason why he has played over 700 games for Liverpool.

James' son, also James, has followed in his dad's footsteps, so I am happy to now have my grandson at the LFC Academy. But the system in place today in the Premier League makes it difficult for any young local lad to make it all the way to the first team level. The Academy is doing a good job and the coaching is working very well, but the way the game operates as a business means that the opportunities for young players have been reduced.

At least at Liverpool today the Academy lads can feel encouraged by the fact that Brendan Rodgers has already proved that he'll give young players a chance if they have earned it. For the first time in some years, the kids have real hope of breaking through. They now have a good reason to believe that if they work hard enough they'll be rewarded with an opportunity to prove themselves at the top. That has got be very positive for all of them and for the club. It boosts morale for everybody.

Young James is ten now and he goes to the Academy on Tuesday, Thursday and Friday afternoons, Saturday mornings and plays a match on Sunday. At the same age, James went to Vernon Sangster on a Monday night and that was that. So the system is a lot more intense these days. The young lad has inherited good genes from his dad and he's got a great engine, so he gets around the pitch well. Plus he's got an opportunity at the LFC Academy, just like all the other kids. So, you never know, he might make a decent player one day. But for me, by far the most important thing is that he enjoys his football and gets a good life.

I like it when people say that our James is a good footballer, but I love it when they say he's a good man. My own mates like him and they enjoy having him around. As a dad, that's what really makes me feel proud!

*Jamie Carragher about to start his last game for Liverpool, with son James and daughter Mia*

**LFC in My Life**

Apart from the three years between 1999 and 2002, when I was playing for Dundee and had a short spell in non-league football, I have spent my whole life since the age of eight at Liverpool Football Club, either as a player or a coach. This is a record that I am extremely proud of and I consider myself very fortunate and privileged to have lived and breathed the Liverpool Way for almost twenty-five years.

To put my amazing experience at Liverpool into perspective, it is worth noting that I have played or worked under eight different managers: Kenny Dalglish (twice), Ronnie Moran, Graeme Souness, Roy Evans, Gerrard Houllier, Rafa Benitez, Roy Hodgson and Brendan Rodgers.

And during my time at the club we have won twelve major trophies:

1987/88 – League Champions
1988/89 – FA Cup Winners
1989/90 – League Champions
1991/92 – FA Cup Winners
1994/95 – League Cup Winners
2000/01 – FA Cup Winners
2000/01 – League Cup Winners
2000/01 – UEFA Cup Winners
2002/03 – League Cup Winners
2004/05 – European Champions League Winners
2005/06 – FA Cup Winners
2011/12 – League Cup Winners

Add to that the long list of great players, past and present, that I have been privileged to encounter along the way, and it is glaringly obvious why I have enjoyed my career at Liverpool so immensely.

I am passionate about the work I do at Liverpool today because of everything that the club has done for me in my life.

Destiny blessed me with parents who were devoted to bringing me up the right way. From the early days of, 'brush your teeth, comb your hair, tidy up after yourself, be polite, respect people's property, do things properly', right through to advising me about my career and financial matters, my mum and dad have been a bedrock of support for me.

In addition to my biological family, I was also raised by my football family at Liverpool. And there can be no doubt that the club has played a huge role in making me the man that I am today. When I first started at the Centre of Excellence, I quickly found myself on the receiving end of the sort of upbringing I was already getting at home: 'get here on time, pay attention, tuck your shirt in, zip up your tracksuit, look the part, open the door for your seniors, do it right'. All of my mentors at home and at the club were on the same page, consistently sending me the same messages and constantly reminding me about the massive importance of having personal pride and self-respect.

So my character was shaped by a set of high standards from an early age. And that provided a great grounding for me, not only as a player and a coach, but also as a person. Thanks to the many good people who have influenced my development, especially Mum and Dad and my coaches – notably Steve Heighway, Ronnie Moran, Sammy Lee, Hughie McAuley, Dave Shannon and Frank Skelly – I have been given every opportunity to build a happy and successful life for myself.

Although I didn't make it as a professional player at Liverpool, I am still here at the club I love and still working in the game I love. Obviously the financial rewards are hugely different when you are a coach and not a player, so I am fortunate that my wife Nikki has a good job that provides a second income. Between our two salaries, we have been able to afford a nice home and a comfortable lifestyle

My life is not about making money; it's more about sharing my experience and knowledge with others to help give them a chance to have a good life, in and out of the game. That in itself is very rewarding.

Regardless of the size of my pay cheque, my motivation is still the badge and what it has done for me. Throughout my entire career, even when I've found myself in situations that I didn't particularly like, my passion for this football club has driven me on. I never want to let anybody down, least of all myself, so I do whatever I'm asked to do and I do it to the best of my ability. My mentality is always that there is a job to be done and it needs to be done properly because this is Liverpool Football Club, and that's the only way we do things here.

My family is unquestionably the most important part of my life and I love spending time around my wife and daughter. Throughout our marriage Nikki has been very supportive of everything I do. She understands my passion for Liverpool and makes allowances for me anytime that I get a bit too carried away with my work. She also knows

that I can be too laid back sometimes, so she is constantly ready to push me to do things that I might otherwise just let slip. Nikki has taught me a lot. We make a good team.

Now that I am a dad myself, I am eternally grateful to my parents because the way they raised my brother, my sister and me could be a blueprint for bringing up any child. Devon now benefits from many of the parenting skills that I have inherited from them.

The way I handle myself as a father has also been influenced by the people skills that football has given me. Even my trips to places like Armenia and South Africa, which exposed me to the realities of human suffering, have helped in a big way, by making me understand what is really important in life. At a simpler level, I often find myself passing on the same snippets of advice I learned as a kid from my coaches. If Devon is ever nervous before some big event, I will automatically quote Steve Heighway: 'That's good. It shows you care'.

It's no coincidence that Liverpool Football Club has a family atmosphere about it; and, like all closely-knit families, people remain an important part of the community even after they have moved on. There is a kind of unwritten law, 'Once a member of the Liverpool family, always a member', and everybody does their best to look after each other.

While producing this book I have experienced some great examples of this mutual respect and support; perhaps none more so than when I first re-connected with Jamie Redknapp. Here is a player who reached the very top in the game and then went on to build a new and very successful career in the media, while I was just one of the young lads who'd cleaned his boots and played a couple of reserve games with him, and now I needed to ask him a favour. I was a bit nervous about calling him because I hadn't spoken to Jamie for many, many years; but the minute I made contact and asked if he could do an interview for the book, he was immediately positive: 'Of course I can help you Yatesy, what do you want me to do?'

The Liverpool Way lives on in the Redknapp household.

I find it reassuring that my ardent passion for LFC, like my commitment to its success, is founded on the same core values that have formed the foundation of the club for many decades, long before I was even born. Many people believe that these strong traditions date back to

*Opposite: Brendan Rodgers talking to the skipper*

the huge influence of Bill Shankly in the early 1960s, while others claim that Liverpool's rich heritage might have commenced even earlier.

I recently watched an excellent video on LFC TV about Elisha Scott, the legendary Liverpool goalkeeper from 1912 to 1934, who still holds the record as our longest-serving player. He was a major part of the back-to-back Championship winning teams of 1922 and 1923, missing just three games of the first title and none in the second. In my opinion, the documentary seems to suggest that this was the era when the Liverpool Way really first started, with Shankly later building upon that outdated but still solid foundation to modernise the structure when he arrived in 1959. Whatever the case may be, there is no doubt that the values we adhere to today are all directly connected to the club's early origins. I am not naïve enough to think that things in life don't change in time – and there is obviously always some new and different way of doing things - but the essential messages are the same now as they were way back then.

When Elisha Scott retired as a player he returned to his home in Ireland and became an extremely successful manager. By implementing his own version of the Liverpool Way at Belfast Celtic, Scott won ten Irish League titles, six Irish Cups, three City Cups, eight Gold Cups and five County Antrim Shields. Quite a legacy!

In recent times, Karl Robinson has also openly advocated the benefits of taking the Liverpool Way values with you to a new club. Karl and I were working together at the Academy when one day he turned around and took me by surprise by boldly announcing: 'I'm going to leave Liverpool and within five years I can see myself being a manager somewhere.' To his enormous credit, today he is the highly regarded manager of MK Dons and has the distinction of being the youngest ever manager in the Football League when he was appointed at age thirty. Karl has already done a fantastic job with the Dons and he often refers to lessons and messages he learned from Steve Heighway.

As somebody who has himself suffered the experience of being rejected as a player, Karl Robinson is an outstanding role model for any youngsters who don't manage to break through into the first team level and are released. He is living proof that there is life after rejection and plenty of scope in the game to turn a negative into a positive. Karl is a shining example of what can be achieved if you put your mind to it.

*Opposite below: Shankly the legend and his adoring fans*

LIVERPOOL
SUAREZ
LIVERPOOL
LIVERPOOL
LIVERPOOL FC
YOU'LL NEVER
ALONE
FC
ALONE
L.F.C.
LIVERPOOL FC
8
LIVERPOOL FC
EST. 1892

Regarding my own future, even though I can't predict where my life in football will eventually take me, I can certainly prepare myself for all the possibilities and try to leave nothing to chance. The really exciting thing for me is that my career is still developing. Unlike a player who has to start planning for retirement when he reaches his thirties, I still have my best and most productive years ahead of me. At age thirty-four, I have already built up lots of experience in a wide range of areas. I have coached young players and coaches, I've been involved in the business side of the game, I've worked on developing coaching programmes and now I'm promoting and delivering them all around the world. With that kind of broad-based knowledge, I could fill several different roles in the game.

But coaching is still my first love. Throughout my entire career at Liverpool, no matter what department I have been working with, I have always tried to keep improving my coaching qualifications. It is important for me that I stay in touch with what's going on in football and keep up to speed with any new coaching techniques or developments in the game.

I am currently doing my A licence. My long-term goal is to complete my Tutor's Licence which, when completed, will qualify me to coach other coaches. I would also love to mentor or advise young players who are in the system, coaching youth players really appeals to me, to have an impact on young people not just on the pitch but off it, is something that I really relate to. I consider myself as a positive role model and now that I am getting on a bit I have lots of experience to offer! While there is no such plan right now, I would never discount the possibility that I will one day get back into full-time coaching here at Liverpool.

Who knows what might happen in a few years time?

Whatever path my current job takes me down, I will continue to get as many qualifications as I can along the way. I love football and I'd like to think that I would be working in the game in some capacity for the rest of my life. I even like the idea of getting involved in TV coverage of football. In fact I would really love the opportunity to have a go at being a pundit, the guy who gives opinions on the game alongside the commentator. That is something that I think I could do well and the role really appeals to me.

It is interesting that any time I stop to think about my future, the old words of wisdom from Tommy Galvin, my first mentor in football, keep ringing in my ears:

'Just stay in the game Michael, just stay in the game.'

# Steve Heighway

*Liverpool FC and Republic of Ireland 1970 – 1981; Director LFC Academy 1998 - 2007*

Mike Yates was always a good player. He was a good player in a very good group, some of who went on to achieve great things. Others, while not reaching the giddy heights of stardom, have had long and successful careers. For the rest, well, it gradually became clear that it simply was not going to happen for them. This realisation comes sooner or later and depends largely on the self-awareness of the individual and his ability to see things the way they really are.

Nobody knew how far Mike would go in the game. Nobody had the genius to see Mike as a potential coach. He gave the playing career every chance and, as with so many young players, you cannot chase the game forever. For the really talented players, the game chases them. So, when it seemed to me that his playing days were coming to an end, it became a question of how could we return him to 'our' system in a mutually beneficial way. I knew Mike and knew his parents and family background. I knew he was trustworthy and of good character. He was always a good communicator and it seemed to me that coming back into the LFC family and coaching kids would suit him. It delights me to see him doing well and forging a successful career. I sincerely hope he can look back and realise how fulfilling a career coaching can be.

The issue of boys not fulfilling their potential and failing to realise their dreams is something that always weighs heavy on my mind. I think that the game needs to maintain a very careful balance between education and football for the gifted, post-16 age group players when they leave school to join a pro club full-time.

Many teachers have often been highly critical of the clubs for 'taking boys in and casting them on the scrap-heap two years later'. This analysis always irked me.

In all sports young athletes make huge sacrifices in their attempts to reach the top, and they do so in the knowledge that few of them will actually make it. For some people it is always football's fault when boys fall short. To label them as failures is a cruel tag and clearly implies firstly that the game has failed them and secondly that they would have been better off not embarking on the journey in the first place. Surely they deserve a better epitaph than, 'Here rests a failed footballer.'

In my view the magic must rest in the development programme created for the players, post-16, within the club. Here the key is one of BALANCE and PRIORITIES. A well-conceived programme should succeed on two fronts:

1. Critically, it should prepare elite players who WILL make it, for a life in football.
2. Simultaneously, and magically, it should also prepare those who will not make it for a life after football, perhaps as early as eighteen.

This is a big ask. Clearly, we cannot sacrifice the technical football programme. All players must have the best chance of fulfilling their potential. For top clubs, Premier League players must be the aim. What a tragedy it would be if gifted players were failing because too much time was spent on 'education'. The core of the syllabus therefore must be the technical, tactical and physical preparation for pro football, through a programme of training and match play.

Running parallel to this should be the 'off-field' element of a boy's development and this requires great thought. An enlightened club should provide training in a multitude of areas, including:

*Me, age 12 & Steve Heighway at Anfield*

- communication skills
- relationships
- finance
- sexual health
- driver awareness courses
- dealing with success, failure and disappointment
- self-control
- computer literacy
- dangers of gambling
- media training
- self-sacrifice

We need to understand that for two years minimum the players generally have five days of 'preparation', one match day and one rest day each week. Assuming 2-hour sessions, morning and afternoon, there are at least 20 hours available for planned activity. This is adequate for providing a comprehensive programme to meet all the needs of the young players.

It used to sicken me to hear managers and hard-nosed senior coaches (often ex-players) say that players were spending too much time 'in the classroom'. How sad! How ignorant! Do they not understand the enormous responsibility carried by the 'developers'? Have you ever heard a manager claim responsibility when one of his players gets involved in a nightclub incident, or beats up his girlfriend, or develops a gambling addiction, or cannot express himself in front of a camera? My view is that some managers and coaches are jealous of the fact that players today are better educated than they were – some even lament the passing of the old apprenticeships and the days when players were put through the 'school of hard knocks'.

So, the challenge is to provide a well-balanced, logical and progressive programme of football and personal development. An elite, international player will need a wide array of skills to help him deal with his success. Likewise, a disillusioned 18-year old leaving the game and re-entering the real world will need a wide array of skills to deal with his situation. There must be no 'failures'.

Consider for a moment Steven Gerrard and Michael Yates. Up to age eighteen their experiences were similar. Now, sixteen years on, they both seem very well prepared for their different lives.

Good luck to them both – TWO SUCCESS STORIES!

# The Final Word

From the age of eight, my one and only focus in life was to be a professional footballer at Liverpool Football Club. Nothing else occupied my daily thoughts. Even my nights were dominated by dreams of scoring in front of the Kop.

I went to school because that is what all kids have to do. My attendance record was exemplary, but my mind was usually elsewhere. The clock could never tick over fast enough for me. I was constantly just waiting for the bell to ring, longing to get back to the world of football that I loved so much.

Each season I put my heart and soul into learning as much as I could about how to play the game better. My young brain soaked up technical information and other facts and figures like an eager sponge. I pushed my body to the absolute limits to get fitter, faster and stronger.

My whole life became shaped by football – the way I thought, the way I ate, the way I slept, the way I took care of myself, the way I looked at other people, the way I behaved, even the way I dressed and cut my hair, everything!

Year after year, with each passing age group, I was successfully promoted to the next level. The longer the journey went on, the closer I felt to fulfilling my dream. I knew that I was within touching distance of having the real thing. I was part of the cream of the crop at Liverpool FC. Everybody kept telling us we had a very good team. I was scoring lots of goals and doing my job well; performing confidently alongside some outstanding young players, including two truly exceptional talents, Steven Gerrard and Michael Owen. There was always a big buzz around our squad and I thrived on it.

Regional honours and trials for England added further fuel to an already burning ambition.

As soon as I reached YTS level, my schoolboy heroes suddenly became my workmates. So many Liverpool Legends, genuine giants of the game, were now an everyday part of my life. I regularly rubbed shoulders with icons like Ronnie Moran, Graeme Souness and Roy Evans; I was coached by Steve Heighway, Sammy Lee, Hughie McAuley and Dave Shannon, some of the best in the game; I learned my trade by watching superb role models of the quality of Steve McManaman, Robbie Fowler and Patrick Berger, all working hard in training; and I was even privileged to play in competitive games alongside players of the calibre of John Barnes and Jamie Redknapp.

In essence, I was fully immersed in the world of professional football. And I was there at the highest level.

By the age of sixteen I was included in pre-season training with the first team squad and, but for a tragically timed broken arm, could have been selected for the club's overseas tour to Norway.

By the age of seventeen I was playing for Liverpool Reserves; and absolutely relishing our home matches played at Anfield. Only one more rung of the ladder to climb.

Before I turned eighteen I was a released player. Or less politely stated, I was a reject. The ruthless world of professional football can be brutal.

To spend ten of the most formative, early years of your life being constantly reminded that you are part of an elite group of young players at one of the world's leading football clubs clearly makes you believe that you will one day become a professional and play for the first team. And, quite naturally, the closer you get to attaining that lifelong goal, the more convinced you become that you will eventually make the grade.

So when that inevitable Day of Judgement comes along and you are suddenly sentenced to life as a released academy player, the abrupt change of status from elite to reject can be totally devastating. Football is the most beautiful game in the world, but it always has this incredibly ugly side waiting in the wings for thousands of unsuspecting young players.

As we have seen in an earlier chapter, many released players become totally disillusioned with the game or, even worse, with their life. Having personally experienced the horrendous trauma of rejection myself, I can attest to the deep depths of disappointment and despair that this can cause in a young mind. It was extremely fortunate for me that in the same instant that Liverpool released me as a player, I was given a golden opportunity to continue at the club by switching to coaching. Had it not been for that future hope to cling to, I might well have drowned in a sea of depression like so many other lads. As it was, I still floated around in a daze of shock and confusion for a while, until I finally accepted my destiny and fell into that new role as a coach.

My family and friends definitely played a big part in helping me to stay on the right track by providing plenty of support whenever I needed it. But, when I think back to those dark days immediately after being released, I can now appreciate that I did a lot to help myself battle through the ordeal.

I now understand that I must have had a really strong mentality to cope with that bombshell experience. In fact, my parents have often commented that they don't know how I ever managed to overcome so many unexpected misfortunes that fate shoved in my face throughout my career. So I suppose

I must generally be a mentally tough person to have coped as well as I have done with lots of setbacks that hit me over the years. Thank goodness!

The really good news for me of course was that I did get to play Premier League Football in Scotland for Dundee, and then I was able to return to Liverpool as a coach. And I think I am very fortunate that I am still here today, enjoying an interesting career.

Over the years, I have been asked on numerous occasions why do I personally think that I didn't get offered a professional contract at Liverpool. And, generally speaking, my standard answer has always been very straightforward: 'I gave 100% effort all of the time but, sadly, I just was not good enough. Otherwise I would have made it!'

However, for the purposes of this book, let's consider a few other factors that might possibly have influenced the outcome.

There is one school of thought that I was unlucky to have been born into an era when Liverpool had such an incredibly strong squad in my age bracket. Any Premier League academy would think they'd won the jackpot if they could produce one player every few years of the extraordinary quality of Steven Gerrard or Michael Owen – but Liverpool had both of them in the same year group. Mine! Clearly the standards they set meant we were all being judged against an unusually high benchmark, but I don't buy into the theory that this worked against me. On the contrary, they helped drive us to a higher level and made us better players. I truly loved playing alongside them and I know that I benefitted from that experience. In addition, of course, I wasn't just competing against Steven and Michael; there was a whole squad of top professionals between me and first team football!

I do have to admit though, I did think for many years that breaking my arm at that crucial time at the start of my YTS, when I was on such a good roll, was a huge setback for my career. And in reality it was! There is a fine line between making it into the first team squad or not, a very fine line indeed, and I was right there on the edge. I felt that if I had got onto that pre-season tour to Norway then that could have been a big opportunity for me to get even closer. Sadly it slipped through my fingers. I needed to keep that good momentum flowing but, after the accident, I just couldn't. Don't get me wrong, I didn't just roll over and die. I did fight back, I got fit again and I played at least twelve games for the Reserves; but, after that disaster, I never ever reached my full potential.

To this day, deep down inside, I truly believe that tour could have been the breakthrough I needed to catapult me up to the next level. But it just wasn't meant to be. However, now that I am older and wiser, I can also be brutally honest with myself and accept that at sixteen I was almost certainly not mentally tough enough to force my way back into real contention. If I were to speculate about what if the same accident had happened to Steven Gerrard, and ask myself if it would have stopped him making it into the first team, then the answer would have to be a resounding no! He would have made it anyway.

That must have been the biggest difference between the two of us back then as young players; he was so much stronger than me mentally and his hunger to succeed was far greater than mine. I know that it's not realistic for me to compare myself to Steven because, with his unique kind of unrelenting determination and his immense natural ability, he was clearly destined to become one of the great Liverpool players. He didn't just want to be the best player over the course of a season; he wanted to be the best player in every single game of football he ever played.

So I might be being unfair on myself to measure my performance against that of a player who has gone on to become one of the greatest amongst the greats, but that was the standard he set amongst our group of players from a very early age.

From my current perspective as a coach, it's very difficult for me to look back over my shoulder and analyse my own qualities as a young player, but if I was really pushed to identify one aspect of my game that I would have improved if I'd had the chance, then it would have to be my competitiveness. As a person, both on and off the field, I was a bit too nice and too honest. I didn't possess enough natural aggression to instinctively want to impose myself on any situation. It wasn't that I lacked the drive to push myself to succeed; I just didn't have the kind of ruthless streak that all people need to occasionally call upon to compete successfully at the highest levels. So, even though I might have been doing all the right things technically, I still needed more steel in my character and a tougher edge to my game.

The unfortunate irony is that I only really fully understood the value of those assets after I had been released by Liverpool.

As soon as I started to play non-league football for Burscough, I had to immediately learn how to look after myself out on the pitch. Playing in the Unibond League I was very much a boy competing amongst grown men; and because I could play a bit, they never hesitated to overpower me physically or try to intimidate me with raw aggression. Things got even rougher when I started to bang in the goals and made something of a name for myself. There was always somebody on the opposition who'd try to stifle my skills with brute force, so I had to toughen up quickly and start making my own presence felt. It might have been a bit late, but I did finally add some more bite to my game.

There was even a headline in a Scottish newspaper article that quoted me as saying: 'At Burscough I became a man.' Definitely a bit dramatic, but it does sum it all up quite well.

Regardless of why I didn't make it as a first team player at Liverpool, and all the many massive implications that short statement contains, I would much rather be the person that I am today, than have to choose to be somebody different to make it to the top as a player.

Everything in life happens for a reason.

And I have been far too blessed to have any cause to complain about anything.

It is not just a cliché to say that my ten years as a schoolboy and YTS player at Liverpool were the happiest, most carefree, enjoyable years of my life. They were!

I owe LFC a huge debt of gratitude for teaching me so much and providing me with such a substantial foundation to build upon for my future.

If I had not been released by Liverpool, then I would never have met my soul partner, my wife Nikki, and we would not now have our precious daughter Devon.

My career as a coach, currently working in the very interesting area of developing LFC International Academies around the world, is now starting to pick up pace; at the same age that I would have to be thinking about retirement if I was a player.

Life is good, my prospects look rosy and I am a contented man.

Of course, I do still have my moments when I dream about pulling on that red shirt, walking down the tunnel, touching the sign and running onto the Anfield pitch to the roar of 45,000 adoring fans.

But would I swap all the wonderful things in my life now for a chance to have played for Liverpool's first team?

Well, with all the amazing experiences, incredible memories and happy times that I have enjoyed so far, along with what promises to be a really exciting and rewarding future for me in football, I can put my hand on my heart and in complete honesty say ....

.... Just stay in the game, just stay in the game!

# About The Author

Born and bred in Liverpool, Keith Miller has been a permanent resident of Barbados since 1978.

Educated at the Liverpool Blue Coat; Liverpool Polytechnic; the Sorbonne, Paris, France; and the University of Valencia, Spain, Keith has a BA in Languages and Modern European Studies.

Keith emigrated to Barbados to take up a teaching position at Mapps College, a boys secondary school, where he worked for fourteen years, including six years as Headmaster. Today, Keith and his wife Sally are the joint owners and managing directors of Miller Publishing Company, best known for their production of the Ins & Outs of Barbados tourist guide and Business Barbados, as well as a wide range of quality books, including several titles for Wisden, the UK cricket giants.

Over the years, Keith and Sally have been jointly awarded the Ernst & Young Entrepreneurs of the Year for Tourism in Barbados and the Eastern Caribbean; the Minister of Tourism's Special Award for Contribution to the Development of Tourism in Barbados; and, most recently, the Barbados Hotel & Tourism Association's Lifetime Achievement Award.

The greatest sources of pride in Keith's life are his three children: Sarah, Steven and Kaylie.

keith@millerpublishing.net